RE-STATEMENTS

OF

CHRISTIAN DOCTRINE,

IN

Twenty-Five Sermons.

BY

HENRY W. BELLOWS,

MINISTER OF ALL SOULS' CHURCH, NEW YORK.

BOSTON:

AMERICAN UNITARIAN ASSOCIATION.

M DCCC LXIX.

CAMBRIDGE:
PRESS OF JOHN WILSON AND SON.

PREFACE.

It is an unhappy prejudice which associates doctrine and controversy. These sermons are not controversial, although they are largely doctrinal. They treat, it is true, of points greatly in dispute, but not in a sectarian way, and seldom with a denominational reference or object. Indeed, they are not designed to unsettle existing convictions, or to disturb satisfied conclusions. Those who are content with other opinions, will find no occasion to read them. They are intended, mainly, for the benefit of that considerable and growing class who find themselves incapable of receiving ordinary statements of Christian doctrine, and are yet unwilling to give up their faith in the Gospel. There are statements in this volume which will be thought destructive, and be read with pain, by some persons of established and confiding faith. But they are serious convictions, reverently held, and are set forth to meet the necessities of doubting and inquisitive minds, that, left to themselves, would abandon Christianity entirely. On the other hand, there are other statements, which may seem retrogressive and superstitious to some of my own immediate brethren. But they, also, are serious convictions, rationally held, and are published to meet the necessities of devotional and anxious minds in our own body, that, left to themselves, would abandon liberal Christianity entirely.

I have long thought that Christian theology, to be truly seen, must be seen alive and at work in the hearts and minds of religious people; and that the usual attempts to separate it from its vital relations, and consider it by itself, are as fatal to the proper understanding of it, as must be the study of the vital organs of man, and their phenomena, in a corpse. The only profitable and decisive discussion of theological doctrines is in connection with the great practical questions of the will, the affections, and the conscience. In sincerely endeavoring to make men like Christ, we find ourselves using the ideas, truths and doctrines, that will alone effect the object, and discarding the errors and superstitions which hinder the work. All the argumentation with error, or supposed error, in this volume, has grown out of an earnest desire to move actual stumbling-blocks out of the way of actual people; all the questioning of popular opinions, out of the necessity of extricating struggling souls from theological embarrassments that would not let them be Christians. It will be found, however, I trust, that the steady object of the volume is to build up, not to destroy; to increase charity, not to embitter differences; to make Christians, not sectarians of any name.

Although hardly any two of these sermons were written with reference to each other, and not one of them with any thought of publication, a certain plan will be observed in their arrangement. I intended, at first, to style the volume by what is now only the running title, "The Re-adjustment of Faith;" but the unwillingness to be thought to claim success in a work in which I am only an humble striver, induced me to surrender the name. A chief effort of my whole ministry has been to meet, not the scholastic, but the practical and spiritual difficulties which, in our day, make faith in Christianity so hard to thousands of the more thoughtful and educated class. My object has steadily been to awaken spiritual apprehension without wounding intellectual laws; and with a profound respect for the understanding, to keep it in its due subordination to still higher faculties of the soul.

If I contribute the smallest addition to the evidence — now slowly accumulating — that the free use of reason is compatible with hearty faith in the Gospel, and that emancipation from superstition and human authority does not involve the loss of a tender reverence for divine persons and things, I shall have abundant cause to rejoice in this work of love.

NEW YORK, *December*, 1859.

CONTENTS.

I.—CONDITIONS OF INQUIRY.

II.—GOD AND HIS PROVIDENCE.

III.—MAN.

IV.—CHRIST.

V.—THE HOLY SPIRIT AND THE CHURCH.

I.

CONDITIONS OF INQUIRY.

I.

CONDITIONS OF INQUIRY.

SERMON I.

UNSETTLEDNESS OF RELIGIOUS OPINIONS A MISFORTUNE.

"Seeking rest, and findeth none."—MATT. xii. 43.

WHAT words can more fitly describe the condition of thousands of religious thinkers in our own day? "Seeking rest, and findeth none." I propose to consider and describe the circumstances which have given over so much of the intelligence of our times to indefiniteness and unsettledness of religious views. I assume that this state of things exists, and that it is to be deplored. It exists, for everybody feels it who seriously thinks about religion; it is to be deplored, for it is a strained, exceptional, and suffering condition of mind.

Few serious and awakened spirits will remain forever content with vagueness and generality. The excellent maxims and the grand ideas which good and wise men have everywhere commended—the worth of virtue, the beauty of goodness, the duty of obedience, the majesty and glory of God, the disinterestedness and sanctity of Christ, do not adequately meet their longing for a more personal faith. The heart cannot be satisfied with truths *about* God and *about* Christ; it wants to know and feel God Himself, not merely to know and feel that there is a God, whom it ought to love, and who has promised to love it; it wants to know and feel Christ Himself, not merely to know something or much about Christianity. The soul must needs be convinced and satisfied that it has attained its right relationship to God, has come as near to Him as it is possible to approach a spiritual Being,—that it has become a true and practical disciple of Christ, and actually is in the experience of whatever power to save there is in the Gospel, before it can be in any true peace with itself.

Now, to meet this want of a personal religious experience, to satisfy this craving for definiteness, this anxiety to come to the point, and to make an end of suspense and generality—in short, "to find rest"—churches, and synods, and creeds, and Christian teachers, have endeavored, in past times, to hedge in from the broad fields of moral and spiritual speculation, a beaten way; to provide specific things to be believed, particular acts to be done, and precise moods and frames of mind to be experienced, which they have either really thought, or at any rate agreed to say, constituted the mental and moral operation called a personal religious experience.

From time to time it has been agreed among the wise and good, just *what* a religious man should believe, just *how* a religious man should feel. Did he believe these things, did he feel these emotions, he was a Christian; otherwise, not. These articles of faith, these frames of feeling, and the particular methods of attaining them—different in different ages and different Churches—have been described with infinite pains, and have given birth to certain conventional terms and certain conventional feelings, which gradually acquired and still possess an immense sway, and to certain modes of religious discipline of the most positive efficiency. Let me not be understood as objecting to this course; on the contrary, it was quite impossible, if Christianity were to produce any positive effect in the world, that its truths should not be systematized by the more thoughtful for the less thinking; that the way of understanding and applying it should not be methodized by those willing to take great pains in its behalf, for the benefit of those willing to take less, or little. The Church has always been an institution whose very purpose was to make a science and a method of what, in itself, was vague and general; to give directness and tangibility to what was circuitous and evasive, and to enable each individual to touch and handle for himself that which, in its sublime elevation, seemed to resist personality, and tended to dwell apart from all private possession. Happy is the age and generation in which the teachers of religion themselves unfeignedly believe their own teachings; the age in which the creeds and methods of religious discipline are so nicely adjusted to the existing intelligence, in such harmony with the experience, the science, and the pursuits of men, that they are heartily and frankly trusted, alike by their administrators and the people they teach. If we desire to understand the great influence of the Catholic

Church, even now, when its power has so much declined in the most civilized countries, we must trace it to the enormous amount of faith it laid up in the days when its creed and its customs were in genuine and unstrained accordance with the minds and hearts of all Christian people. There was nothing arbitrary or forced in its dogmas when they were adopted. They then entirely met the best sense of Christendom and truly expressed its wants. And the same is true of orthodox Protestantism. Consider the significance of that word orthodox—*the right doctrine.* By what strength of conviction alone, by the aid of what an overwhelming public sentiment only, can any doctrine be pronounced orthodox, entirely and exclusively right? Yet orthodoxy never acquires her right to use that title without reason. At the time theological sentiments or usages have the self-confidence to assert themselves to be *orthodox*, they are truly so; that is to say, they best express the convictions and wants of the Church, or of the efficient and substantial *body* of Christians; as compared with the heterodoxy they denounce or assail, they form the safe and judicious way of thinking, and express the highest and calmest wisdom of the time. So long as THE Church can maintain the emphasis of the definite article, she is rightly and truly *the* Church. She holds the confidence and salvation of the people in her hands. It is only when the criticism or opposition of a growing intelligence succeeds in bringing the definite article into popular suspicion, so that it is no longer used even by its own chief representatives, Popes, Cardinals, and Archbishops, without a consciousness of presumption, that *the* Church becomes only *a* Church, and Catholic is fitly changed into Roman. Consider the enormous testimony to its original sway, contained in the very word, the *Catholic* Church; the WHOLE, only, and all-embracing Church! What power of faith, what unity of opinion, what repose of sentiment, are implied in the possible assumption of such a title! And just so with the permitted use of the self-assumed title of *Orthodox*. There was no presumption in either of these phrases at the time it was adopted. The Roman Church was truly the *catholic* Church, and afterwards the doctrines of the Reformation were truly the orthodoxy of Protestant Christendom. No Church could possibly take either of these titles without general consent; and general consent, so long as it can be maintained and enforced, is admirable justification. The Catholic Church was right in seeking to maintain its unity and authority to the utmost. Just so long as its self-confidence was complete, its mission was a providential and a holy one. And the orthodoxy of the Reformation—the mother of all the great bodies in Protestant Christendom in our day—was right in defending its creeds and discipline, its exclusive and special character, to the utmost of its power. It has proved this right, by really being the principal source of the religious life of Christendom during the last three centuries; as the Catholic Church proved it by being the principal source of the Christian life of the world for the fourteen previous centuries. Nor, indeed, can any Church do much for the world, or take the place of these great institutions, until by general consent it is able to say, without arrogance or serious dispute, "I am the true Catholic Church; I am the real Orthodoxy." For consider, that the whole office of the Church and of religious institutions is, to relieve men of that vague, indefinite, suspended, and unsatisfied frame, in which mere individual thinking leaves them—leaves them at the mercy of the wild ocean of general speculation—leaves them to the homeless, harborless, uncompassed, and unruddered navigation of their own limited experience and observation. Nobody can tell *us* any thing of the perils, the storms, the icebergs of that Atlantic. We have providentially in our generation and day been thrown upon it. The winds of doctrine that have tossed us hither and thither, the latitudes of polar cold, the dreadful length of the voyage, the immense uncertainty of the harbor, the beclouded heaven, the fog-clothed headlands—oh! how often have these, the necessary experiences of all heterodoxy, taught us the inadequacy of mere individualism to bring us Christian peace and rest! How have we sighed for the pilotage of an authorized Church; for the chart of an established creed; for the methods and discipline of a fixed and defined religious life! Our sighs and longings, my brethren, are the honest groans of a nature made to find repose in a loving and settled faith; and they unquestionably are the very pangs by which Providence is seeking to bring forth a *new* catholic Church—a *new* orthodoxy—that is to say, a creed and a ritual which shall have the honest consent of the great bulk of the people—shall express its new or fresh conceptions of Christianity and of Christian faith, discipline, and worship, in a way to match the experience, the wisdom, and the wants of a new era, and so to secure the uncompromised, the unfeigned, and the hearty confidence of Christendom.

If any imagine that the intellectual condition in which the Christian world now is, is one of comfort to itself, one in which any real catholicism, or any real orthodoxy exists—a condition in which the teachers of religion are in sincere and simple satisfaction with their own creeds—or in which the administration of religion is efficient, and meets the wants of society—I must think them very poor observers. It is no comfort to me to think this; to know that doubt, equivocation and vacillation, describe the general condition of enlightened Christendom; that scholars, thinkers, statesmen, men of science, are everywhere openly or indirectly, by what they say, or do not say—by what they do, or do not do—bringing the Church and its creeds into suspicion or contempt. It is no comfort to me, because I am heterodox and have to sound my own perilous way in the great deeps of speculation and religious inquiry, to know that the whole world is shivering on the brink of that terrible sea—distrustful of its old charts, ready to fling overboard its pilots, and quenching the very stars with the mists that rise from its own turbulent and yeasty intellect. I may see that this is inevitable; that it has been of periodical occurrence, that it is the only way to a better faith. Thank God, I believe this—as I believe that the original Deluge of water which swept away a race of God-defying people; or the modern deluge of population which is now sweeping away with melancholy haste a race of effete idolaters from this continent—are providential decrees, laden with beneficent consequences. But I should not like to have been out of Noah's family in the days of the original flood; nor to be *in* the family of the Red-man in the days of our own; nor, however necessary destructive transitions may be for society and humanity, whether of a political, social or religious sort, are they to be considered as comfortable, useful and saving, for those who are the instruments and victims of them. It is a misfortune to be a doubter, a dissentient, and a questioner; a grave calamity to be at odds with the Church and the creed—an unpropitious birthright, to be born into a revolutionary and skeptical era! And no man is fit to occupy the position of a useful reformer who wholly enjoys his post.

To destroy ought to be a work of reluctance; to doubt, a matter of pain; to be in suspense and without clear footing and an open road, a ground of serious anxiety. The stormy petrels of social and religious reformation, who enjoy the heavings of the ocean over which they scream, and plunge into the dark troughs that yawn in the once smooth and safe sea with delirious eagerness, are not birds of good omen. God made them, and they have their mission; but they are not the doves that hover peacefully above a subsiding deluge, nor the birds of passage that safely wing their way over commotion to stable and happy shores. The true mediator between the past and the future—old opinions that no longer satisfy, and new opinions that are yet too vague to supply their place—is the man who is too honest to affect a confidence in the old which he does not feel, or a certainty and definiteness in regard to the new which he has not attained—but who deplores while he nobly occupies, his attitude of transition—who tenderly preserves all that was precious and nutritive in the past, while he yearningly anticipates the faith of the Future, and honestly admits the unsatisfactoriness of the Present. If our revolutionary fathers had hated the English constitution as much as they hated colonial dependence; if they had enjoyed the conflict with their own Saxon blood, which they bitterly lamented but solemnly undertook; had they not known that the cause they fought was a necessary evil, we should have had, in place of Washington and Hamilton, and Jay and Madison and Adams—temperate, cautious, high-toned and serious patriots—leaders like the fillibusters and border-ruffians, and wretched pipers on popular passions and prejudices who now disgrace the land—propagators of wars with weak powers—and instigators of sectional strifes. Warriors that love the sword they draw and the blood they drink; reformers that revel in the prejudices and hatreds they arouse; doubters that glory in their denials and their skepticisms—are men, who, if they do any good, do it as the hurricane, the locust and the lightning do good—in the overruling of Him, who maketh the wrath of man to praise Him, and out of evil still educes good.

I suppose, my brethren, that a great and painful indefiniteness of opinion respecting the doctrines of Christianity and the methods of the religious life, exists in our generation among thinking men of all sects—secretly in most, openly in many, and characteristically in our own liberal Body. Compare the sacred literature of our day—the published sermons of all denominations, the religious newspapers of all sects, with the Bodies of divinity, the articles of faith, the catechisms and creeds of fifty, a hundred, and five hundred years back. Notice the contradictions, the inconsistencies, the vacillations of theological opinion in all statements of our time; how vague the language chosen, how uncertain the note struck, how many the loopholes of evasion! Examine the children of the Sunday-Schools of all orders, and see whether they are indoctrinated in any positive system. Try if you can get a definite declaration of theological faith from your intelligent friends of any denomination. Question the professed teachers of religion, and notice how slowly, how guardedly, how vaguely they answer direct inquiries! I do not set forth these undeniable facts with undivided pleasure. They indicate discontent, without establishing improvement. They furnish opportunities for reform, without yet revealing the wisdom to use these opportunities. Movement is not always progress, any more than revolutions are always reforms—as Mexico and Central America might admonish us. I must know the causes of agitation and the direction of movement, before I can praise them. Men are as much in motion when they run away from truth, as when they hurry from error; and the procession moves as swiftly from the funeral as it hastens to the wedding. The religious dissatisfaction and unsettledness of the day will be good or evil, according as it is used. Nor, on the other hand, am I complaining of this indefiniteness and uncertainty, this restless but undetermined activity, as if it were anybody's fault, or could possibly be avoided. It is an actual, a real experience; as real as a fog at sea, or a mist on land. The theological mind of the world is actually, and by reason of a change in human circumstances, in an unsettled state. Nobody seems to see far ahead, or to be certain where he is. The needle is violently disturbed, the stars obscured, and the position of the ship unknown. The brave and honest men of the Church know that they are seekers after fixed truth, rather than present possessors of it ; and the more distinctly they avow their inability to answer direct questions, the more truthful they probably are. What I complain of, is not that doubt exists ; not that doubt is courageously avowed—above all, not that a positiveness and definiteness of opinion which does not exist is not feigned for popular effect. But I complain of the seamanship, which imagines that theological fog and mist, however honest and unavoidable, are the desirable weather for the Christian voyage ; of the folly, which undertakes to stay on the vapory banks of a spiritual Newfoundland, sailing back and forth in the mist, and considers it a return to stupid coasting to attempt to get into sunlight and clear water, and take a straight course for a harbor. We live in times when, because exact political and religious truth are hard to attain to, it has become the fashion to call the endless search for them more valuable than their actual possession. Thinking is mistaken for the results of thought ; liberty for the uses of freedom ; the chase for the game. The sportsman who hunts for his amusement may hold this opinion ; the pioneer who hunts for his dinner and his life cannot accept it. To be ever learning and never able to come to the knowledge of the truth, may suit amateurs of wisdom, but not her genuine lovers. They wish not to pursue a goddess, and embrace a cloud; but to overtake the solemn and substantial mistress of their hearts, and possess her forever. And I must think the mood so common with the intellectual adventurers of our day, which pronounces eternal change the only fixity; the right to think, the only thing certain connected with thought; and the love of truth, more important than truth itself, very unfavorable to any proper earnestness of conviction, or any real progress of character.

Let us, then, distinctly recognize the fact that the dimness and uncertainty of our theological and religious opinions is not due to the essential obscurity, or the fluctuating and evanescent character of religious truth itself; that although men's views about the Gospel change, that Gospel itself is the same yesterday, today, and forever; that though the mind of particular generations or bodies of men become honestly unsettled by historical events, or change of intellectual position, so that their views of Christianity—as of other great and valuable interests—lose their clearness and require fresh statement before they can have efficacious influence; yet that this unsettledness is an evil to be deplored and corrected, and toward which an incessant vigilance is to be directed, that a speedy escape from it may be realized. I am fully convinced that as precise and definite a statement of Christian doctrine as was ever made, will yet be made again, a statement which will express the essential truths of revealed religion, in a manner to meet the experience, wants, and faith of the Christian world at large, and which will produce that unity of faith which it is now the fashion to describe only as a unity of spirit. The Church wants not only unity of spirit, but the bond of a common faith; not because agreement is so desirable, but because *truth* is so important, and agreement is only common success in the attainment of universal truth. Those indeed who imagine that religious truth has no outlines or boundaries; that in her case one thing is as true as another; that all formulas are equally erroneous or equally veracious, may be permitted to doubt this result. But, I cannot see why truths about God, the source of all truth, should necessarily be left in perpetual vagueness; nor why Christianity alone, of all systems of opinion, purely because it is divine, should therefore be absolutely indescribable. There may be that about it which is past finding out, which is true of every thing, a grain of sand, or a sand-fly, but that its characteristic features and truths are of this nature, ought not to be acknowledged. Vagueness and the claim of infinite obscurity are convenient covers for indolence and weariness. So long as this round world was not circumnavigated, it might be imagined to be shaped like a tortoise, or an elephant, or a man, or to be a boundless plane, or it might be safely asserted that its form was past the possibility of human discovery and determination; but the time came very soon when positive knowledge banished this indolent speculation, and silenced, by actual disproof, the convenient assertion of the unknowable shape of man's present abode. And so it is with all knowledge. Laziness and fatigue pronounce clear views unattainable in regard to all very obscure subjects; but industry and curiosity, and the love of truth, are perpetually bringing within the realm of positive science what long lay hopelessly out in the fields of crude speculation. So, I doubt not, it is destined to be with Christian theology. Christianity is intended to be accurately understood; and because successive ages have failed to define it satisfactorily for their heirs, we need not conclude that no successful and exhaustive statement of it can yet be made. It might as well be concluded that, because the Chinese, Ptolemaic, and Copernican systems of astronomy supplanted each other, a new system would presently drive out the satisfactory and self-evidencing system we have now attained! The time comes when the positive and complete truth is known about things; and, contrary to sentimental expectation, their interest, instead of diminishing, is only enhanced by the clearness with which they are known. It will be so with the Gospel; and to hasten this, should be our earnest and prayerful endeavor.

I believe, my brethren, that the time is approaching when a Christian theology will be more truly within the reach of the world than it has ever been since the days of the old Catholic Church. Oh! that the crystallizing minds would appear, to bring into shapes of all commanding beauty the tremulous fluid into which the old theologies have dissolved! Doubt, speculation, license, have had a long enough era. Religion as a life, a consolation, and an inspiration, is losing its power, because the vessels that used to hold it are broken, and there are no new buckets to drop into the well. Meanwhile, a mixture of worldly prudence and morality is doing the work of absent faith. It is fortunate that we have so decent a substitute. But it would be blindness indeed, not to see that worship, that faith, that "peace in believing" are left now with the ignorant and the unthinking, while the intelligence and power of the world are running after substitutes for religion in place of religion itself. It is not in criticism of others, but of ourselves among others, that I say this; for I think it cannot be denied, that the most acceptable administration of the Gospel in our day, is that in which morality is dressed out and flutters in the plumes of faith; not that in which faith itself carries morality with her on the wings of worship and steadfast and clear conviction, and merges it in a living piety. Is it ever to continue so? Is there to be no more quietness of mind, positiveness and certainty of conviction, absolute knowledge of God, and satisfied communion with Christ, in the Church? Nay, is there to be no Church? but a mere figment of a church—a church without a creed, and without a worship—Mr. A.'s church, or Mr. B.'s church, and not the Church of God, or the Church of Christ; ordinances barely tolerated—opinions utterly at variance—with nothing tangible and settled to lay hold upon? I am sure this state of things should not, cannot, continue. It is more than human nature can bear. It leaves the finest and tenderest souls in the world in a state of ruinous exposure. They fret themselves nearly to madness, for the want of religious repose. It frightens the religious-minded back into what is now a superstition, the Roman, no longer the Catholic Church; it drives the strong into absolute scepticism and silent despair.

Brethren, let us be up and doing. Make up your

minds that definite and settled opinions in theology, if not within easy reach, are possible, are desirable, are worthy of intense inquiry. Shake off this lethargy which allows you to remain in eternal suspense, this indifference which you call liberality, this apathy you name candor. For my own part, I believe that the sober, historic Unitarianism of five-and-twenty years ago needs only to be rigidly examined, Scripture in hand, experience in full view, to prove the basis of a much nearer approach to a statement of doctrine in which universal Christendom can agree, than any thing else which has been presented for ages. What has gone beyond it, has fallen into Deism; what has kept behind it, is still in motion; what has gone one side of it, is compelled, sooner or later, to fall into its track. It needs, I doubt not, some finer and more generous statement, to win the ear and heart of Christendom; but I feel a mighty confidence that, the first time now that Christian theology clears her trumpet and utters a not uncertain note, the voice of Channing will be the dominant of the strain. If, as a body, we could distinctly affirm, with a good conscience, that positive, historic faith—leaving the frigidness of rationalism and the indefiniteness of sentimentalism aside—I think we should start the Christian world from its theological dreaminess, and *articulate*, in wholesome, credible, inspiring words, the truth that now sticks and sputters in the throat of Christendom.

God grant us the utterance which our languid organs refuse, and give us the blessed privilege of speaking the word which would set chaos in order, and for an ecclesiastical ruin furnish Christendom with a Church!

SERMON II.

SPIRITUAL DISCERNMENT.

"And even things without life, giving sound, whether pipe or harp, except they give a *distinction* in the sounds, how shall it be known what is piped or harped?"—1 COR. xiv. 7.

THE apostle uses this illustration in dwelling on the importance of distinctness in religious ideas. Undoubtedly there is a great want of distinction in the sounds of the pulpit. Religious ideas and experiences are vague and confused, as they fall on the learner's ear. But this is not wholly, perhaps not chiefly, the fault of the teacher; it is quite as much the want of a disciplined ear in the hearer as of a careless finger in the performer; and it is also, still more than either, the essential difficulty of the subject. The music of divine truth is the most delicate and difficult music to read or sing. Leaving, however, the peculiar figure used in the text, I wish now to enter into a consideration of the grounds of the confusion and perplexity which involve religious ideas; to show how and why religious language is so obscure, and religious doctrine so contradictory; why it is that, in regard to spiritual things, we find it so hard to keep definite, tangible, and distinct notions; and then to exhibit the advantages and importance of making all the distinctions and seeking all the definiteness which is possible. No one, for instance, who reads St. John's gospel or Paul's epistles, can fail to feel baffled and discouraged by the seeming contradiction and confusion of ideas and terms in those sacred pages—faith and works, God's grace and man's obedience, free-will and strict dependence, all running into each other, until it seems almost useless to attempt to say whether one thing is not as true as another. In like manner, Christ's work, and God's work, and man's work, in human salvation, seem inseparable, and each to occupy the other's place. The prospect presented to the unpractised eye is certainly that of a dissolving view, in which different objects contend for the same space.

I purpose now to explain the grounds of this obscurity and confusion, rather in the way of a fuller statement of it, than in any philosophical method; and next to give some hints for the gradual correction of it; to show how discrimination and clearness are possible, and why greatly important.

Man, by constitution and circumstances, is so mixed up with nature, with society, with history, with the universe, with Christ, and with God, that it is never easy to see or to say where he ends and they begin, what he is in himself, and what he is only in them. His powers and their powers are so blended and co-operative, that it demands a perhaps impossible discrimination to assign to each its precise place. Thus, who can say exactly where man's power begins and nature's ends in the work of husbandry? how much of human industry and skill, and how much of natural fertility and divine chemistry enter into the products of the farmer's fields? Was it this hoeing, or that shower; was it this good seed, or that warm weather, that added so much to the crop of corn? "Paul may plant and Apollos water, but God giveth the increase." But God will not give the increase if Paul does not plant and Apollos does not water; and He does not need to claim the credit of Paul's industry or Apollos's faithfulness. Again, you attempt to move a heavy body; you apply a lever; you call on the laws of science, the powers of nature, to assist you. Is it you, or is it gravitation that has moved the weight? How much is it you and how much is it nature? Nature could not have moved it without you, and you could not have moved it without nature. So if you study closely the philosophy of human activity, you will find that man's highest results come from the skilful advantage he takes of nature's powers. He sets his sails for her mighty breezes, and lo, commerce is born! his mills against her powerful currents, and behold manufactures arise! he shuts up heated water in strong prisons forged in these mills, and his bulky vessels move swiftly up against the strongest tides, or run against winds and waves; and so man conquers nature with her own weapons. Which have we most to admire as we look at a locomotive drawing a tremendous train with a bird's swiftness and ease—the skill of man, the vast powers of nature, or the Creator of nature and man? Who shall assign the precise part which each has in this magnificent result? You have said nothing to the purpose, when you say to God, as the author of every thing, belongs all the praise. It is true, yet not at all the truth it is profitable to consider; for God has chosen to distribute and discriminate powers and responsibilities. God might make locomotives, as he has made water and heat and iron; but he does not. Nature, too, might grow railroads or magnetic telegraphs, as she does grow forests and gravel-pits and the metals, and all the various things from which railroads and telegraphs are made; but she does not; and man's work is deliberately and providentially made real and distinct from her's. Yet it becomes man to be cautious how he uses nature, or how he overrates his own part or powers in their partnership, or she will punish his presumption and mortify his pride.

And as with nature, so is man mixed up with civilization, in a way to make it very difficult to say what he does or knows or feels in his own individual and independent right, and what only as a citizen, an heir of the past, a creature of his time and his circumstances. He perhaps thinks he owes his personal safety to his own strength, or courage, or good fortune, and little estimates the rivers of blood, the generations of disorder, the slow and expensive experiments which that civilization has cost, which now throws its laws, its affections, its customs around him! The stranger observes not the police that observe him and watch and defend his way through the city; nor the indomitable will behind them; nor all the vast political machinery that quiets and controls a great metropolis; and he imagines that his security or his unimpeded freedom are due wholly to his own good behavior, or prowess, or excellent fortune. And in part they are due to these, but how much more to the social order which embosoms him!

In the same manner man is mixed up with his fellow-men. What he does as a single, isolated intelligence, and what he does as a creature of affections, a son, a brother, a child, a friend, a lover, a rival, a seeker of social position or public sway—what he does as a private person, and what he does as a social being, are so inextricably mixed up that nobody can say offhand, or perhaps after the utmost deliberation, what the same man would have been, brought up alone, (if such a bringing up were human or possible,) and, in society. And yet man is the same being, in or out of society. And so is the cunning instrument the same in the empty house, where no skill exists that can touch it, and under the hands of the most accomplished performer. Man has all his powers before society touches him, or after it has ceased to touch him; but those powers are as if they were not, till brought out by his social relations.

And in a not unlike way are we all mixed up with Christianity, or Christ. Do we suppose the world is the same world now as that to which Christ came? No. His truth, spirit, gospel, has entered into it as leaven, and modified it; or as a vital principle, and organized and fashioned it; until no pious soul can tell how far it is Christianized by the inherited and unconscious influence of public sentiment. The common religious faith of the world, which it costs us no trouble to believe, which indeed it costs us much trouble to disbelieve, is the best part of our Christian inheritance. If our faith in God's paternal character, in immortality, in man's brotherhood with man, in the sanctity of truth and chastity, of womanhood and childhood, were a matter of individual option or research, depended upon argument, and had to be attained as we attain our calling or profession, by arduous personal labor, the world would be a hopeless world. But these are the happy, blessed prejudices of our age—for prejudices may be true as well as false—and we act upon them as a collective society, taking it for granted that other men think precisely as we do upon these fundamental points, in which assumption we are fully justified. This, however, does not at all alter the fact that the personal, individual character has just as much to do for itself as though Christianity were just born into the world. What Christianity does for us spontaneously, is just so much pure gain; but it does not diminish our private responsibility, nor lessen our freedom. Men are wicked in the most advanced states of society and the most Christianized communities, and all the grades of faithfulness and unfaithfulness are as distinctly marked in an elevated as in a low state of society, in the nineteenth century as in the ninth, or the first, or before the first. And so although Christianity is a part of modern civilization, it is also, in another sense, a fresh revelation to every man who penetrates through its history and social life, to its original facts and persons, or brings himself, by independent efforts of mind and heart, into direct, in place of merely common or universal relations with it.

And finally, I may add, that man is so mixed up with God, who is his Creator, the original inspirer of his intellect and heart, the informer of his understanding and the light of his conscience, that it is a most difficult thing to say what he does in his own character, and in the strength of his nature and will, and what as in and from God. Who can nicely distinguish between thought and the objects of thought, or love and the objects of love? What are the inspirations of genius? Is its light its own, or reflected? Is the saint's holiness his own or his Lord's? Is our religious strength intrinsic or communicated? We must answer, if we speak with candor, both. We can judiciously adopt no theory in any supposed honor of God, which flings up what God has taken infinite pains to fix fast—man's freedom and separate existence. God does not want man merged in himself, otherwise He would never have given him an independent existence. Man feels his freedom, knows his responsibility—feels and knows this, as the basis of all his knowledge—and whenever theology or philosophy has sophisticated the simplicity of this truth, he has been landed in a dreamy fatalism, or an immoral pantheism, which is very similar to materialism or atheism in its last results. Yet man's selfhood is not an existence out of God, such as makes all approaches from God strange, supernatural, or foreign and remarkable. When you hew a piece of clay or wood from nature's breast, and fashion it into a ball which obeys the motions of your hand, it still continues to feel all the forces of nature as much as ever. Gravitation has not lost an atom of its power over it, and in its utmost departures from its original place or mother-rock or tree, it carries the control of nature with it. The globule that madly dances in the rapids of Niagara is as much in the meshes of law, as the dew-drop that falls in the stillest night of August. So man, a spirit, the intelligent moral offspring of God, has in his nature permanent relations with God—blood-relations, so to speak. God is near him ; his nature leans back upon his Maker. There is no nearness which place or sense could exhibit or establish so close as this spiritual relationship. The English mother that has sent her own heart's blood to beat beneath St. George's cross in the trenches before Sebastopol, is nearer to the young ensign as he keeps his midnight watch, though the ocean and two seas intervene, than his companion that shakes with the same cold, or languishes with the same fatigue. Thoughts of home, communion with the unseen and absent, are more natural to the soldier than the foreign sky that blazes over his head, or the soil that is so palpable to his pickaxe or his weary limbs. Absent do I call the souls that yearn towards each other ? I am too bold. I know not that they are not more truly present to each other than ever the bodies that make them visible can be ! And surely God is not far from our prayers, from our thoughts of Him, from our need of Him ! The truth is, He is so near, that, like the babe whose eyes are blinded by the bosom that presses and feeds it, we cannot see our Parent. Divine influences, suggestions, support, are as natural to the soul as the influences and fructifications of the sun to the earth, and the earth does not know that the sun is not a part of herself. In like manner, God's spirit, power, will, is operative over millions that do not distinguish it from their own soul ; but it is not the less distinguishable because it is not distinguished. Men do not spontaneously study the operation of their own minds, or separate their various powers by careful analysis. Yet these powers are separable, and it is immensely instructive and disciplinary to separate them. So, God in us is not naturally distinct in our view. We confound Him with our own nature in its highest activity ; but Christian meditation and experience succeed in putting God, as it were, away from the soul, that it may the more gratefully and adoringly contemplate Him, and so bring Him nearer than ever. Moreover, because God is in us, and is the light of our conscience, and the warmth of our heart, and the energy of our wills, He is not us and we are not Him, any more than the light in our chamber is the sun, or than our chamber itself is the sun. Yet confessedly, it is not easy to say where God's suggestions and our own thoughts, God's strength and our own vigor—where ourselves and where He begin and end ; and therefore we find it equally natural to say, that we can do nothing without God, or that we can do all things ; that we have great power, or that we have none at all—just as we fasten our thoughts upon the fact of our freedom, or on the fact of our dependence—just as we include God's never-denied aid with a filial self-appropriation, or exclude it, that we may the more consider and magnify it.

The all-important fact to keep in view is, that God's influence is a natural influence, not an unnatural one, and is applied spiritually, and in accordance with the laws of our souls. It is from looking for God out of the soul, and expecting to see Him with the eye of sense, or else with the eye of faith regarded as a different eye from the eye of the soul, that so many miss Him forever, though He be so nigh.

Our various relations, my brethren, with nature, society, humanity, Christ, God, are, as we have seen, inevitable, and, up to a certain point, independent of our recognition or furtherance. So close are they that to a great extent, men do not separate or discriminate between themselves and the forces of Nature, Society, Christianity, and Deity, but confound themselves with the universe, or rather come only to a very low consciousness of their independence. Yet all intellectual progress, and I may add, moral progress, depends upon discrimination. We must put things in their places and keep them there. No man enjoys nature or can use nature's powers to great advantage, until he sees that he himself is not a part of nature, or nature of him; that nature has an existence independent of him, and is the proper subject of curious and profound study. The native familiarity of man with nature, as if she were the mere extension of his own person, is fatal either to wonder, curiosity, knowledge, or the use of nature. Those tribes and races, therefore, that live most in the bosom of nature, really know and care least about her—have the least enthusiasm for her charms, the least knowledge of her powers. It is only when man distinguishes accurately between himself and nature, his powers and hers, and his destiny and hers, that nature becomes charming, instructive, and greatly serviceable to him.

All the great discoveries of nature's powers, all the great poetry in praise of nature, the whole department of landscape-painting, are modern, and have come in with the ages that have lived less in immediate contact with and dependence on nature, and since nature lost her place as man's superior or equal.

And so with society. Man is a social being. But the benefits of society, the recognition of its powers, charms, uses, origin, value, are dependent upon man's recognition of his *un*social or independent destiny—his strict individuality, his personal accountableness, his capacity for an inner solitary life. Men were not most sociable when they lived most together. The Indian, who dwells in tribes, is the most reserved of human creatures ; and society developed none of its perfections, while it continued a mere instinct, or coarse necessity. Society, to be valuable, must be the common relations of uncommon people ; the agreement of opposite and unlike experiences ; the deliberate and intentional intercourse of those who live for the most part separate from each other. A valuable social circle is constituted by the individual and distinct values of the various persons who compose it, each with his own experience and views. Therefore, the highest sociableness will belong to a community in which private homes are most sacred, and the best society will be composed of those who most value solitude. People who live together constantly have neither zest for, nor improvement in, their intercourse, and therefore out-of-door nations, and people who make society their rule, lose the self-respect, the moral elevation, the domestic happiness, the highest uses of friendship and affection, which are the noblest fruits of man's social nature. I might add that the philosophy of society, in its political, economic, and domestic aspects, is the discovery of those who are not betrayed into the natural but perilous error—not the error of our age—of setting social man above individual man—humanity above the soul. While man contemplates the destiny of the race, the progress of society, as the grand concern, instead of considering the destiny of the private soul as the fundamental interest, society itself cannot advance wisely or swiftly. Christianity which cares nothing for society, but loves each man infinitely, is the real source of the triumphs of modern civilization. In a still greater degree does the enjoyment and use of Christianity depend upon its being carefully and consciously distinguished from what is natural and spontaneous in man's own religious nature, or from natural religion. That it is practically mixed up with these we have seen. And many persons of intelligence suppose that all attempts to separate between natural and revealed religion, natural goodness and Christian goodness, the light of conscience and the light of the Gospel, are a waste of time and feeling. But as a mere matter of fact, it will be found, that other things being equal, Christianity is positive and influential, just in proportion to the distinctness which it acquires in the mind of its disciple; to the care with which it is separated and distinguished from other good things. It is no reason for thinking ill of natural religion that it is not revealed religion, nor of morality that it is not piety, nor of reason that it is not faith, nor of a sound spiritual philosophy that it is not the Gospel. But there is just as little reason for mixing up and confounding all these good things. I wish to have a distinct and separate sense of obligation and love towards all my friends, and I do not disparage one by not mistaking him for the other. The Catholic

Church succeeded wonderfully in blending life and religion together, faith and daily usage, pleasure and worship, philosophy and the Gospel, and it won the whole world to its side by the success with which it confounded differences and obliterated distinctions. The world became the Church, but the Church became the world. Sabbaths and other days were all on a level —equally sacred and equally secular—morality and piety were charmingly melted together. But with what result? Piety became superstition, virtue a formality, worship a spectacle, and faith an absurdity. The return to any positive moral power lay in the painful process by which the Reformation untwined this tightly-braided cord of Catholicism, and distinguished among things different; and all the triumphs of Protestantism, the universal improvement of private and public morality, of public education, respect for the individual, have grown out of the increasing care taken to keep the Church and the world apart—religion and other interests distinct subjects of thought and attention. The confounding of all days as alike holy and unholy, all rites and ceremonies as equally binding, all opinions as equally true, all names and authorities— Moses, Jesus, Socrates, Confucius, Swedenborg—as alike venerable, though many think it a very superior style of philosophy, and indicative of a very high tone of character—experience, I think, will prove to be a very dangerous amalgamation of truth and falsehood, of things real and things fanciful. And so men will find that their own religious improvement, their own Christian life, is very dependent upon the distinctness of their religious views, the exactness of their historical knowledge of the Gospel, the precision of their acquaintance with ecclesiastical history, the definiteness of their ideas about natural and revealed religion—in short, upon the amount of time, interest, patience, and thought they give to this supreme subject. A man needs not merely to have his religion as a sentiment, *in* him ; he must be able also to put it *out* of him, as a theory, that he may contemplate it, systematize it, study it, fit it to himself and himself to it. To leave it mixed up with every thing else in his soul, not distinguishable nor differenced, is like having any thing else we need to know, to use, and to improve, in the same confused and unmethodized condition, whether it be the lawyer's library, or the physician's medicine-chest, or the mechanic's tool-box.

And finally, God ought to become more and more a separate, distinguished, and solitary Being, in the knowledge and reverence of the human soul. God is in man, God is in nature, God is in Christ ; and there we look for Him and find Him ; but if we look truly, we find Him so vastly greater than man, or nature, or Christ, that in them though He be, He is far more out of them, and in Himself alone. The vast ocean is in the bay, is in the tidal river, is in the clouds, big with its exhalations, is in the spray that dashes in our face as we stand upon the shore. But neither bay, river, cloud, nor spray, is the ocean, or gives the least idea of its power, vastness, depth, and majesty. The huge leviathan that plays in its waters is a minnow, the vast navy that rides on its bosom a chip, in the immensity of its circumambient wastes. So do we live and move and have our being in God, the unexplored, boundless, spiritual element, the beginning and end of our existence, without the right to imagine that we have begun to know, much less to measure and fathom our glorious and all-hallowed Creator. It is a weak error to suppose that we draw any nearer to God by losing our awe of His majesty, by becoming familiar and accustomed to his face. We have truly lost God and gone away from Him, when we cease to tremble before Him ; when our awe and dreadful love and wonder have decreased or given up their edge. The child that cowers before the thunder as God's voice, has a nearer view of Him than the man that uses His name as a familiar household word, identical with nature—is a thousand-fold nearer than the careless being who uses that solemn term to give emphasis to his anger or his folly. Profanity is hardly more shocking than the familiarity of many Christian prayers, which approach the Deity as if Christ had let down his dignity to the level of man's pretensions. Moreover, there is a real danger that the paternal character of God, now so much dwelt upon, should be made a cover or shroud of that eternal glory and awful majesty in which the First Cause forever dwells. God, known in his real character, must inspire unbounded veneration and awe. The better He is known the more of holy and delicious fear He must excite. The soul will approach Him with shudders of joy and tremblings of adoration, and rejoice that He is thus ineffable and fearful. Woe to the heart that has ceased to fear God ! Christ himself was as far from that familiarity as the most conscience-smitten sinner could be, and every man's real spiritual weight and moral elevation may be estimated by the grandeur and solemnity of his feelings towards his Creator. "He had a great idea of God," it was said of one of the most profound and sainted among religious reformers; and every man who wishes to be a Christian, or a deeply religious man, should see to it that God becomes every day a holier word on his lips, a greater idea in his mind, a more brooding and awe-inspiring affection in his heart. It should shock him more and more to hear that sacred name profaned, or lightly spoken, or confounded with Nature, Humanity, or Christ. The substitution of Christ for God constitutes, I know, the religion of millions. But it is only the latest and least offensive remnant of idolatry: the proof how little God's vast and undefinable, yet separate and peculiar glory and majesty, are yet understood. Christ was a creature—a glorious and holy creature, yet a creature—and therefore as incapable of claiming God's place as He is now shocked at the worship he receives. We may still hear him saying of his idolaters, what he said of his crucifiers: "Father, forgive them, they know not what they do!" Let us worship neither Humanity, nor Nature, nor goodness, nor Christ. Let us worship the alone, the infinite, the eternal, the ineffable One.

SERMON III.

PARADOX—ITS PLACE IN RELIGIOUS STATEMENT AND EXPERIENCE.

"He that is not with me, is against me."—MATTHEW xii. 30.
"For he that is not against us, is on our part."—MARK ix. 40.

THESE are, in both cases, the sayings of our Saviour, and they seem on their face to be flatly contradictory of each other. They appear to have direct reference to a common principle, which is first emphatically affirmed, and then just as decisively denied. "He that is not my friend, is my enemy," is the first assertion: "He that is not my enemy is my friend," is the second. Now, in an inquiry where to place, in respect to the divine acceptance, those who are neither the friends nor the enemies of Christ—neither for him nor against him—the common position of men, perhaps—the question, according to ordinary views of scriptural interpretation, would be decisively settled on the authority of the Saviour, if either *one* of these texts, to the exclusion of the other, had been found in the record; and it would be settled in directly contrary ways, according as one or the other had been omitted. Certainly, there can be no more important question, for those who acknowledge the divine authority of Christ, than to know whom he considers under his protection, and on his side. And if any one of us were about to appear at his bar, and should be compelled, on the review of our lives and the careful inspection of our hearts, to say to ourselves, "Well, if I have not followed Christ, I have not opposed him; if I was not pious, I was not blasphemous; though I did no good under the inspiration of his precepts and example, I was careful to do no harm; I always respected religion, though I never felt its power; if I did not pray, I did not swear; if I did not love my neighbor as myself, I did not hurt him, and felt no malice towards him; though I did not love God with all my heart, I did not profane his name or doubt his existence and attributes; and if I did not profess Christ, I did not deny him"—if, I say, we were compelled thus to soliloquize, it would be a very vital and imminent question with us, how, in view of this history and internal condition, our Judge would count us, whether among the sheep or the goats. And if we could then hear ringing forth from the judgment-seat, in clear and undisputed tones of the Saviour, "He that is not against us, is on our part," we should feel as the prisoner feels, whose straining ear catches the foreman's "Not guilty;" while that other saying, "He that is not with me is against me," in the mouth of our Judge, would be equivalent to the verdict of guilty, without recommendation to mercy.

But these sayings of Jesus are *both* in the record, and they either neutralize each other, or else suggest some important discriminations, both as to the nature of truth, the essence of religion, and the modes of our

Saviour's speech. The text is only one among many verbal contradictions, and even moral paradoxes, to be found in our Saviour's mouth. I shall ask your attention to three points, one respecting the language, another the theoretical doctrine, and the last, the practical application of our religion. Our text is a case of paradox; and the doctrine of paradox, whether in language, thought, or character, is worthy of the most careful consideration.

1. And our first point respects the folly and danger of pressing our Lord's language, on any occasion, with too literal a force. If he could say, as in this instance, the very reverse on one occasion of what he said on another, the impossibility of believing that he could contradict the spirit of his utterances, compels us to admit the necessity of interpreting him, in all cases, with careful reference to the circumstances. There is not the least reason to suppose that the company of disciples who heard our Lord give utterance to the two conflicting sayings brought together in our text, felt any incompatibility between them; because, in both cases, his words were qualified and limited by the immediate circumstances. Words, we are sometimes in danger of forgetting, are not the only language. Actions, tones, circumstances, speak equally loud; and the same words, uttered on two different occasions, might mean, and be felt to mean, two directly opposite things. In like manner, opposite words—words grammatically and etymologically interpreted directly contradictory of each other—may, under different circumstances, be unequivocally understood as having an identical meaning. When the author of the Proverbs says, in one sentence,

"Answer not a fool according to his folly, lest thou be like unto him," and then in the very next breath, "Answer a fool according to his folly, lest he be wise in his own conceit," the very boldness and bluntness of the contradiction, and the nature of the reasons given, teach us at once that there is perfect identity in the spirit and meaning of the contradictory directions, and that the real counsel is, in both cases, to answer a fool discreetly, and in such a way as to bring down his conceit, without lowering our own dignity. Indeed, the bolder verbal contradictions are, the less liable are they to be mistaken. And perhaps he, who is most firmly and unequivocally settled in his spirit and principles, is the very one to hazard the greatest seeming inconsistencies of speech. Of all beings in the world, Jesus is the least able to bear a literal, prosaic, scholastic interpretation; and chiefly because no being before ever had so much, so profound, so universal, and so novel truth to convey through a narrow and imperfect vocabulary. Christ invented no language. He had to employ the one in popular use, and one whose terms had all been appropriated, and in a manner perverted by the imperfect knowledge and ideas of those who had used it. Moreover, what he said was addressed to the intelligence of his contemporaries, and we read it as if it were directly addressed to ours. There is hardly any one, besides Christ, who could bear this. And he bears it, not because his words had any conscious reference to future times, but because, speaking of universal truths, and in the spirit of God addressing the inmost soul of man, he has less that is local, peculiar, and temporary in his thoughts, than any other moral teacher.

But while this universality makes him intelligible, as no other ancient is, even to the latest posterity, as no other sage is, to the humblest mind, it forbids any other than a generous, spiritual, and sympathetic interpretation of his language. Those, therefore, who follow him with grammar and dictionary, and Jewish antiquities and patristic lore, into the record of the New Testament, and expect to find in each particular text a mine of exact and scientific doctrine, capable of being stated in one age for all ages, and to become the foundation of specific doctrines of equal authority with the great general truths and holy spirit of his teaching and life, are not half as likely to reach the presence of the Saviour as the most ignorant and unlettered Christians, who derive their ideas of Christianity from the well-known facts, the uniform precepts, and unmistakable spirit of our Saviour's life. If there be any thing unprofitable in this world for Christian food, it is the chaff of textual criticism. No text of the New Testament, by itself alone, can, in its literal meaning, claim to be authoritative. It is authoritative only when and because it emphatically, compactly, or more luminously conveys the general and recognized spirit of our Lord's whole character and instructions. It is not to abate reverence for the words of the New Testament, but to exalt reverence for its spirit, that I dwell on this point. We must honor the *word* of God, which is Jesus Christ, even more than the words that he spoke, whenever there is any conflict between the letter and the spirit of our Lord's instructions. But let us pass to another consideration.

2. Our text is not merely a verbal, but a moral

paradox, and the apparent contradiction in it gives the authority of Jesus' own name and practice to the use and value of paradox, while it shows the feeling of his mind to be precisely like ours, in respect to the two-sided character of all truths—a principle whose recognition is of vast importance to the understanding either of Christianity or of our own mental and moral experiences. The mind, in regard to most important subjects and inward states, is forever swinging between opposite points, and it seems sometimes almost indifferent to us whether we affirm or deny a given proposition ; there is so much truth in the denial, and so much truth in the affirmation. Thus, there is a very small difference between the philosophy that asserts the eternity of matter, and that which asserts its non-existence. Very severe cold has the effect, and produces the sensation, of excessive heat. Starting from the same place, and going in precisely opposite directions, two men would finally meet on the other side of the globe ; and ultraisms in opinion and sentiment are as sure to meet as physical extremes. The Roman Catholic and the Unitarian have more sympathy than any of the intermediate sects of Christendom. In regard to many questions and many people, you must have observed, it is a matter of great hesitation with us whether we shall go wholly for or wholly against them ; and sometimes it is a matter of pure accident, to which our very conscience seems to drive us. The extravagance of another person on the right side of a controversy, often repels the man who had previously elected that position for his own, to the very opposite ground—not from any caprice, but because it is the instinct of our nature to conserve the balance of truth. This accounts for our frequent experience of antagonism in the ordinary intercourse of life. The strength of this disposition is proportioned to the independence and courage of the mind. If our companion state a truth in a strong way, although his might be the very side we should most naturally adopt, we are at once impelled to take the opposite side, in order to complete the unity and harmony of the principle. The world calls it the love of opposition, but it is rather to be called the love of wholeness. Thus the moderate conservative will find himself a reformer in the presence of ultra-conservatives, and the reformer a conservative in the presence of ultra-reformers. The abolitionist keeps the pseudo anti-slavery man from adopting his own ideas, by the necessity the mind feels to restore the equilibrium and maintain the proportions of truth ; while the secessionist keeps the indifferent citizen from upholding slavery. There are always two great parties in politics and religion, and each has part of the truth in its keeping, not necessarily just half, but the complement of the whole. No government could stand long without an opposition ; and those who suppose what is called party spirit, or even sectarian spirit, to be wholly wrong and bad, mistake the conditions under which truth is maintained. Truth is too large to be surrounded by any one man or any one party. It is viewed from opposite directions by different intelligences or representative parties, and each is likely to mistake its own prospect for the whole landscape ; but as the roundness of the globe prevents any altitude from overlooking its whole circumference, so the roundness of every truth prevents any observer from taking a complete survey of it, at one moment and from one point of view. It is not merely the *extent* of *truth*, but its *shape*, which produces this difficulty. To make a perfect day, there must needs be morning and evening, light and darkness, within the compass of twenty-four hours; and if we pursue the day within the polar circle, where the sun does not set for six weeks, in seeming to gain something, we really lose the day entirely, for it is composed of the rapid and bounded contrast of daylight and night-darkness. So, if we attempt to keep in view, at one time, the opposite sides of any truth, so as to have no shadow to the object we look at, instead of feeling and enjoying the truth, we become critics of it, which is the way to destroy its real power and vitality. Just as nothing but scientific or idle curiosity drives a man within the polar circle to see a day without contrast, all light or all darkness, so nothing but a dissecting and destructive metaphysics enables a man to hold both sides of a truth in his view at the same time; and then it is not the truth he holds, but its image, just as we really never see, in fact, the whole heavens at once, however good an idea our wooden orreries may give us of their shape.

The progress of the world, therefore, has always been that of a ship beating up a river by short and constant tacks, between the opposite shores. We are very much distressed at this various and contrarient course. We could desire to have truth permanent, unchanging. And so it is; it is only our view of it which changes. The very reverse of the operation takes place in regard to our view of truth of all kinds, which occurs in the passing of a panorama, where we are fixed, and the picture moves. Truth is stable, and it is the spectator that passes round it. It is equally true of the race and the individual. The whole race is but one man, and all history his biography. The history of the universal human mind is essentially the history of every mind in it. Now, the varieties of opinion in the world on all subjects are but the different reports of man, looking from many different positions at the central object of all intelligence. Truth is like the water on the globe, never increased, never diminished—some of it in the sea, some in the clouds, some in the earth, some in the rivers, and some in the tissues of the organic structures, but always the same in all its various forms, always making its circuit, always returning to the ocean. See it as ice, vapor, fluid—see it in its protean forms, and it appears unlike itself. But it is always true to its own laws, unchangeable, and not to be annihilated or increased. It is so with truth. And probably if, at any given time, the mental tendencies and faiths of the whole race, from all quarters of the globe, could be collected and compared, it would be found that, though the separate nations were in error, the race held firm hold of the truth ; that the conservatism of one country was balanced by the radicalism of another—the superstition here by the skepticism there —the over-excitement of this land, by the apathy of that—while all the elements of essential wisdom always remained, partitioned and scattered in fragments, but always to be regathered and formed into a whole. This or that candle may go out, this or that hearth grow cold, but there is always *fire* in the world.

When it is winter in the northern hemisphere, it is summer in the southern, and the same amount of light is always playing upon the earth's surface. The mind has its tides, like the sea; thought its agitations, like the ocean; truth its dark and its light side, its outline and its shadow; and we are presumptuous when we doubt that variety of sentiment, conflict of opinion, and even contrast and seeming contradiction, are perfectly compatible with the eternal and unchanging nature of truth itself. The real progress of the world consists more in the *interchange* of thought than in the creation of it, and the advancement of the human mind more in the participation of each, in the thought and experience of all, than in the discovery of new principles, or the publication of new views. Indeed, there is nothing new under the sun, but new combinations. It is the rapidity with which we get about the earth that constitutes the peculiarity of our modern civilization. Rapid and constant locomotion, or the ease with which we pass through other places or physical space, is civilization; and so, rapid and constant change of spiritual place—or the ease and rapidity with which we pass through other men's minds, or mind itself, is true intellectual and spiritual culture. And it is so, simply because truth is round and surrounded by Humanity, and the intercourse of minds is the circumnavigation of truth. The traveller in other countries sees the world, and is freed from prejudices by his observation of all sides of civilization. In like manner, the student sees truth, because he is a traveller in other men's minds, and is freed from moral and spiritual prejudices, from intellectual pride and complacency—from a sense of popish infallibility, and from that stupid dogmatism, which men mistake for the love of truth, when it is only the sloth, timidity, or short-sightedness of their own natures.

As it is with the race, so is it with the individual. The history of every honest, aspiring and courageous mind, that lives not a parasitical life, but in the strength of its own root and stalk, is a history of intellectual, moral and spiritual vicissitudes. Truth is as jealous, capricious and shy a mistress as was ever wooed. She eludes her lover as a hunted deer her pursuer. Her votary must follow her in all the circuits and involutions of her flight—now doubling on her track, now making the north star, and now the Southern cross, her beacon—now on the earth, now in water or wood, and again in the sky, but always having it for her purpose to lead her wooer through every parallel and point of latitude and longitude in her domain, that he may view her and her possessions from all quarters of the moral compass, and see her full shape and whole fortune—and so be the more in love with his holy, heavenly bride, his destined partner for eternity. Be not alarmed at the inconsistencies of your own opinions—at the violent contrasts in your own mental and spiritual moods—at the necessary action and reaction of your religious experience—if you are only alive and truly devoted to the pursuit of truth, duty and God. If these varieties and changes are the work of your own mental and spiritual activity, and not of mere passive acquiescence in the forces that you encounter from without, you are truly blessed alike in your doubts and fears, your faith and your skepticism, your assent and your dissent, your orthodoxy and your heresy, your mood of quiet and your mood of unrest. Nay, startle not at the suddenness and violence with which opposite convictions crowd each other out of place. It was for the safety and relief of your brain, and your spiritual sanity, that the overstrained cord that was pulling you in one direction, however legitimate, gave way, and allowed you violently to fall back upon the opposite side, with a painful shock, that disinclines you for a time to the once so attractive quarter.

The religious man, who has no vacillations in his views, who is not sometimes inclined to Calvinism, sometimes to Rationalism, sometimes to Catholicism, sometimes to Quakerism, has an imperfect activity, a dull imagination, and a timid love of truth; for all these faiths have embodied great and interesting spiritual facts, which the free and earnest explorer will encounter in his own experience, and find more vividly portrayed in the history of these sects than in himself. It is for the spiritual integrity of every individual to have sympathy enough with all the religious opinions of the world to understand the ground of their attraction. If he has not, it does not discredit them, but his own experience. The more there are of carefully understood forms of spiritual faith in the history of the Church and of the human mind, the better. And when great spiritual instincts embody themselves in honest and grand institutions and creeds, they are like light-houses on dangerous rocks, by the side of deep channels, at the mouth of safe harbors. They show us a safety and a danger lying close together, and enable us to shun the one and seize the other.

Under the diversities and vacillations of truth with reference to the seeker, there will be an ever-growing fixedness in the thing itself; so that his experience will be like that of an elm, which strikes its roots into the ground the deeper, the faster it multiplies its branches, and the further it extends its limbs; so that the more tremulous and waving its top, and the more variable and fleckered its shade, the larger its bole and the more unshakable its foundation. For the pursuit of truth does not at length bring us into consistent and harmonious views, so that we finally grasp the comprehended sphere in our hand. But it leads us to the glorious conviction that the truth-loving and piously-aspiring spirit is a part of truth, in harmony with God and God's wisdom, beyond the reach of harm from the unknown, in subjection to truth, not with the mastery of it; fed by it and upheld by it, not feeding and upholding it; its guest, not its host; its child, not its protector. It is heavenly wisdom, coming not in the form of dogmas and creeds, but of a spirit and temper, that finally settles and tranquillizes the seeker of truth. His horizon does not close, his voyage is not over. The ocean lies at his feet. He is as eager, as curious, as doubtful about the forms of truth, as ever. But the spirit of truth is in his heart. The comforter has settled in his bosom; and as the dove, that knoweth not whither she goeth, takes wing with sure but blind instinct for her passage to her winter home—no feather ruffled and no anxiety in her untried pinions—so the soul, once given up to God and God's truth, discharges itself of all anxiety about results, and follows freely and safely where truth calls out of the dark. In simple teachableness, pure candor, holy aspiration, ineffable faith, there are fixtures and certainties enough for her. She changes her sky, but not her mind. She changes her view, but not her vision. She is one with God, under all varieties of experience and changes of opinion, and expects, under the immortal lease of His favor and His truth, to pass in one glorious identity of spirit through infinitely varied forms of truth and experience.

3. My brethren, there is another and more immediately practical suggestion of our conflicting text, on which I have left myself little time to dwell. When our Lord said, "He that is not with me is against me," and then "He that is not against us is on our part," he seems to have set up two finger-posts upon opposite sides of the entrance-way of life. The narrow way of life runs right through the ordinary paths of men, like a railroad cutting across, or running into and going parallel with, the common roads. It is straight and narrow; they, wide and crooked. It follows only the shortest way to its destination; they, the sinuosities and facilities of the country. But all are tending, perhaps, to the same important destination. Religion has no interests of its own—no interests separate from the great and real interests of men—and, therefore, men find it convenient to use its track every now and then. The common road and the heavenly road occupy the same general way. The interests of the worldling and the saint are often, perhaps, for the most part, the same; therefore, it is very often impossible to say whether those who are in the narrow way are there for the whole passage, or only for that part of the way that

falls in with their own road—whether they are there as volunteers, or as compulsory travellers. Jesus, then, might well say to mankind, as they now were in and now out of his way, that they were both friends and enemies ; both opposed to and in agreement with him. And what it is important and practical to say, to those who are not avowed, chosen, thorough followers of Christ, is that they know not how much of the Saviour's road they are using all the time, and how much easier and better it would be to take his way wholly and deliberately. You are mistaken, my brethren, in the purposes of God and Christ towards you. You mistake the position and nature of the way offered you in the Gospel. It is infinitely more within the reach of your ordinary experiences, infinitely better adapted to your common wants and interests and habits, than you suppose. You are often in it when you do not know it, and it is the easiest and pleasantest part of your journey. It is on account of this inter-threading of the way of life with your ordinary way, that Christ says of those who do not deliberately take it, that they are *in* it, and that they are *out* of it. Oh ! think what sorrow and shame it will be to us to find that we have been all our mortal life nearly right, and yet wholly wrong—in the very footprints of our Master one moment, and then off into the track of Satan—mistaken for his friends one hour, proving his enemies the next ! Oh ! it is enough to make the flint weep blood to witness the blindness of beings with a religious nature, without a religious purpose—with a shrine for Christ in their inmost souls, and no Saviour in their hearts—with God beckoning them, and they not seeing the divine invitation! Oh, brethren, remember Christ cannot call you his friends—will not call you his enemies—or rather, does call you his friends, even when he must see you to be his enemies! Will you not relieve him, who died to save you, from this suspense? Oh! give the Saviour of your soul some other reason for calling you his friend, than that you are not his enemy, and leave him no reason for thinking you his enemy, because you are not *with him.*

MARCH 9, 1851.

SERMON IV.

THE ABSOLUTE IN MORALS AND FAITH.

"And it came to pass, when Jesus had ended these sayings, the people were astonished at his doctrine. For he taught them as one having authority, and not as the Scribes."—MATTHEW vii. 28, 29.

THESE words conclude the account and report the effect of our Lord's Sermon on the Mount. "The people were astonished at his doctrine." Fortunately, we possess the exact means of knowing what it was that astonished them, and what it is which the Evangelist thus describes as *doctrine.* Were we without the transcript of the sermon itself, we might naturally infer, from the astonishment it created, that it contained some extraordinary disclosures touching the mysteries of religion ; some novel facts, or some undiscoverable and peculiar account of the terms of salvation. Considering what ordinarily excites the enthusiasm of Christian believers, and what is most eloquently dwelt upon in those discourses intended to ravish the hearts, or move the consciences, or excite the marvelloving imagination of novices in religion, we should certainly expect to find in this astonishing sermon of the Founder of our faith, some systematic statement of the evangelical creed of Christendom, some gracious unfolding of the Gospel plan, some description of the perplexity caused in heaven by the conflicting justice and mercy of God, and of the extrication from that desperate extremity by the interposition of the Son of God, gloriously taking on himself the sins of the whole world. Surely that central dogma of the Atonement, round which the affections of ages have clustered—that doctrine to doubt which is evidence of the most hardened heart and the most hopeless depravity—will be found to have a prominent place in this discourse, and be the principal cause of the astonishment felt by those who, for the first time among created beings, received the great corner-stone of Gospel truth. And, as part and parcel of this sublime doctrine, doubtless the great teacher will most unmistakably declare himself, to the amazement of his hearers, the equal of Jehovah, the partaker of the Godhead, the second person of the Trinity.

What ought to be our astonishment—surely not less than that of those who heard this address, though for very different reasons—to find in this discourse, the only long and completely reported sermon of Jesus Christ, no reference whatever to the fundamental doctrines of Christianity, no Trinity, no Atonement, no natural or total depravity, no scheme or plan of salvation whatever?

But surely you are now expecting me to say, since the so-called evangelical scheme of Christianity is not found there, that we do unquestionably find the Unitarian scheme of theology laid down! Doubtless we shall have a distinct account of the special commission and coming of Jesus Christ; a particular unfolding of the doctrine of Human Nature; a special revelation of the Immortality of the Soul; with some distinctions touching the nature of Christ and his relations to God and to man; which will constitute a credible, simple, and compact body of divinity! If the hearers of this sermon were not astonished at the disclosures of the Trinitarian scheme, surely they must have been astonished at the disclosures of the Unitarian scheme, and we shall find evidences of it in the discourse itself!

When, however, we turn to the sermon and examine it, we find as little evidence of its author's having our scheme in his mind as the Orthodox scheme. There is not *a doctrine,* according to the ordinary acceptance of that word, of any kind whatsoever, in the whole sermon. The entire discourse is an attempt to heighten and enforce the well-known obligations of piety and morality as they were recognized by the pure and good under the Jewish law; to remove whatever technical obstructions or limitations the essential and eternal principles of morality there suffered, and to carry out, without reserve or equivocation, the spirit of the old commandments. The sermon on the mount has no other object than the substitution of absolute morality in the place of technical morality. It aims to remove the partialities and compromises from Jewish law, and to give a broad and universal effect to the spirit which underlies the Mosaic dispensation. There is, therefore, strange as it may be, not one word in the sermon on the mount on the subject of the Immortality of the Soul; nor one word upon the organization of the Church; not one word upon the obligation of the Christian rites, nor on any other of the topics which one might naturally expect would have prominence in a manifesto of such dignity and such fundamental authority. When we read, therefore, that at its conclusion, "the people were astonished at his doctrine," we are puzzled, first, at their astonishment, and second, that the ground of their astonishment should be termed *doctrine*. For we find nothing to startle, nothing peculiar and novel in the way of opinion or dogma ; and nothing corresponding to what we usually call *doctrine*.

In regard to the term *doctrine*, it must, I suppose, be conceded that the ordinary monopolization of this phrase by theological dogmas is wholly unscriptural and misguiding. *Doctrine* means simply *teaching*, and its general, I might almost say exclusive, use in the New Testament is in application to the precepts of Christian morality. We have seen that it was the doctrine of duty, the enforcement of a more careful, thorough, and hearty performance of moral obligations, which constituted the real teaching of the sermon on the mount ; and I could give you a thousand illustrations besides, that false doctrines in the New Testament language almost uniformly refer to errors of practice, not to errors of opinion. Heresy in our Saviour's time was loose morality. The doctrine of devils was the doctrine which allowed men to practice lying, stealing, drunkenness, and lust. Sound doctrine was the doctrine which enforced the greatest integrity, purity, disinterestedness, and mercy ; not that which laid down the most orthodox creed. Speculative opinions had not then risen into the vast and overshadowing importance which has since been allotted to them. Metaphysical distinctions, theories of salvation, opinions about the modes of spiritual existence, the nature of divine persons, all that has since passed under the name of theology, found small place in the mind or the instructions of our Saviour and his apostles; and the reason why we have continued to dispute about them so long, and have been able to defend any and all sides of opinion out of the Scriptures, is, that the New Testament having nothing directly to say on the subject, but being occupied with entirely different matters, can throw only an uncertain, oblique, and chequered light upon the issues we insist upon forcing before its bar. This is sufficient to account for the eternal disputes in theology. We insist upon carrying a question of speculative science before a judgment-seat devoted to practical morality, and are very much astonished that the court is on both sides of every question we raise, having neither jurisdiction over the matter in dispute, nor interest in its settlement.

The sermon on the mount is full of doctrine, understanding that word in its true Scriptural acceptance, i. e. of teaching on moral and religious duties, but of no other kind of doctrine.

But what then astonished the disciples? Doubtless, in great part, the thoroughness and strictness of the morality; for the sermon on the mount is a declaration of the eternal, unchangeable morality of Heaven and earth, eternity and time. There was enough in a teaching which laid bare the hollowness and partiality of the ordinary, technical morality into which Judaism had sunk, to inspire profound astonishment and reverence. But the main ground of astonishment was not so much the energetic tightening of the cords of duty, as the entirely new basis upon which our Saviour's teaching reposed, "for he taught them," is the evangelists' artless account of the effect of Jesus's discourse, "as one having authority, and not as the Scribes."

At the first blush, we should be almost tempted to reverse the phraseology of Matthew, and say, of Jesus's teaching, that he rested it not upon authority like the Scribes, but upon self-evident truth ; but let us not be too hasty in our rejection of Scriptural language. The peculiarity of the teaching of the Scribes was that they quoted chapter and verse for every thing they commanded or enforced. They did not pretend to base any instructions in morality or religion upon their own knowledge or experience. Like other lawyers, they went to the books and cited the authorities, and they, like many of their brethren in every age, could split hairs, and make exceptions, and limit inferences, and use special pleadings, to make the Scriptures—their law-library—teach pretty much any thing they chose. On the other hand, our Saviour's teaching was peculiarized by a disregard of these authorities. His sermon on the mount is a severe criticism upon the legality of the Scribes ; he pulls their special pleadings in pieces ; he shows how the spirit of the law had been sacrificed to the letter, and bases his own instructions not upon old documents, however sacred, but upon the absolute, irrepealable character and claims of moral truth and duty. The difference between him and the Scribes is, that while the Scribes teach by an authority outside of themselves, to the total disclaimer of any standard in their own hearts, or the hearts of others,

Jesus teaches by an authority within himself and within all men—speaking out of his own heart and conscience, to all other hearts and consciences, and thus resting his doctrines upon the immovable basis of impersonal, universal, unchanging moral truth.

We might at first, considering the prevailing notions of the Christian world upon this subject, conclude that the authority in Jesus, which so astonished the ancient disciples, was the authority of his commission as a divinely appointed messenger from God. But whatever authority of that kind he possessed or claimed at other times, he had produced no credentials at the time when his authority was so forcibly and fully recognized, except those of entire moral conviction and profound earnestness and directness of moral appeal. There is not a word of claim, in the sermon on the mount, to any external authority whatsoever. The hearers recognized an authority which, however it may have been felt by Jesus, was not asserted by him in any formal manner. He spoke as one having authority, not as one claiming it ; as one having that authority in himself, not in his office ; and his right to be trusted and obeyed rested on a basis which does not allow itself to be questioned, namely, the moral instincts of humanity.

My brethren, there is an inherent and absolute authority in all truth, which makes it, in the end, unconquerable and victorious. The truth is mighty, and will prevail. What is founded on error, has rottenness for its corner-stone ; and although it may temporarily be upheld by foreign aid, yet, deserted by its supporters, it always finally tumbles to the ground. Man's nature is in harmony with God's nature, in whose image it is made; so that there is not one truth in heaven and another truth on earth; one right for God and another right for man; one beauty for angels and another beauty for mortals; but the true, the right, the beautiful are universal in their nature and absolute in their authority. The principle of gravitation which governs each particle of dust on our globe, controls the suns and stars of the firmament, and exerts just as decisive an influence in the remotest fields of space, as it does here in our houses. The same arithmetic we use in our little domestic calculations is applied to the relations of worlds, and our geometry is the same which God used in meting out the bounds of the universe. Science is man's knowledge of God's ways; and God's ways are truth. We do not undertake to quarrel with the laws of nature. Our ignorance oftentimes puts us in opposition to them, and a very expensive position we find it to be, because they never yield, and in the end, of course, we must. And truth is none the less true because it is undiscovered. Before it was known that water would rise to its own level, you can imagine the vast and unnecessary expense at which the old aqueduct builders sprung their arches over the long plains and the deep valleys, to maintain the level deemed necessary to the distribution of the fluid. The magnet turned to the pole just as unfailingly in the long ages when commerce was steering her uncertain path by the stars, as it has, since its invaluable property was discovered. Electricity was just as ready to run our errands a thousand years ago as to-day, and steam to drag our burdens ages before as ever since its power was understood. There is no change in the laws and properties of things. Truth is unchangeable, whether it be physical or metaphysical, material or spiritual, scientific or moral. The authority of truth is thus absolute. We are obliged, in the progress of knowledge and experience, to come round to it. All progress is the triumph of truth; all improvement the concession of experience to the unchanging fact. The wisest man is the man who is most in sympathy with nature; who follows most closely in her footsteps; yields most readily to her intimations; catches quickest her whispers; sets up least his own will, or prejudices, or notions, against her instructions. Therefore it is that true philosophy is such an humble observer. She sits like a child at the feet of nature, and closely watches what she does, and only after the most patient accumulation of numerous observations, undertakes to report a law. Presumption, theory and pride, frame their own general principles, and then hunt up facts to support them, and are necessarily kept in real ignorance all their days, amid a great show of knowledge. True science knows that man invents nothing, but merely finds out what God has invented. We cannot make things true by any amount of effort; we can merely discover what God has made true from all eternity. And I suppose it would take a deal of argument to persuade a sound natural philosopher that there was any thing arbitrary in nature; or that even the laws of matter were not founded upon absolute and supersensual necessities; so that the facts of nature, or the truths of nature, are very much like the truths of mathematics.

But what we thus readily recognize in regard to physical or scientific truth, we are somewhat more slow to perceive in regard to moral and spiritual truth. The absolute, unchangeable authority of morality is one of the latest observations human creatures make. And yet, by a universal instinct, we feel the native eminency of moral truth over intellectual or scientific truth. We recognize the *usefulness* of intellectual truth ; but all know that moral truth rests its claim not on its usefulness, but on its sanctity, its inherent obligatoriness. God is a moral being, a being in whom justice, rectitude, goodness reign supreme. He has made man a moral being, and wound his nature up with the same moral weights that move his own divine life. The laws of duty, then, are not strange impositions to the human soul. If you go into the most barbarous regions, you safely take it for granted that right and wrong are well-known distinctions among the people, and no amount of disregard of right or practice of wrong changes your conviction that human beings are everywhere *moral* beings. Men have very different degrees of vision ; and some, living in constant darkness, lose almost or quite the power of sight ; but it is nevertheless true that man is to be described as a creature with the use of his eyes, and, using his eyes, he always knows the difference between black and white, straight and crooked, smooth and rough ; nor is there any difficulty in establishing general rules or principles in respect to the laws of vision. It is just so in regard to right and wrong, good and evil, just and unjust. Under all the superficial diversities, whether of tribes, ages, climates, civilizations, there are discoverable to the candid mind a few general principles of morality, uniformly recognized, if not obeyed, and which it takes no authority outside of the human heart to bind cogently upon the conscience of all men. The will, through indolence and neglect of discipline, may be too weak to carry out the edict of the conscience, but the conscience will respond with almost unvarying consent to every appeal made from the ground of absolute morality. We must not mistake the weakness of human character for the blindness of moral vision. People know their duty when they do not do it, and pay the homage of their hearts to virtue, when they are too irresolute to render it the obedience of their lives.

Now, it is upon this grand eminence of absolute morality that Jesus Christ stands in the sermon on the mount. That mountain was God's holy hill of everlasting moral truth, a truth corresponding to man's nature because the original mould of it. And when from this ground of absolute truth Jesus spoke to the disciples, their natures answered from all their moral depths, with echoes that shook and astonished their souls. What is it, my brethren, that gives sanctity and power to all moral truths, if it be not the moral nature? If you stand in the midst of a plain, and blow the far-sounding trumpet with the lungs of a Stentor, you get back no response! But a gentle whisper, breathed from this same instrument among the hills, brings back echoes that roll and thunder upon the ear of the trumpeter, until his own voice is drowned in their peal. The moral laws of God, urged upon beings without a moral nature, can produce no effect. But what prodigious effects may we not expect when moral truth meets moral beings; when moral obligations come home to the moral debtor? Thus, when Christ presents his claims, the claims of eternal justice, mercy, truth, and duty, the human soul sees its own signature at the bottom of the notes he presents for payment. It sees and feels that its own nature endorses these claims, and that it must escape from itself, and learn to hate and despise what it is compulsory upon it to love and honor, before it can repudiate the obligations of its Saviour.

And if moral truth has its high authority in the very nature of man, so that he who utters it nobly and faithfully needs no credentials but the truth itself, which is a cipher to which all men hold the key, so, again, the possession of the truth is the true and self-sealed commission to declare it, investing its holder with sacred and all-commanding powers. It is the nature of all truth to clothe its discoverer with a certain measure of confidence; and this confidence will be proportioned to the dignity of the truth he sees committed to his hands. There is a time when all great intellectual discoveries, whether the law of gravitation, or the circulation of the blood, or the efficacy of vaccination, or the power of steam, or the true theory of government, is in the hands of a minority, perhaps a minority of one; but it is impossible for this minority to feel that modesty and uncertainty becoming its numbers, and the vastness of the majority which disputes its pretensions. For great discoveries or high truths bring such a flood of light into the mind of their possessors, that, in regard to them, they are not left to think or suppose; they *know*, and their position is not that of their opinion against the opinions of other men, but of their knowledge against other men's ignorance. And it is this mighty vantage-ground of positive knowledge against negative prejudice which enables them so rapidly to conquer the world.

But this is peculiarly true of moral and spiritual knowledge. To him who is greatly flooded with moral and spiritual wisdom, his attitude towards moral truth is not that of an inquirer, a speculative philosopher, but that of an adoring disciple and sworn champion. The conscience, the heart, know the things whereof they affirm. The truths with which they are conversant are objects not of probable reality, of preponderating evidence, but of positive knowledge. The soul sees God, feels immortality, knows with absolute certainty the obligations of duty, the policy of virtue, the blessedness of justice and mercy and humanity, and in submitting to them yields to no calculation of chances or overplus of motive, but to an entire, hearty, and all-gracious moral necessity. Thus, if you study the basis of our Saviour's teaching, and examine the solid ground of his calm, perfect, serene, and never-yielding authority, you will find it in the self-evidencing nature and imperative character of his moral and spiritual knowledge. I believe, therefore have I spoken. He knew the things whereof He affirmed. The words that I speak are not mine, but my Father's. Christ never explains the grounds of his authority, except by asserting it, and conquers doubt and objection only by awakening in other hearts that moral nature, in the perfect activity of which his own deep, absolute, and victorious convictions rested.

You must all have observed the oracular character of the sermon on the mount, and of the Scriptures in general. Truth, especially moral truth, is, of its very essence, oracular. It issues from its shrine, to find the argument that upholds it in the hearts of its hearers. Would you know, my brethren, the truth of Christianity; would you receive and enjoy the blessed life and light it offers its disciples, do not waste your time in side-issues, or strifes about evidences and critical questions, but admit the words and the character of Jesus directly to your hearts. Christ puts himself on a new trial before every human soul. Behold the man! If he speaks what no man could speak unless God were with him; if he reaches depths in the human heart that are elsewhere unfathomed; if he awakens and gives distinctness to dispositions and affections of a divine beauty and blessedness; if he reveals the wants and capacities of the soul to itself; if he communicates vigor and sanctity to the conscience, unfelt before; if in his light, life wears another and more glorious and consistent meaning; if he purges the moral and spiritual eye until it sees things that are invisible; if he rouses the spiritual nature until the great truths of God's paternity, man's brotherhood, the soul's immortality, become self-evident, all-commanding, and, finally, native and visible truths to the soul's celestial vision—then I say, that to such a glorious and divine master, thus offering himself at the judgment-seat of humanity, we cannot say, Away with him! away with him! Crucify him! crucify him! Nay, rather we shall say, Let me die with him, for he is the lover and Saviour of my soul.

Such an authority we can all understand and honor. It is upon this authority, whatever may be the theories of theologians, that Christianity is sustained this day. The world, while it is disputing upon the subject, knows, in its deepest heart, the truth of the gospel. Its truth has been tested and tried. Jesus outlives and commands all other teachers, philosophers, and sages, by the twofold superiority of his moral nearness to God and moral nearness to man. He knew what was in man, because man is at his deepest heart a moral being; he knew what was in God, because God in his most sacred essence is a moral being; and he knew both these, because supereminently he was the blossom of conscience, the consummate flower of absolute morality. This glorious, eternal eminence is his throne; from it he rules the moral world, as the moon sways the tides. From this high mountain he pronounced his sermon, and no wonder that it came to pass, "when Jesus had ended these sayings, the people were astonished at his doctrine. For he taught as one having authority, and not as the Scribes."

MARCH 26, 1854.

SERMON V.

CHRISTIANITY AN HISTORICAL RELIGION.

(PREACHED ON EASTER-SUNDAY.)

"This Jesus hath God raised up, whereof we all are witnesses. Therefore, being by the right hand of God exalted, and having received of the Father the promise of the Holy Ghost, he hath shed forth this, which ye now see and hear."—ACTS ii. 32, 33.

THIS day commemorates the resurrection of our Saviour from the dead. Yesterday he lay in stark and hope-destroying coldness—a pierced, bloodless corpse within the tomb. To-day he rises in perfect life, in moving, speaking, substantial existence, to astonish and delight, and to recover, his scattered and broken-hearted disciples; to retrieve the defeat of his crucifixion, and accomplish a perfect triumph over his enemies. Let us thank the old Mother Church and her English daughter for keeping this and the other great historic facts of our religion steadily before the world, by the festivals and holy-days of the Christian year. The disuse and even censure of these natural and affectionate customs, by Protestantism, which is so needlessly afraid of forms and seasons, accounts to a great degree for the dangerous dissociation into which the principles and sentiments of our religion and its actual facts and persons have fallen. Since the world has seen into the spiritual import of Christianity, it has wilfully disparaged its external history, and fancies itself capable of receiving and maintaining its precepts and spirit, without any aid from its facts and the positive form of its bestowment. Thus, society, to a large extent, has broken utterly loose from that beautiful framework of religious events and seasons, called the Christian year, which for so many centuries formed the calendar of ordinary life; and I very much fear that the same spirit which has discarded holy-days and seasons is rapidly discarding holy books and means of grace; abandoning the habit of familiarity with the Scriptures; of secret prayer; of studious self-discipline and self-searching in the light of Christ's example.

It was, perhaps, necessary to make a protest against ecclesiastical control, and to rescue ordinary and secular life from the regulation of priests and popes; necessary to take a stand against a superstitious and barren veneration for forms out of which the spirit had ebbed; but now that we are emancipated from Church tyranny and the bigotry of externals in religion, I see no reason why we should not voluntarily and from our own sense of need, and not at the bidding of priests or of superstitions, resume all we can of the usages and customs, the times and seasons, founded in the actual history of our religion. For either our religion had a history or it did not have; either we have the record of that history or we have not. If our faith be a fable, a beautiful but baseless tradition, in heaven's name let us say so. If our Bible is an unhistorical, undependable book, come to us from none know where, and sustained in its present position of pseudo veneration, only by the toleration which scholars pay to the ignorance and superstition of the people, let us know this, too, and say it. If, on the contrary, Christianity be a part of credible and universal history, to whose investigation honest, great, and courageous men have given patient, learned, and profound attention, and with results essentially satisfactory to their faith ; if the New Testament is an historic document in all its main facts and statements, which the most searching scepticism has not yet shaken from its essential credibility, and which every day only more confirms in its place of authority, then should we not pronounce unacquaintance with its pages, disregard of its facts, carelessness or indifference concerning its history, a great folly and misfortune, and not compatible with the moral and spiritual prosperity of any soul? And yet, under the general emancipation of the mind of this country and the world from authority, aided by the spirit of self-reliance which democratic institutions engender, and by a popular literature which has made standard works and solid reading very much neglected ; still further assisted by the tendency to scientific and mathematical studies, which the subjugation of the soil, the mining and manufacturing, the road-making and boundary-drawing necessities of the age have promoted, to the neglect of ethical, historic, and spiritual explorations, we have a wide-spread and deep-rooted skepticism, indifference, and neglect, united with a profound and measureless ignorance of the subject itself, touching the whole supernatural and historical character of Christianity. That part of the Gospel which accords with the doctrines of natural religion and universal morality we gladly and commonly accept; but the positive religion of the miracle-working, crucified, risen, ascended Son of God, with all the tender and affecting personalities of that peculiar, special, historic faith, we, as a generation and a race, as Americans and as citizens of the nineteenth century, have a disposition to reject, or what is worse, to treat with indifference or neglect.

Day before yesterday, the citizens of the village where my kindred dwell, were laying in the tomb a venerable man of over eighty years, of spotless life and character, a universal benefactor, and an honored and beloved friend—the first and most esteemed of their people. And I will venture to say, that not one person in the hundreds composing that intelligent New England community, gathered at the grave's mouth, knew that it was the anniversary of our Lord's death and burial, or would have attached, if they had been told it on the spot, any special interest to the tender and comforting coincidence. They are not knowing or thinking to-day that this is the morning of the Resurrection, and finding consolation and assurance in the glorious fact that it is not possible that any of his disciples, any more than himself, should be holden by the pains of death.

Is this well? Does a faith stripped of historic reality, disunited from its original facts and persons, promise to live and work in the human heart and life? Is it not asking too much of human nature to cherish in pure spirituality what God chose to communicate in a positive form? Can we afford to lose what is so fitted to win and impress the heart of childhood; to shape and attach the affections of youth; to captivate the imagination of the poetic and quicken the stolidity of the calculating, as the embodiment of religious ideas, truths, and doctrines, in an historic, personal, and ritual form? I seriously think, the loss of the church year, of the festivals and fasts of the Church, Christmas and Easter, Good Friday and Lent, a great detriment to practical religion—a loss to the sentiment of reverence, and to the public sense of the historic reality of Christianity, which is already, in conjunction with other causes, producing very alarming consequences in this country. You may not be aware that there are not half a dozen Protestant churches in the country, out of the Catholic, and Episcopal, and Lutheran communions, in which the great seasons of historic importance in the Gospel find any regular notice or commemoration, and that, imperfect as our own attention to these seasons is, it vastly exceeds what is common, and is indeed very exceptional. What, then, may we suppose to be the state of positive, historic faith, in the country at large? Is it not easy to be accounted for, why, in a sense of gasping weakness, a thirst for sensible images and external aids, the love of something positive and symbolic, shapely and protecting, so many worthy and tender souls, as well as so many strong and earnest ones, have gone from the communion of Protestantism into the Catholic Church, and from all other forms of Protestantism into the Episcopal Church? I frankly say, that notwithstanding all the doctrinal defects, and the notorious pulpit dulness of the English Church, it seems to me the most respectable form of public religion now on the globe; the best worth taking as a model;

better adapted to human nature and human wants, and with a better apparatus for self-perpetuation and extensive popular influence than any other of the existing systems. And it is for the reason that it best succeeds in blending the great facts and events of Christianity with the regular life of the people, keeping their religion always before them, drilling it into their daily habits and affections, and giving them the support of numbers, exactly agreeing with them in opinion, usage, and season.

At how few palpable points, on the contrary, except by purely and expressly personal application, and through a sanctified will, does our religion touch our daily habits and ordinary career? It gives us no book of prayer which is consecrated by universal use, and can be carried home, like a private chaplain, to become the authority and helper in domestic worship. It has no express teachings to be communicated at a well-understood season to all children. It has no rites of universally-conceded sanctity and importance. Do we baptize our children? It is a matter of private caprice; some will, others will not. Do we take the communion? It is a peculiarity which a devouter or more courageous few venture upon, but not a general dignified custom, toward which all are pressing. We have no season of confirmation, when youth, awakening to the sober responsibilities of life, are girded with strength by the special interposition of the Church. Our worship, too —how bald, how at the mercy of the taste and talents of the accidental occupant of the pulpit! how difficult to join in, when we do not even know what it is going to be! And with all the diversity of doctrine, usage, opinion—with all the slackness of authority—how can we expect to throw around the minds and hearts of our people the blessed restraints, and hopes, and fears, the supports and consolations of a positive, revealed, unchanging religion? God knows, we are not answerable for this unhoused, unnatural, and disembodied faith. It has come of a deep and grand necessity of the human mind, which felt instinctively, that at whatever cost, it must have *freedom*; that religion itself must stand aside, if human nature could not take a long breath in its presence. But we have now got freedom, abundant, generous, thorough freedom, so far as political or religious bonds are concerned, and now we want religion, faith, reverence, humility, teachableness, worship—want it immensely, immediately, and in great measures.

To get it, I am persuaded that we must turn to an historical faith in a revealed and supernatural religion. The world never did, and never will be able to live on natural religion—not that natural religion is not the very object of revealed religion, but religion and *a* religion are two different things. That the people may have religion, they must have *a* religion; just as that they may have government, they must have *a* government. And if we must have *a religion*, must it not be an authoritative, divine religion, not one made and shaped and set up by men like ourselves, but revealed and authorized by God himself? Such a religion we have in the gospel of Christ—an historical, precise, actual revelation. It is confessedly not a worship, as Judaism was, in which the sacred rites are literally and exactly prescribed, but it affords the materials and guides for a worship, in its positive facts and injunctions, in its ministry, its simple rites, its weekly worship; and, above all, in its extraordinary and affecting blending of all its truth, doctrines, and precepts with the person of Christ. This is the wonderful, providential peculiarity of our religion—well called Christianity, not merely because revealed by Christ, but because actually communicated by the facts and special developments of Christ's personal history and life. No man need fancy he can make a satisfactory summary of Christianity, or describe our religion, by stating the *principles* of the gospel; it were as easy to give an idea of a diamond, by announcing its mineral composition to be of pure carbon, and showing a bit of charcoal as a sample. Christianity is Christ born of Mary, Christ working miracles of love and mercy in Galilee, Christ dying on the cross, Christ rising from the tomb, Christ ascending into the open heavens. Mix with these facts the great truths of natural religion and eternal morality, and you have the gospel; but if you take the great truths of nature and the soul away from this connection, and think you carry the substance of the religion with you, you might as well take home the multiplication-table as the only absolute part of a difficult problem in mathematics, or an architect's plans, and expect to eat and drink and sleep in the paper house so skilfully and completely drawn in your portfolio.

My brethren, if you want to become practically religious, and to receive the substantial supports of religion, you must become Christians in the sense I have thus given—Christians, in that you are students, lovers, disciples of the historic, actual New Testament

Christ. You must know and love the records of his life ; you must associate your principles with his person and example ; you must run your faith into the form of his words, and fashion your calendar by the dates of his career. In this way alone can you realize any thing like the aid and support of a positive faith ; an external, palpable religion, a helpful and supporting worship. Because the imperfect and outworn creeds of Romanism have so successfully availed themselves of this law of the mind, do not imagine that the truth does not need to learn wisdom from the long and wonderful experience of the Mother Church. If any man believe in freedom, in progress, in essence, as opposed to dogmatism, fixity, and show, I more. And let none imagine that this solicitude about the external apparatus, the positive form of faith, the historic truth of Christianity, grows out of the least distrust of freedom or of human nature. It is a free human nature, a free, emancipated, and independent thought that prompts and enables us to look candidly at the wants of our souls—to elect what is good and necessary in the experience of the past, and to carry it with us into the future. If freedom or progress in religion, politics, or domestic life, means a thoughtless commitment of ourselves to the current of events, a blind sweep on the tide of the times ; if it involves the admission that "whatever is, is right," and safe and good ; if it implies disrespect of past experience, disconnection with our predecessors in faith and virtue—an ignoring of old wisdom and old truths—then I pronounce freedom and progress opposed to reason, enemies of humanity, and foes of God. But if freedom and progress mean the right and duty of the human soul to improve upon the past, to select and carry with it all that is sound and strong in ancient faith and practice, while we anticipate all we can of future good, and embrace eagerly all new truths, then it is of God, and is rational, Christian, and divine. Such a wise and holy progress will never succeed in leaving historic Christianity behind ; will never outgrow Christ ; will never long be able to dispense with the outward forms and helps of a positive worship, or the inwoven strength of the Christian with the secular calendar. At present we are in a chaotic and most unsatisfactory state. We entertain certain wild, spontaneous, undigested notions of freedom of thought, conscience, and affections, which, carried out fearlessly and to their natural conclusion, would land the country, the age and the church, in universal lawlessness, anarchy, and impiety. The state, the church, the home, would lose their sanctity, and no government, no worship, no marriage terminate the mad dream of untrammelled liberty in general license. Rapidly are we travelling that road. Our good men are no longer holding themselves responsible for the government, general or local, but are in fatal recklessness saying we wash our hands of the blood of the country or the city. Our most gifted and bravest religious thinkers are dwelling in exciting harangues upon the superiority of insight to revelation, of natural to revealed religion, of a free and spiritual over a regulated and embodied faith, while the few who dare to brave the instinctive, but ever and ever more feeble protest of society, are throwing doubts over the sacredness of marriage, and undermining the last stronghold of virtue in the American home. All this is natural, necessary, inevitable It is an inexperienced freedom, trying its rights; an emancipated human nature, seeing how far and in what directions it can safely go. But already the wounds and injuries which society experiences, so obvious in the crimes, the disorder, the impudence, the unhappiness of our social state—our children rude, irreverent, and presumptuous—our family relations unsatisfactory, cruel, and irksome—property and life unsafe—literature morbid, passionate, and violent—amusement spiced with crime and indecency—government suspected and convicted of bribery and corruption—religious institutions in the newer parts of the country neglected and despised—the best wit, literature, and art of the time thoroughly alienated from the Church, so that, as a rule, authors, historians, artists, statesmen, are neither church-goers nor professed believers in historical religion—all this, I say, necessary, unavoidable as it was as a tremendous reaction upon old world superstition and tyranny, shows us that we have misunderstood freedom, wronged human nature, and very much neglected the true conditions of domestic, social, and political independence. I do not say this, God knows, in any despair, or with any doubt of our recovery. When we understand the source of evils, and are alive to their existence, they are already half conquered. And *we are* beginning to see and confess that unregulated liberty, undisciplined freedom of thought, unhoused and unformalized faith, human nature setting up on its own account, without God and without Christ, are all, necessarily, failures. We are beginning to see that religion is not a spontaneous, self-protecting plant; that faith is not safely and wisely left to its own growth; that it will not answer for men to say or to think that it is of no consequence what they believe, or to cast themselves in a fascinating sloth upon their good and generous intentions.

No, no, my brethren; you must wear the voluntary yoke of a positive religion, a religion that exacts some reading, some study, some inquiry, some time, some sacred seasons from you—a religion which asks attention as a religion, and not only as a sentiment or a principle. You must not imagine that Christianity is everywhere and nowhere; every thing and nothing; a vague sentiment; another name for virtue; the mere synonyme of goodness and truth. It is a religion of facts, an historical, positive faith, supporting and illustrating and embodying its doctrines in the incidents of Christ's career, and demanding for itself visible incarnation in a discipline, a worship, and a church. I believe, and I assert it in full knowledge of all the supercilious sneers of advanced thinkers and emancipated spiritualists, transcendental or socialistic, that the decay of faith in historical Christianity and the visible Church is at the root of the chief evils of our country and age—is the thing most to be dreaded and regretted in the tendencies of the times—the chief enemy of our political, domestic, and personal happiness.

A lively faith, based on investigation, in the historic truth of the single event commemorated by this Easter morning, the resurrection of Christ, would change the condition of many a man's whole philosophy of life—his whole views of morals and piety—his whole theory of family government and the religious education of his children. For if the resurrection be a literal fact, the whole miraculous character of the Gospel is established; and that established, the relations of Christianity to human life, of Christ to man, become pregnant, practical, and imperative beyond all reckoning. It is no wonder a visible Church, a permanent ministry, a formal worship, a systematic discipline should be established, to enshrine, preserve, communicate, and apply such an astonishing and all-important relation as this. Our whole attitude of resistance, curiosity, suspense, hypothesis, towards Christianity, of proud self-reliance and self-satisfaction, is changed into an humble solicitude to receive and apply the divine grace, instruction, help, and salvation in Christ our Lord, by the simple reception into thoughtful and willing minds and hearts, of the great central fact of Gospel history, the resurrection of Christ.

That resurrection, as a Christian minister, I announce and proclaim to-day as a fact, a pure, proven, historic fact, a glorious fact, worthy of God, its author, and most welcome to man, its object. If it be not a fact, fling your Bibles into the fire; for they are deliberate teachers of falsehood. If it be not a fact, the apostles are conspirators in a fraud, and Christ is an accomplice of their crime. If it be not a fact, history is itself a common liar, and the learning and faith of ages are but proofs of the worthlessness and folly of human testimony and human inquiry. But if the resurrection be a positive fact, we have a religion indeed. Christ is our master and Saviour in no rhetorical sense, but truly and literally. The Church is not an institution standing in men's breath, a prejudice of past ages, and soon to be a memory of which wiser generations are ashamed, but a God-founded, eternal, and authoritative institution, standing with the family and the State, permanent and essential parts of civilization, ramparts and dykes which freedom must respect, lighthouses and harbors which human nature must support and endow, even with her last dollar and her last strength!

APRIL 12, 1857.

SERMON VI.

"THE WORD OF GOD."

"And the seed is the Word of God."—LUKE iii. 11.

IN sympathy with the season, I addressed you last Sunday morning upon the preparation of the spiritual soil for the seed; the opening and softening of the ground for the great Sower's hand, ever ready to fling its treasure into the open furrows. I propose now to follow up the analogy then traced between the showers of spring and the mild and subduing influences of God's providence, with a contemplation of the resemblances between the natural seed and the Word of God. But I must first enter upon a careful examination of the phrase, "the Word of God"; for in its perverted use lies the stronghold of modern error, the great obstacle to the progress of natural and simple opinions in regard to the will of our Creator and the teachings of our Saviour. At every step, the truth, as it beats in men's hearts, is blocked by some knotty text, which is assumed to call itself the Word of God, because it is contained within the covers of the Bible, no matter by whom it was said, on what occasion, or for what purpose. It is time this melancholy and obstinate superstition, which crowds and chokes the truth, were treated according to its deserts.

It was neither to the New nor to the Old Testament that Jesus referred, when he said, "and the seed is the Word of God." Not a page of the New Testament was then written, nor was it to his purpose to name the old Jewish Scriptures. It was of that Word, ever sounding in men's hearts, of God's voice heard in the conscience, felt in the soul, and illustrated and signalized in his own spirit and convictions, that our Lord spake, when he named "the Word of God." Free your minds at once from the narrow and modern sense in which the phrases, "the Word" and "the Word of God" are customarily used. "The Word of God" is not a printed or articulated sign of thought; a sound made by the lips, or suggested by a cipher. And it is a misleading and perplexing habit we have acquired or inherited of confounding *the words* of the Bible with "the Word of God," the literal syllables and sentences of the sacred book, with the mind, and will, and spirit of God, written in our natures and republished in our Scriptures. It is in the true interest of the Bible, and from a profound reverence for its essential truth and holy significance—from an ever-increasing devotion to its study, and an ever-growing feeling of its permanent connection with the progress of civilization, and pure morality, and sound religion, that I feel it necessary to discriminate with great and unqualified plainness between a true, and a superstitious, veneration for the Scriptures. The Scriptures are holy, but they are not holier than conscience, than reason; and those who attempt to make them so, desecrate God's Word in one place to honor it in another. The Bible is the *Word* of God, as the conscience is the voice of God ; but the *words* of the Bible are not the words of God, any more than the decisions of the conscience are the decisions of God. The mind, the will, the spirit of God, whose inspiration informed our consciences without making them infallible, has produced the Bible without making it perfect. He who studies the holy book in all its parts will discern a divine communication, a sacred teaching, an unmistakable guidance, running through and shining out of its complete tenor, as a river runs through a broken country, or as an expression of benignity, of law and order, of justice and mercy, runs through the diverse and often contrasted and puzzling effects of external nature. We must fasten upon the general effect, not the particular detail.

As it will not answer to separate and fragmentize nature, and pronounce each and every part, taken by itself, to be indicative of the benevolence of its author—as there are deserts and disorders, defects and contradictions, cruelties and monsters, poisons and miasmas in nature, which no doubt have their providential use, but of which no one is to be regarded as having a right to represent any portion of the divine design and character, any more than the grumbling drum or shrill fife in a grand orchestra have a right to assert an excellence of their own, distinct from that they owe to combination and a disappearance in the general effect ; so it will not do to consider each and every Old Testament story, or Jewish ordinance, or prophetic curse, or local argument, as in itself an expression of God's mind and heart, whether it be the deceptions of Abraham, the cruelties of Joshua, the debaucheries of David, the imprecations of the prophets, the historical mistakes of the evangelists, the imperfect science or rhetorical rudenesses of any of the sacred writers. It is with the Scriptures as it is with nature. " By the Word of God," says St. Peter, " the heavens were of old and the earth standing out of the water and in the water." Yes, and every thing upon the earth, and above and beneath it, was created by the Word of God ; but we do not on that account deem it necessary to admire, and curiously consider and maintain, as of equal value, and beauty, and instructiveness, all parts of nature—the disgusting and repulsive, or violent and cruel—as we do the lovely, attractive, mild, and generous operations and exhibitions of her hand ! We believe, and truly, that all parts of nature, duly understood, have a divine significance. We know that what are poisons to some creatures are the chosen medicines of others, and that the offal of the nobler beasts is the banquet of the meaner ones. But we rightly leave the poison to its true proprietor ; the offal to its natural owner. And it is precisely this that we ought to do with whatever contradicts our reason, or wounds our moral sensibilities, or shocks our Christian instincts and spiritual tastes, in that half-human, half-divine record of God's doings and judgments we call the Bible.

We are not to grieve the Holy Spirit by forcing ourselves to approve or justify any thing there which we do not approve elsewhere, nor are we at any time to think the words of the Scriptures have any authority against the general spirit of the Scriptures. There is no single text and no combination of texts, that has any right to control our judgment or opinions, when brought into antagonism with the ordinary and plain tenor of the whole book. The first thing to be assumed of the Scriptures is, that being the Word of God, they speak common sense, support common morality, breathe charity, uphold virtue, respect reason, are friendly to humanity. We are to assume, therefore, with all boldness, the impossibility of their teaching contradictions, cruelties, partialities, terrors, and riddles ; and if any knotty text, or harsh and bloody imprecation, or verbal absurdity, is brought to confound us and our reason out of the Bible, we are to treat it precisely as we do the things which offend our instincts in nature—spiders, or cobwebs, or bad odors, or toads, or tornados—get out of the way of them as soon as possible, as being offensive to our moral taste, our better knowledge of God's truth and God's language. We will not conceal the slaughter of the Canaanites by Joshua, nor David's curses on his enemies, nor Paul's quarrel with Peter, nor Peter's denial of Christ ; but neither will we approve them, nor quote them as authorities for our own conduct, even if they are recorded as having been done by divine commandment. We do not believe any of them to have been acceptable to God. We know that good men have honestly thought themselves acting under divine command, when they were really obeying only their own passions ; that even Paul verily thought it doing God service to blaspheme the name of Christ. But we are not going to resign our own enlightened sense of God's character, enlightened by this very Word of God, to bow before certain words which certain people, without any authority from Christ, have chosen to call plenarily inspired. For our part, we are too jealous for God's honor, and truth, and wisdom, to call any thing inspired which is not obviously true and good ; and if this is called presumption—if this is thought setting ourselves above the Word of God, or setting in judgment on God's Word—we can only reply, that it is base cowardice which makes us set the words of any book higher than the word of God in our souls ; that we cannot do it in reality, and do not do it, but only pretend to, emptily thinking something is to be gained by flattering an imaginary jealousy which God might have of human reason, that light which lighteth every man that cometh into the world, and which God himself kindled.

" The Word of God," in the use our Saviour and his apostles make of that phrase, never means the text and language of the Scriptures. It always means the mind, and will, and spirit of God, however made known. When an order or commandment from God—whether by a vision, a mental impression, a dream, or a conscientious impulse—is received, it is not the words or signs by which the direction is given, that are entitled to the name of " the Word of God," but the thing to be done, the truth to be welcomed, or communicated. The Word of God, moreover, is not the arbitrary command of God, but the wisdom of God ; it is a spirit, a temper, a truth ; not a regulation, a requirement, or precept, owing its value purely to its source. God being considered and assumed to be perfectly holy, true, pure, good ; his word is this holiness, truth, purity, goodness, considered as in any way communicated to men. Thus the creation, considered as full of wisdom, truth, and order, and divinely arranged to teach these to man, is just as much "the Word of God" as the Scriptures, for it is distinctly and repeatedly said that the world and the heavens, the earth, and all that in them is, were made by the Word of God. The truth is, the Word of God is God himself, speaking in any of his chosen tongues, whether by His works, His son, or His spirit in our souls.

Hear what John says: "In the beginning was the word, and the word was with God, and the word was God." This word was made flesh, and dwelt among us, full of grace and truth. Christ is the Word of God, and we must properly distinguish between our reverence for Christ and our reverence for his words. It is only as his words help us to see *himself*, his heart and soul, that we really reach the Word of God in him. He was greater, wiser, holier, than any thing he said, and it is to get at *him* that we study his actions and history as well as his words and precepts. The soul, too, is the Word of God. "Say not," says Paul, in the epistle to the *Romans*—"say not in thy heart who shall ascend into heaven, (that is, to bring Christ down from above,) or who shall descend into the deep, (that is, to bring Christ up again from the dead.) But what saith it? The word is nigh thee, even in thy mouth and in thy heart." Since the Protestant Reformation it has been convenient for the Church to cultivate a superstitious and exclusive veneration for the letter of the Bible, which is really fatal to any true and Scriptural idea of the meaning of the phrase, "the Word of God;" i. e., the truth, the wisdom, the love of God, considered as in any way declared to man. I pronounce this servile deference to the letter of the Scriptures a gross superstition, an insult to the divine reason, and to Christ's own authority. It is a miserable perpetuation of the Jews' soul-crushing worship of the very letter of the Mosaic law, which Christ in vain resisted and reproved. It is not only most dangerous to the progress and growth of the truth, to our perception of the real meaning and intent of God's Word, but it is quite as perilous to the real authority and sacredness of the Bible itself, with men of intelligence and courage.

The Bible owes its continued authority and influence to the fact that it *really contains* the Word of God; that in its various records flows down the full and vigorous river of God's truth and grace, in the history of a race peculiarly and providentially fitted to receive special communications from on high. Nothing can ever change or destroy the sublime merits and religious influence of the Mosaic dispensation; nothing outlive the strains of David's glorious harp; nothing take the place of Isaiah's exalted prophecies; much less can the record of our Saviour's life and conversations ever cease to win the profoundest reverence and gratitude of mankind. But the habit of confounding the words of the Scriptures with "the Word of God" will create secret scepticism as to the whole truth of a book, which it is falsely and superstitiously asserted claims to have been written page for page and word for word, by God or by God's immediate interposition. Every error, extravagance, inconsistency, mistake, contained in a volume, made up of the works of fifty different writers, in twenty different periods of history, is at once made an objection to the credibility and value of the book itself—a course as rational as to hold the fountains of the Hudson river answerable for the litter and offal discharged by the brooks and streams, the canals and sluices, that empty into its current ; or for the discoloration caused by the successive soils over which it flows ; or to pronounce it not a great, or beneficent, or God-given river, on account of these superfluities. Is it not navigable ? does it not fertilize the banks it flows through ? ventilate the city ? beautify and refresh a hundred towns ? Does it ever dry up, or fail to be healthful, nutritive, and benignant for all ? Is it not the great feature of the country through which it runs ? All this ; but there is feculence, and float, and cloudiness in its waters ! Shall we fill it up, then, and abolish it ? So would the narrow sceptics, the products of the narrow credulists, do, when they discover verbal errors, chronological mistakes, or even moral imperfections in the Bible. "What !" they exclaim, "the Word of God with errors in it ! We will have nothing to do with such an absurdity !" The Bible, we answer, is not "the Word of God," and the Word of God has and can have no errors in it. Well does Agur say, "Every word of God is pure. * * * Add thou not unto his words, lest he reprove thee and thou be found a liar." (Proverbs xxx. 5, 6.) But the Bible *contains* the Word of God, and much beside, as the Hudson holds its own waters and also the feculence and litter contributed by many poorer sources to its flood. God's Word is not responsible for the stuttering and stammering of those who have tried to speak it. Happily all their impediments and roughness of speech have not been able to conceal from the willing and reverent ear his real and genuine intent. The New Testament is the criticism and correction of the Old, and the life and character of Christ is the criticism and correction of what his disciples have said about him. The soul of man is a perpetual and lawful criticism, under a providential development, of all that has been previously thought and said. Life, experience, the unfolding of Providence, the progress of Christianity, all are bringing the Word of God out into purer and nobler relief from the mere words of holy writ, until finally, there shall not be one cloud of prejudice, superstition, or literality, to hide the noble, generous, humane, and welcome proportions of God's eternal Word.

Turn now to the analogy instituted in our text: "The seed is the Word of God." How instructive is the figure our Saviour here uses upon the point we have been examining! "And the seed is the word of God." The Word of God was sown by that great husbandman, our Lord, in the souls of men. The truths he taught and exemplified touching the paternal character of God, the sanctity of conscience, the beauty of holiness, the relations of loving service between man and his brother, the community of the race, the glory of self-sacrifice, the superiority of the soul to death—these were the Word of God, the precious seed he sowed in the hearts and souls of men. The mere words that contain these truths are the husk around them; the narratives in which they are found are often like the dead stalks and leaves with which the living germs have been harvested. These seeds are not to be eaten, nor are they to be stored away; they are to be planted. Their efficacy does not lie in the preservation of their present shape, nor in their power to propagate themselves, but in their fitness to *grow*—to draw nourishment from our hearts, and to become what other seeds become, plants, such as our Father hath planted. When the Word of God enters into the soul, it is meant to draw life from the soul; to have the thoughts, and affections, and experiences of men, act upon it; and while, like a living germ, it preserves its identity, and shapes the nourishment it draws to its own kind, it is itself affected and meant to be affected by the properties of the soil to which it is confided. The Word of God was sown in human nature, on its appropriate soil. The precious seed did not despise the ground it entered, nor could it have any growth except in that soil of human hearts.

Religion—from the Latin *religare*, to bind together—implies two parties. Man is as necessary a party to it as God; the juices and chemistry of the soil, as the vitality and power of the germ. The Word of God respects the soul of man, as much as the soul of man, the Word of God. Our relations with our Maker are reciprocal. He does not want slaves for his subjects, or bastards for his children, or a blasted and poisonous soil for his seed-ground; and therefore all those servile and debasing feelings which would prostrate our nature, vilify our reason, resign our freedom, abandon our judgment, in the presence of God's Word—as if the truth, the authority, the goodness of God, were to be honored by our self-contempt—are grounded upon a grovelling superstition. The soil for God's Word is freedom, reason, knowledge, trust, love; not self-contempt, timidity, cowardice, ignorance, creeping and self-falsifying. This is the barren rock, the sandy wayside, the shallow top-soil; not the deep, rich, generous loam. God's seed wants all man's powers, faculties, tastes, passions, as the noble soil for its growth. And there never was a greater and profounder mistake, than that which has made the human intellect stand a trembling coward in the presence of the divine Word. Reason shrinks abashed before the very light that kindled it, and all the sacred affections and natural instincts of men creep into their holes, like newts and bats at the rising of the sun. Let human infirmities, sensual passions, selfish thoughts, and malignant feelings, be afraid of God's Word; let them feel their inability and their folly in attempting to judge it. But for reason, conscience, humane feelings, universal sympathies—for them to think they are not on a level with God's Word, being indeed God's Word, too—for them to think they have not as good a right to question the Scriptures as the Scriptures to question them—for them to feel abashed and humbled in the presence of God's spirit, or God's truth—for them to meet the messenger of the Lord with bandaged eyes, and to think it an honor to his message to listen to it in chains—this is, indeed, a veritable part of the worship of the crocodile and the serpent—of the horrid fascination of the ugly—the worship of mere power, more venerable as it is more arbitrary.

It is to inspire fresh confidence in reason, in conscience, in our highest instincts and sympathies, that the Word of God comes to us, just as it is to bring out and turn to use the vigorous properties of a noble soil, that good seed is sown. Nothing has falsified and perverted religion like fear, distrust of natural conscience, and instinctive sentiments of right. What is luminous, courageous, aspiring, and generous in man, is the great interpreter of what is divine and eternal in God. The Gospel has too often been an acorn planted in a flower-pot instead of a field, and shivering its petty vessel before completing the first stage of its own gigantic destiny. It has been belittled by the dwarfishness of its receivers. Thus the Word of God has been bound, until men seek free thoughts, free speculations, free hopes, and free aspirations, anywhere rather than under its sad and enslaving influence. As if the Word of God were not in highest and noblest sympathy with all thought, aspiration, generous faith, and high resolve ; as if the oak loved the winds and storms of the sky, the wild motion of its own swaying branches, the fitful changes of the clouds, more than the Word of God loves the fresh play of human faculties, and human speculations, and human hopes.

If there is any time when we ought to be free, strong, brave, determined on the use of our own God-inspired natures, it is when we seat ourselves to the study of the Scriptures. Every particle of mind and heart and conscience, every instinct of truth, every experience of life, should then be in active exercise ; for the word is seed, and a dead soil, to which light and heat are denied, out of which vitality and richness have gone, can do nothing to quicken or nourish the germ ! To hide our doubts, to quench our curiosity, to force our faith, to try to believe what is not credible—do you imagine this to be an humble, acceptable frame of mind ?

Does the Word of God ask to be treated with gallantry, forbearance, and politeness? Ah! this is what degrades it, like a courtier's false courtesy to the woman he means to betray. No; the Word of God asks our manhood, our experience, our largest thoughts and grandest feelings, to judge it. It says, Come, let us reason together! It puts itself upon trial. It asks to be received into the genuine, hearty, and robust faith of our souls, like the truths of nature, science, and life. It wants a warm strong soil for a vigorous and aspiring seed; and until we learn to read the Bible and study religion, in the great exercise of all our powers, in the fullest light of all our experience, in the most rigorous application of common sense, God's Word, and God's truth, and Christ's cause, will be in the eclipse they now suffer—will be not the light, and help, and glory of the strong, the resolute, the thoughtful, and the free, but the refuge of the superstitious and ignorant; the policy of the prudent, the machinery of a priesthood; the useless and decaying heirlooms of a venerable past; the source of convenient prejudices for governing the weak-hearted and the feeble-minded. The seed is the Word of God.

Will the day ever come, my brethren, when the sacredness we now superstitiously confine to the Scriptures shall be extended to the soul of man, his reason, his affections, his conscience; and to Nature herself—each of them a book of God, all volumes of one work, truly coherent, equally divine, and not intelligible except in connection and harmony with each other? The faculties of man are divine seeds sown in the soil of his nature and circumstances. Reason, conscience, instinct ! what nourishment and growth do they not find in our human lot ! but how, under all circumstances, they preserve something of their original type, and what a divine independence and indestructibleness they possess—how incapable of long perversion and long concealment they are ! We are often under the foolish mistake that reason has some power to choose its own arbitrary conclusions ; conscience and will, some authority to settle their questions by caprice. Men, no doubt, are capricious and arbitrary, but reason and conscience are never so. It is by acting against reason and conscience that we exhibit our wilfulness and folly. When figs produce thistles, and thistles figs, we may expect reason to bear folly, and conscience to countenance immorality. No ! reason and conscience are seeds sown in us, having a divine and peculiar type, and destined to produce a peculiar fruit. They may find a bad soil, a poor nurture, little sun and little rain, and they will produce very imperfect fruit ; but then it is not their fault, but the fault of the soil they find. They are always good seed ; always sacred and divine in their rights, and no more liable to abuse and perversion than the written word, being themselves the unwritten word—the elder Scriptures in men's hearts. When we want to know what God made us for, we are to study the seed he planted in our nature, and we are not to believe any account of our origin or destiny, be the same what it may, which contradicts the Word of God, spoken in our mental and moral constitution. With the brave Paul, we should say, Though an angel from heaven preach another Gospel than this, let him be accursed.

As the faculties of man are planted in his nature, so are the truths of revelation and the doctrines of the Scriptures planted in the Church, to grow there, and show what they are by what they come to. And they have grown! grown and outgrown many of the prejudices of men. Every now and then, becoming used and attached to the stage of growth reached at some highly luxuriant season of faith and practice, perhaps centuries ago, men have said they had attained their exact maturity, and must not grow any further! Further growth, in short, became troublesome. Their roots had struck down into the earth and invaded the foundations of men's dwellings, or their branches had towered and spread till they threatened to push over some interest that once asked their shelter. And then, what a clamor about latitudinarianism, and going too far, and getting out of people's reach, and radicalism, we have had! The truth is, *seeds* are nothing unless they *are radical*, and all growths are poor unless they are broad and wide, that is, latitudinarian. The Word of God, in Christ's life and character, is the most vigorous seed in all history. Its root is the oldest, and its head is likely to be the largest. It is a tree whose leaves are for the healing of the nations. In God's name, let it not be given over to the pruning and hacking of theological horticulturists. Let it not be shut up in a conservatory of moral herbalists. It is not a sensitive plant, but a vine native to all countries, stronger than any winter, and which asks only freedom and room, to bear continually richer and nobler fruits for all peoples.

Let nature teach us confidence in God and in God's protection of his own Word. The seed is the Word of

God—aye, that natural seed that men are now planting in their gardens and fields. God speaks to the earth, in the significant language of these tiny seeds, finer than the monotonous dots of the telegraphic tongue, which in every minute and indistinguishable shape, we carry in our hands, and sow and plant in the soil. How dead and unmeaning they look—how similar in form, and taste, and smell, and appearance ! and yet how miraculously each keeps the specific secret God has committed to it ! how loudly all finally tell the precise word he spake to them ! "Go," says the Almighty to the seed which is his Word, "cover this field with golden wheat ; go make that gay with tasseled corn ; stand here in glistening flax ; spring up yonder in bursting bolls of cotton, and far down under the sun, in bristling ranks of juicy cane ; become the orange grove of Louisiana ; the nutty wood of Illinois ; the luscious pineapple of Cuba ; the oak forest of Canada. Be always what I sent thee to be. Speak out, in language that every eye can read, the word which ungrown, no man, prior to experience, as he beheld the seed, could interpret !"

Do we ever sufficiently consider, that all the culture, soil, sun, rain in the world, could do nothing to feed or clothe us, without those wondrous and divine germs, those words of God, that by a mysterious organization unfold themselves from specks of darkness into plumes of beauteous vegetation—into gorgeous flowers and lustrous fruits, spicy shrubs and mighty forests—in every form pleasant to see, and every flavor goodly to taste, and every medicine potent to heal, and every lesson significant to read and saving to learn, because it is the Word of God in his own great print.

Let God's Word in our faculties,—let his Word in his Scriptures, have equal freedom with his Word in nature! Let them all have free course, and be glorified. He will see to it that every seed produces its own kind, and that his Word, while it shall never cease to grow, shall never outgrow the intention of him that spake and it was done, that commanded and it stood fast.

MAY 9, 1858.

SERMON VII.

PRIVATE INTERPRETATION.

"Knowing this first, that no prophecy of the Scriptures is of any private interpretation; for the prophecy came not in old time by the will of man; but holy men of God spake as they were moved by the Holy Ghost."—2 PETER i. 20, 21.

PROPHECY has two offices and signs: first, the foretelling of future events; second, the outspeaking of forgotten, neglected, or unknown truths. In this it corresponds with inspiration, which has a twofold character, in that it communicates, first, a *knowledge* not otherwise possessed or attainable by its subject, and second, in that it communicates a spirit far above the level of the prevailing spirit of an age or neighborhood. Inspiration, religiously considered, contemplated as part and parcel of revealed religion, must have both these attributes—a knowledge beyond the times, and not possible on any other theory than that of special illumination; and a spirit which is absolute in purity and truth. In this respect, it is distinguished from the inspiration of genius, the poetic, literary, artistic inspiration, which, in its purity, and truth, and beauty, we feel to be truly divine and immortal. We have no need to disparage that inspiration, or to say that it is not from God, the creator, the author of all genius, the fountain of all beauty, and the original of all truth. But we must and may say, that it is positively and definably distinguished from religious inspiration, in that while one depends upon felicitous organization, propitious circumstances, and is the natural development of the original powers of its subject, the other is independent of these circumstances—often in direct antagonism to them—and is the result of a power external to its subject, which uses him as its instrument and organ. It is not necessary to the completeness of this idea to accept such vulgar and demeaning notions of inspiration as imagine its subject to be acted upon by God, as a pen is acted upon by its holder, and which, in the modern necromancy, present us with individuals possessed as by devils—speaking, acting, knowing, they cannot tell by what power external to themselves. Inspiration, in its scriptural form, does not use human beings as if they were machines. When God used fig-trees, or loaves of bread, or dead bodies, or swine, to illustrate his power, he made fig-trees act like fig-trees, loaves like loaves, swine like swine. He used machines as machines ; but when he used men, he used them as men ; and if he inspired them, they became inspired men, not inspired machines. He inspired their souls—their whole manhood—not their memory, nor their fingers, nor their toes. Of course, their inspiration then became in a manner subject to their human attributes, suffered their limitations, but it also had their intelligence, their sanity, their self-consciousness, connected with it ; and usually, instead of making them eccentric, crazy, odd, unintelligible, just in proportion to the degree of it they possessed, did they become calm, wise, intelligible, sensible, and universal.

The ordinary popular view of religious inspiration, which makes man the mere tool or pipe of the Almighty, with all its mechanical defects, is truer to the reality of the case than the so-called advanced view, which confounds religious inspiration with the possession of superior natural insight and purer gifts of mind and heart. The man who sees no difference in kind between the inspiration of Paul and the inspiration of Milton, because they both agree in possessing souls vastly elevated above the common herd, ought to be consistent with himself, and pronounce Milton greatly Paul's superior. Milton was utterly incapable of Paul's mixed metaphors and offences against taste and propriety ; was possibly his superior in mere intellectual faculties, in poetic imagination, and general culture ; and in power as an exact reasoner. Perhaps, in general elevation of mind, in rigor of conscience, nay, in moral and spiritual excellence, he may have been his peer. But Milton was not marked out, selected, and used by God, as the organ and instrument of a positive revelation—as the missionary and founder, under his master, of the Christian Church—and he did not possess inspiration in the sense in which Paul possessed it, in the least degree. Paul had, in connection with his supernatural knowledge and impulses, something of Milton's inspiration also, though to no such high degree ; but Milton had nothing of Paul's ; and the consequence is, that while Paul's writings have entered into and become a part of the religious life and sacred study of the whole world, and will continue for ages the revered depository of ever-fresh wisdom and help ; Milton's works —great, glorious, immortal as his fame is—are confined to the appreciation and use of a select class, and belong to the delights, not to the uses, of the world ; are the luxury, but not the bread, nor the medicine, of men.

Prophecy is another name for inspiration, and what is true of inspiration is true of prophecy. The sacred writings, both old and new, contain literal predictions of coming events—predictions which natural sagacity could not have surmised or guessed. But these predictions were made by men who, to the supernatural knowledge of the future, added as extraordinary a moral and spiritual elevation above their times. And, now, men of extraordinary moral and spiritual elevation venture to call themselves prophets, when they are wholly without the other quality or sign of their office—the power of predicting future events. It is only when these two distinct attributes meet, that we should grant the name or authority of prophet ; and I venture to affirm that they never have met, except in connection with the positive revelations of the Jewish and Christian Church. I know very well the pretensions made by or for various seers, of whom Swedenborg is the most respectable. But, when the human race, in its deliberative and mature judgment, acting with the gravitating power of its own instincts of need and truth, rejects any claim to religious inspiration, be sure that no clique of eccentric, or excellent, or ingenious persons, however persistent, will be able to make that claim good.

And this brings us back to the text, and the significant description it furnishes of the true method and test of prophecy. "Knowing," says the Apostle Peter, "this first, that no prophecy of the Scriptures is of any private interpretation; for the prophecy came not in old time by the will of man; but holy men of God spake as they were moved by the Holy Ghost."

Does not the text seem to place us on Roman Catholic ground? We have heard, from our youth, a great deal of the right of private judgment. It was the battle-cry of the Reformation: it is the fortress of Protestantism. The right to read and judge the Holy Scriptures, each man for himself—what so distinctive, what so precious to our liberal Christianity? And is it an attack upon this privilege that Peter makes in the text? Are we to call in synods, consistories, creeds, churches, popes, to tell us what we may believe and what we must reject? what is the true and what the erroneous interpretation of every prophecy of the Scriptures—prophecy here having both senses of prediction and lofty teaching? Were it so, Protestantism should at once enter the confessional, and ask, upon her knees, absolution from her sins; for she has exercised the right of private judgment more and more, and clearly intends to maintain it. She is not only heretical, but contumacious, if private judgment be an apostolic forbiddance.

I need hardly tell you, however, that the right of individual search into the meaning of the whole matter and teaching of the Scriptures, is not only a right demanded by our self-respect, but commanded by the Old and New Testaments themselves, in many passages. "For whatsoever things were written aforetime were written for our learning, that we, through patience and comfort of the Scriptures, might have hope."[1] "Continue thou in the things which thou hast learned and hast been assured of, knowing of whom thou hast learned them, and that from a child thou hast known the holy Scriptures, which are able to make thee wise unto salvation, through faith which is in Christ Jesus."[2] "But whoso looketh into the perfect law of liberty, and continueth therein, he being not a forgetful hearer, but a doer of the work, this man shall be blessed in his deed."[3] "Search the Scriptures; for in them ye think ye have eternal life, and they are they which testify of me."[4] What does Paul say of the Bereans? "These were more noble than those in Thessalonica, in that they received the word with all readiness of mind, and searched the Scriptures daily, whether those things were so."[5] "Yea, and why even of yourselves judge ye not what is right?"[6] "Let the prophets speak two or three, and let the other judge."[7]

It is not at all against the right or duty of the private soul to search and try the Scriptures, and come to such conclusions as earnest and accurate investigation warrant, that the apostle is speaking in the text. It is not as a rebuff to inquiry, but as a help to it, that he sets up his most important principle. What he teaches is not that private men should not interpret the Scriptures, but that they should not put private interpretations upon them, if they expect to understand them. He means to say, that the Scriptures contain a religion for the public, for all men, as well as for each

[1] Rom. xv. 4. [2] 2 Timothy iii. 14, 15. [3] James i. 25.
[4] John v. 39. [5] Acts xvii. 11. [6] Luke xii. 57. [7] 1 Cor. xiv. 29.

man; that they were not written by private men, in the indulgence of caprices and eccentricities of their own; but inspired by God, written by holy men of old, who spake as they were moved by the Holy Spirit—written in accordance with a plan, in subjection to a design, under the animation of a spirit, which contemplated the common, public, universal wants of humanity; not intended for local, national, denominational, family, individual appropriation; nor to be warped and moulded, pieced and pared, modified and adapted to temporary, partial, local views and feelings; used to carry out personal ends and aims, to elevate particular persons, to indorse private plans, or to give way before the weaknesses, the peculiarities, the special necessities of this or that individual; but to be received by each, and understood by each, in their absolute, universal, impersonal, impartial, unchangeable character. The private interpretation of the Scriptures, which Peter denounces and forbids, is like that interpretation which, in the Roman Church, would furnish a selection for the use of the laity, lest they should discover how little countenance the common and general teachings of the Bible give to the peculiarities of that Church; or that interpretation which would, in the Episcopal Church, conceal the fact, that in the apostolic age *all* ministers were *bishops;* or, in the Baptist Church, would have a new translation of the Bible for the sole purpose of mentioning the private interpretation of that sect, touching the subjects and mode of baptism; or of the teachers of the Tri-personality, who would maintain a corrupt text, and resist all new translations, because sure to be unfavorable to that unscriptural dogma; or like those interpretations of Unitarian rationalists, who, because they dislike miracles and supernaturalism, would make it out that the apostles themselves did not believe in them. Any interpretation of Scripture is a private interpretation, which is adopted and maintained to shield a private interest, whether the slaveholding divine proves the identity of Hebrew serfdom with South Carolina negro-holding; or the aristocratic governments of Europe keep the people down, in favor of the honor of all kings and the sanctity of all anointed brows, with texts of Scripture; or the judges of Salem yield to popular outcry against miserable women, because of Saul's trouble with the witch of Endor; or, when any ingenuity, or learning, or position is abused in twisting the universal, common, and ever-applicable general sense of the Bible into apologies, warrants, and excuses for private and wrong ends, or personal and partial objects.

The doctrine of Peter, that no prophecy of the Scriptures—meaning, I repeat, both prediction and instruction—is of any private interpretation, is admirably accounted for by him in the text; for he says, the prophecy came not in old time by the will of man, but holy men of God spake as they were moved by the Holy Ghost. The will of man is not the source of the religious truth set forth in the Scriptures; nor, if one might say it without irreverence, even the will of God. There is something deeper than will. Will, by its essence, is something free; and if free, then liable to change, carrying in it the possibilities of arbitrariness or caprice, the limitations and characteristics of personal existence. But the Holy Spirit, the eternal truth, the law which governs God's nature as well as man's, is not free ; it is fixed ; it is not arbitrary, but absolute. It cannot be strengthened by will, nor weakened by want of it. It carries its own authority in itself, and needs no warrant and no argument to maintain it. It is the ground of a common rational and moral nature, shared by man with God, that makes any intercourse between them practicable, renders revelation possible, and forms the basis of all religious obligations and hopes. When the Holy Ghost speaks, it must speak in the only language common to God and men. It must speak in terms of reason and conscience, of the impersonal reason and the impersonal or public conscience. If any thing pretends to come from God, which is irrational, immoral, or merely of private and temporary importance, we pronounce the pretension false. And if any thing which has come from God is interpreted in an irrational, immoral, private, and local manner, we pronounce the *interpretation* false and fleeting.

Oftentimes, it is true, absolute truths and permanent principles are draped by revelation in decaying costumes and perishable colors, precisely as the eternal moral law of the Jewish Scriptures was hidden in the ritual of the Hebrew people ; and it then becomes a difficult work—a work of time and experience—to separate the permanent from the perishing, the precious jewel from its worthless setting. Indeed, it was against the Jewish prejudice of private interpretation, the obstinate pride of birth and race, which chose to consider the local and temporary wrappages of universal and eternal truths as essential parts of their religion, and so to reject Him who came to publish (to make public and universal) their hitherto *private*, because merely national, religion, that Peter first used the language of the text. We need not wonder that the glorious universality of the moral law, the sublime doctrine of the unity of God, the absolute truth and permanent reality of the Mosaic revelation, gave it power to uphold and make authoritative the external staging and mere mechanical apparatus of the Jewish local code and ritual; nor need we deny the providential, and, so far as the Jews were concerned, the authoritative, charactei of their national law. But it is perfectly easy now to distinguish what was designed to come down, from that which was designed merely to bring it down; the unchanging message from the accidental messenger; the living water from the muddy channel; the public and universal truth in the Old Testament, from the national and limited religion of the Jews.

"Private interpretation," as thus illustrated, not only of the Scriptures, but of all true and sacred and worthy things, is forbidden, not only by God's own word, but equally by the general constitution, the social and affectional nature of man, his sympathetic, and even his æsthetic, connection with his race and with his Creator It is favored only and always by human selfishness, blind passion, egotism, and sensuality. See how the great significance of nature, its commonwealth of truth, beauty, and happiness, meant to lie open to the use, enjoyment, and instruction of all men, and to give breadth, purity, disinterestedness, and elevation to their whole being—see how this great letter-book of God is spoiled by *private* interpretation. One set of divines, to carry out and support their private interpretation of the Scriptures—the interpretation which those private scholars, St. Augustine and John Calvin, gave to them—must have a private interpretation of nature, according to which they declare it a world in ruins, manifestly lapsed from its original beauty, a world in which neither the mineral, vegetable, nor animal kingdoms are as God made them, but all awry and askew, the crust of the earth a jumble, the woods and fields, nay, the very sky itself, a snarl of discordant and perverted elements! Is this what the common heart proclaims? Is this what David felt when he exclaimed, "When I consider thy heavens, the work of thy fingers, the moon and stars which thou hast ordained, what is man that thou art mindful of him, and the son of man that thou visitest him?" Or Christ, when he taught, "Behold the fowls of the air, for they sow not, neither do they reap, nor gather into barns; yet your heavenly Father feedeth them. Consider the lilies of the field how they grow; they toil not, neither do they spin, and yet I say unto you that Solomon, in all his glory, was not arrayed like one of these." Or Paul, when he said, "For the invisible things of him, from the creation of the world, are clearly seen, being understood by the things that are made, even his eternal power and godhead; so that they are without excuse, because that when they knew God they glorified him not as God, neither were thankful." Is that what every sensitive child, every poet, nay, at his best and happiest hours, every human heart has felt about the beauty and glory and divinity of the external world?

It is mere private interpretation that introduces these vain imaginations. And it is equally private interpretation which represents human nature as essentially corrupt, disordered, and perverted. No mother thinks it of her child; no lover of his mistress; no man of his friend. The imperfections, the limitations, the inexperience, the weakness, the faults of human character, those who love human nature best, are readiest to see and feel; and they see them with sympathy, compassion and tenderness. They are not anxious to hide them from God himself. And, blessed testimony that it is, we cannot find a word to express all that is sweet and noble, unselfish and tender, in our relations with our fellow-beings—a word the very use of which is itself worth a thousand of the arguments of private interpreters, who demean and disparage our nature—we cannot find a word fitly to describe the highest duties and the greatest privileges, and the most common properties of our being, except the very word that names us—I mean, the word *humanity.* Look further at the perversity of private interpretation of the Scriptures—of the Scriptures alike written on parchment and in the human heart, both inspired, though, in different ways, as we have seen. Here is this great and glorious world about us; this wide and magnificent world; this green and teeming earth, with all the wealth of our culture added to the products of its spontaneous fertility, the beauty which God the first shaper, and man his agent and the invited continuer of his work, have given to it! To how much perverse private interpretation is this common possession and inheritance subject! How greedy the scramble, how incessant the ingenuity and toil to seize upon, fence in, and appropriate as much as possible of this free territory! How common the delusion that *private* property in the planet, the exclusive ownership of a bit of the world, and a large bit, too, is the secret of its best or only enjoyment! Far be it from me to spurn the very idea of property. It would be to deny the very principle I am proceeding upon; for property and the sense of it is universal, therefore legitimate and true—a Scripture. But it is not the only, nor the whole, nor the most important truth, and immensely remote from being the beatifying truth. It is a necessity, a condition of social existence, and therefore to be submitted to. But he who keeps his soul freest from that lust, least open to its fascinations and delusions, who is least anxious to own and appropriate the planet, or any part of its product, beyond a reasonable defence against dependence, and a reasonable provision against want, is the richest man! Private property! there is not a greater delusion in the world than that which ascribes any considerable part of the happiness of life to the things that a man possesseth in his exclusive right.

And equally fatal is that private interpretation of the eternal Scripture, written in ourspiritual constitution, which makes men think themselves wise in their own thoughts, strong in themselves, independent of their race and their God. Man is really wise, only as he is in communion with his race, and with his Saviour and his Creator. Intellectually, those who study originality in the sense of peculiarity and private unlikeness of opinions, are eccentrics—comets, not planets. The true originality of mind is that which goes back to the origin, to the divine fountain, the source of all fresh thoughts, and which exhibits thoughts not new in themselves, but only new in the freshness of their pristine lustre. There is nothing less vulgar than the thoughts which are common to all men. Common sense is not the sense which is common, but the sense which is *in* common—the sense which, once distinctly set forth, is most commonly seen and felt to be sense. Common sense! it is to all other sense what the ocean is to the lakes and ponds: the medium of intercourse, the source of health and purity, the immense reservoir of practical and life-directing wisdom. The Lucullus, who spends a fortune on his private fish-pond, might as well think to substitute it for the Atlantic, as the dainty doater on his ingenious notions think to make them take the place of the great common thoughts that enrich and sustain the intellect and sanity of the world.

And what is true of thought is true of feeling. Private interpretation is the bane of the heart. Narrow sympathies, exclusive tastes, a self-humoring, self-coaxing spirit, how it belittles and impoverishes life! The man who mistakes *himself* for his race, *his* family for God's family; who interprets all claims and duties by their relation to his own private feelings or domestic interests—how he shuts himself out of the kingdom of humanity—how poor the bargain he drives with his race! This is his proposition: "If you will not ask me to love you, I will not ask you to love me!" As if the flower should say to the sun, if you will not expect me to shine on you, I will excuse you from shining on me! What can a man do for the world, compared with what the world can do for him? What can a man give, compared with what he can receive? His own single heart can make all hearts pay it tribute. It is indeed more blessed to give than to receive; to love than to be loved; to love God, than to have him love us; to love man, than to have all men loving us. But the rivulet cannot pour into the sea more than it receives from the clouds, nor they, more than they drew from the ocean. And the heart that would love much, must have a universal sympathy, must draw in a mighty and ceaseless love from all within its reach.

Ah! my brethren, suffer yourselves to be moved by the Holy Ghost. It is no spectre that will steal upon you in the dark and whisper riddles, but a bright, glad spirit, clothed in light, that pronounces universal truths in everywhere intelligible language. The Holy Spirit is the friend and ally of reason; for reason came from the same fountain. It is the elder sister of conscience. It is the original of humanity. It is always generous, rational, wide, common in its precepts—not sectarian, provincial, temporary—never odd, wild, fitful. It is calm, clear, solid, like the crystal throne of God. It will rebuke all your egotisms and self-seeking, your prejudices and partialities. In its light you shall read the Scriptures into the sweetest and noblest utterances of immortal truth; you shall understand Jesus Christ as the liberator of conscience, the emancipator of mind, the Saviour of the heart. God, the all-in-all, shall prove to be, not your Father only, but *the* Father, the All-father, as the Germans tenderly call him. You shall not any longer, see men as rich and poor, black and white, learned and ignorant, but as members one of another, brethren, children of God. You shall not be chained and imprisoned in private interpretations of any kind, but have the freedom of universal truth and universal goodness and universal love, for your joy and glory and habitation forever.

FEBRUARY 13, 1859

SERMON VIII

DOCILITY.

"Whosoever, therefore, shall humble himself as this little child, the same is greatest in the kingdom of heaven."—MATTHEW xviii. 4.

"Take heed that ye despise not one of these little ones: for I say unto you, that in heaven their angels do always behold the face of my Father which is in heaven."—MATTHEW xviii. 10.

THE disciples had been asking Jesus, who was the greatest in the kingdom of heaven. He, anxious to reprove in them those first risings of ambition and jealousy which prompted the inquiry, took a little child and placed him in the midst of them, and replied, "Whosoever shall humble himself as this little child, the same is greatest in the kingdom of heaven." The difference between the kingdom he came to establish in men's hearts, in which the virtues and graces are the only nobles, and that kingdom which the Jews in general sighed for, and in which they looked to be princes, was such that he could not hope for any understanding of it on the part of those who did not place themselves before his instructions in the docile attitude of children. It was indeed the humble origin and position of the first disciples, a lowliness of state which had done little to encourage the conceit of knowledge, or to stimulate the pride of opinion, which made them alone open to the approaches of the Gospel. Well was it asked, Have any of the Scribes and Pharisees believed in him? Certainly not. They were all too deeply committed to prevailing systems of opinion, and too closely interwoven with the web of ecclesiastical authority and prejudice, to be able even to contemplate the possibility of any truth in Christ's teachings. Therefore he was left to the grown-up children of the day for his earliest and only teachable followers, to the plain and simple day-laborers, the fishermen and tax-gatherers, the common people, who heard him gladly. They did not know enough, perhaps, to mark the inconsistency between what he taught and what was taught in the synagogue; and with their simple souls bound in the cords of no social or scholastic necessity, they only knew that it sounded true and sweet, and moved their hearts and consciences, and awakened their veneration and confidence, as nothing they had ever before heard had done. It must be confessed, my brethren, that minds and hearts like these were just as easy to mislead as to guide aright; for superstition and error seek their disciples in the identical places where truth finds her best followers. A child's mind, by its very openness and simplicity, its irresisting and pliable state, like a virgin soil, is equally prepared to receive and give quick growth to tares and wheat, truth and falsehood. Doubtless the false Christs had obtained their followers from the same class of persons—the child-like, uncommitted, unoccupied minds of Judea—from which the true Christ obtained his. But this proves nothing against the worth of their simplicity, though it might rightfully weaken the value of their testimony, considered merely in the character of legal evidence. But Christ neither asked nor needed such evidence. He asked and needed just what he found in them, an unresisting medium, through which to convey his truth, a yielding clay in which to stamp his image. And it is what Christ *left* the apostles, not what he found them; not their faith in him, but what that faith did for them; what he put into their minds and hearts, and rapidly recreated them to be—those strong-souled, pure-hearted, heroic, heavenly-minded men they became after two or three years of intercourse with him—able, by their deeds and writings and testimonies, to give the world its majestic and lovely and authoritative idea of the Saviour—it is this that makes them the grand and permanent witnesses of Christianity.

Christ's followers were all, or mostly all, for a long time, of that humble, child-like class, whose judgment is, by general consent, regarded as weak; who, by their approbation or discipleship, lend no authority to the opinions they adopt. It was the effect their adherence to Christ had upon their characters, the sacrifices it inspired, the good sense it developed, the spirit it infused, the elevation it communicated, that gradually made their testimony so valuable. The more ignorant they were, the wiser it proved their teacher, when they improved so rapidly under his hands; the more credulous and excitable their hearts, the more credible the prophet who planted such unsuperstitious and rational opinions only in their all-believing minds; the less distinguished, intelligent, trained, disciplined, logical they were, the more of all these must he have been who could so soon, from such crude, unfurnished men, have raised up a band of truly dignified and noble, and venerable followers. And this has always been the evidence Christianity has sought to stand on, the evidence of its fruits. It has never, from the first, appealed to cultivated, scientific, philosophical minds, and begged their examination, scrutiny, and testimony in its favor. But it has appealed to the changes it has wrought, the temper it has communicated, the lives and characters it has produced, wherever it has been, on any grounds, accepted heartily and in a confiding spirit. No candid person will deny that Christianity has for the most part owed its triumphs to the teachable and receiving temper of those whose power to judge of its evidences by scholarly inquiry, logical tests, and historical investigation, was weak and without claim to respect. But, in this particular, it is on a level with all other great and important things. The practical faith of the world, in all the truths of nature, government, economy, science, rests not upon logical and statable foundations, but upon experience. We do not use wheat, because Liebig has discovered just how much gluten, farina, starch, sugar, there is in that grain, and what a wonderful adaptation it has to the human constitution; nor tea and coffee, because modern science has found a chemical nourishment for the brain in the phosphates they contain; but because experience has proved wheat the most wholesome and permanently useful article of human food, and tea and coffee pleasant and salutary drinks. We do not navigate by the stars, because astronomers have proved their fixity of place, and can unfold the laws of the stellar system; but because experience, from the earliest time, made them the natural and necessary and reliable guides of ocean travellers. Theories are built upon experience; and long after we have adopted opinions, customs and beliefs, scholars, thinkers and theorists come in to tell us *why* we have adopted them; and then we begin to think them and their reasons to be the causes or foundations of our opinions and usages, which, in fact, preceded them and their evidences.

The Gospel, as a religion, asks from men, who hope to profit by it, the same childlike spirit now it did in the early times. It appeals no more to the inquisitive and speculating, the logical and reasoning faculties, now than then—not because the finest understandings, the most scientific minds, can refute it, or that it has any thing to fear from them, but neither has it any thing to hope from them. We make a great mistake when we suppose Christianity to be on trial, or that God has submitted his Gospel, any more than his other universal gifts and mercies, to human reason, to decide for or against it. He planted Christianity in the moral world, just as he planted wheat in the natural, to grow, with or against the consent of men; to be a great and unspeakable blessing to those accepting it, to do vast services for society, to cheer and save men. And here it is, doing its work. Skeptics and infidels do nothing to overthrow it: they only overthrow themselves by their assaults; philosophic believers and learned apologists do nothing to uphold it: they merely satisfy their own minds, and may satisfy the minds of a few others, by their investigations. But we might just as well think the stars shone by the permission of astronomers, or spring came by leave of the almanac, or conjugal and family life existed by social contrivance, or poetry were a trick of fanciful scholars, or truth the result of an agreement among philosophers, as to think religion, and the Christian religion, a conclusion of learned theologians and writers on evidences, and the best wisdom to which religious thinkers had arrived. Christianity came into the world by nobody's leave, and it stays here by nobody's leave. It sprang up a living fountain, by the Word of God, out of the heart of Christ; and it has flowed on a river by its own divine affluence, fed from the will and the love and the wisdom of God. There is, indeed, not only no harm, but great good, in examining its origin, and early circumstances, the genuineness of its records, the secondary causes of its spread; but all such examinations, when successful and favorable, have been made by men already believers in it—by those who had felt its power and loved its sacred influence. An impartial, unprejudiced explorer of its truth never existed, and never could exist. The man who could say it was a matter of absolute indifference to him whether Christ were an impostor or a prophet, whether the Gospel were true or false, would be a man not to be believed, or, at any rate, not to be trusted with such an inquiry. It is impossible, in respect to matters intimately connected with the affections and the moral and spiritual nature, not to have the intellect and the judgment anticipated by the heart and the great instincts. There are glorious prejudices, holy and awful truths, which precede all ratiocinations; and he who pretended to examine into the reality of his own existence without a prejudice in favor of it, or into the reality of right and wrong as fundamental distinctions of the utmost significance, or into the existence of virtue, or the genuineness of Christ's character, or the holiness of God, with the same sort of candor and uncommitted judgment with which he explored the evidences for and against a scientific theory, or an historical hypothesis, or a matter of literary criticism, would be so obviously self-deluded, and out of just relations with himself and truth, that we should at once pronounce his inquiry worthless, and his conclusion vain.

It being settled, then, that the great thing the Gospel wants, is not our testimony for its sake, but our submission for our own—not to triumph over our doubts, but over our affections, that it may bless our lives and characters—you will appreciate the godly jealousy it has of mere curiosity and criticism and acumen and intellectuality, and why it tells us still that we must become like little children, if we would know and feel its power and become heirs of its kingdom. We, in our conceit, imagine that it is because religious truth and Christian faith are afraid of our knowledge and criticism and shrewdness and knowledge of the world, that it asks us to lay them aside when we come into its presence. It is not afraid of what these will do to *its* prejudice, but what they will do to *our* injury. It does not want them dazzling our eyes, and dangling their superficial impertinence before our higher and holier powers. It wants to speak to our deep moral instincts, our permanent and sacred affections, our spiritual nature; and therefore it bids our noisy logic and lip-wisdom, our intellectual attainments, all be quiet, that our souls may receive its simple and sublime communications, and feel its glorious power. After we have caught its lesson, and drunk in its spirit, we may try it as we please, by history, science, philosophy, and it shall stand every test; but none of these shall help us in advance. There is no denying that this is precisely the course which superstition and imposture, delusion and folly, would take, if they were seeking possession of the human soul. They would say: unless you believe before you examine, you cannot receive the testimonies we have to offer; unless you will exclude the prying, curious, suspicious temper you bring for your protection against imposture, you will see and hear nothing, you will learn and know nothing. And the reason why they say this, and why this counsel has dangerous influence in the case of superstition, is because it has lawful power in the case of genuine truth. Superstition addresses a sound principle when she makes this appeal, but uses it in a perilous way. Let me illustrate the distinction. An exquisite picture—Murillo's Madonna, if you please—is to be exhibited, and you are taken into a room to see it, in which the light is carefully shut out from all quarters but one, and from that only just so much admitted as the artist knows to be suited to the revelation of its highest beauty. In this precise light you see its wondrous loveliness, and feel its charming and exalting truth. You recognize the painter's claim to his great reputation. Again: a picture-dealer wishes to give a factitious appearance of age, merit, value, to a pretended original. But he, too, wants the light excluded, the special quantity only admitted, and the picture looked at only in a very carefully arranged way. He aims to deceive, and succeeds. Are you, therefore, to deny that a special light and a carefully directed light is essential to the perception and enjoyment of the picture of real merit? And so it is plain enough that the spirit of confidence, frankness, and simplicity, in which alone the highest truths are to be seen, is the spirit most open to abuse, and of which error takes most advantage. But until a rich soil is undervalued because it is favorable to weeds, or a sweet disposition because it is easily betrayed, or a believing spirit because it is taken in with facility, we must not deny that a child-like docility is a proper condition for the reception of the Gospel, because it is an equally natural condition for the reception of that which is only imaginary and unreal.

In an age of light and thought and criticism, of shrewdness and common sense, the best results of worldly experience and intellectual culture are those which teach us not to rely upon such experience and culture for our deepest and most saving convictions. It is very certain that wisdom, which is the bright consummate flower of knowledge, is very like, in its tastes and even its conclusions, to that unconscious simplicity or docility of mind which precedes all knowledge. The wise old man is again a child. He has the humility, teachableness, modesty, and faith of a child. How beautiful and touching it is to see the soul, which has been strained out of its place by worldly experience, the biasses of party and the pride of opinion, settling back, with the relaxed efforts of a weakened bodily vigor, into the more natural feelings and childlike opinions of youth! I know that we are sometimes accustomed to attribute this return to early tastes and feelings to a decline of the faculties, to the loss of intellectual vigor, to weariness and weakness of mind. But what is that strength of mind worth which merely sustains us in unnatural and eccentric postures of thought? what that originality which separates us from homely and universal truths? what that brilliancy which is due to the sparks struck out by our conflict with wisdom? How plain is it to riper souls, that half the smart and noisy and striking thought of the world is false and hollow, while the unshowy, sober, and substantial sense dwells with the unpretending and the unobserved! Moral qualities are infinitely more essential to the perception and estimate of facts, than intellectual qualities. It is desirable, indeed, to have acuteness, sagacity, discrimination, in the observer; but how much more to have candor, the love of truth, and the strictest scrupulosity in stating it. What philosophers, or men of science and learning, could have filled the place of the apostles in reporting the life of Christ? They would have obtruded their theories and schools of philosophy, and tried to make a fine and striking and coherent story out of the case; and what would have become of that inimitable portrait of Christ and Christianity we now derive from their transparent sketch? illiterate, unskilful, broken, and confused, but with the most precious proofs of nature, reality, and genuineness in its very defects.

My brethren, it is so with the understanding and reception of the religion of Jesus Christ. If you desire to know what this blessed Gospel is, to receive it, understand it, and live in and from it, you must approach it in the spirit of little children—you must lay aside your pride of understanding, your worldly wisdom, and dearly-bought experience. They belong to a quite different class of pursuits—are valuable only in a very different sphere from that of religious experience. If, after eighteen centuries' experience of its fruits, we have not made up our minds to trust Christianity—if we are disposed to be wary of it, and to stand on our reserved rights—we are practising the same folly that a bright and confident youth would be guilty of, who should go to see the master-pieces of art, architecture, sculpture, painting—and at once set up his raw taste and judgment against the testimony of time—stand before the Apollo, or the Moses of Michael Angelo, or the Transfiguration, or the Parthenon, not to correct his own ignorance, form his own taste, and drink in the humbling lessons of beauty and truth they embody, but to indulge his self-opinion, criticise their defects, and dispute the verdict of ages. Is it to lay aside reason, to shut the eyes and open the ears, to bow to mere authority, that we are recommending in respect to our religious faith? Not at all. The reason is never so sound and active, the eyes never so clear, the judgment never so reliable, the man never so much in possession of all his powers, as when he says to himself, I am a child before God—an ignorant, dependent child, who feels his profound need of instruction, his inadequacy, by mere self-directed thought, to penetrate the secrets of faith, hope and charity; and who thankfully, humbly, trustingly opens his soul to the lessons of the Great Master. W do our souls despite, we really disparage and despoil them of their highest worth, when we deny them the sagacity to know and take their humble place in the presence of a personage like Christ, their true attitude of love, reverence, and trust, before a religion like that of the Cross. It is a more than earthly faculty, this faith that humbles and exalts the soul. It rests upon a sublimer evidence than that of sense ; and, because it cannot interpret into propositions intelligible to all minds the grounds of its confidence, do not suppose those grounds to be fanciful or unreasonable. When the soul of the thinking, disciplined, scientific, and all-accomplished man, makes itself like a little child in the presence of its Maker, sits at the feet of Jesus with an air of waiting and tender discipleship, admits the reproofs of the Gospel with an unresisting penitence, and unaffectedly feels that humility, lowliness of mind, love, are profounder acquirements than all that the schools and academies can bestow—then we have a glorious and most instructive union of the highest intelligence with the most childlike faith. How beautiful, how affecting, how suggestive is this spectacle. "Let not the wise man glory in his wisdom ; neither let the mighty man glory in his might. Let not the rich man glory in his riches ; but let him that glorieth glory in this, that he understandeth and knoweth me."[1]

"Take heed," said our Saviour, in illustrating in the context, the necessity of a childlike spirit and temper in the religious inquirer and Christian disciple—referring, doubtless, to the humble origin and poor, mental furnishing of his then chosen disciples, which made

[1] Jer. x. 23.

them objects of contempt to the learned and great—"Take heed, that ye *despise not one of these little ones* (these children in worldly wisdom and scholastic accomplishments); for I say unto you, that in heaven, their angels do always behold the face of my Father, which is in heaven."

Oh, my brethren, there are diviner and purer sources of wisdom than any within the exclusive control of the educated and the great. Whatever dependence the mind may have on learned teachers and books, the soul has immediate access to its source, and its source has direct communication with it; so that, informed by the spirit of truth, the meanest faculties have bloomed into wisdom, and the most uneducated and unfavored persons discovered an all-furnished nature. Exactly what our Lord means by saying that *their* angels always behold the face of his Father, I know not; but that every man, in a lowly and humble temper of soul, has a messenger from God, waiting to instruct him—an infallible and heaven-inspired teacher, I fully believe. Whether it be that these our angels are our own souls, which, as they came from God, and indeed have never left him, may be considered as really still before his throne, gazing into his face, and ready to report to us, in the first lull of passion and wilfulness, at the first moment of humility and teachableness, what they see and know; or, whether we are blessed enough to have each a guardian angel, who is charged with our salvation, and forever waits for the opportunity to catch our now preoccupied and diverted attention, who shall say? But the practical truth is the same. Every man carries in himself the seeds of eternal truth, the hints and suggestions of a divine life and character. Would he heed his own heart, would he allow his conscience to be heard, would he obey his better instincts, he would be wiser in one hour than all the learning of schools and the experience of the world can make him. Irreligion, selfishness, inveracity, pride, sensuality, jealousy, hatred, envy—who ever unlearned these in the world, or in the library, or in society, or the company of the famous and the brilliant? An angel from heaven must teach them: the soul must see their falseness and folly for itself. It is a moral and spiritual light that can alone illumine the path of salvation. All our darkness is a bandage we wilfully bind over our own eyes; all our difficulty, is made by our self-will. Were we willing to know and to do the truth, it would flood our souls. Had we the simplicity of apostles, we should share their illumination. And it is this principle which accounts for the wonderful re-creation of the soul, sometimes produced suddenly by powerful religious influences. It takes no more time to open the eyes of the soul than the eyes of the body; and the prospect is always ready. There is no such wonderful change in life possible, as the change from self-conceit to humility, from pride of opinion to utter teachableness, from the attitude of one that turns his back upon divine truth, to that of an earnest pupil; and that change is a change of will, which may take place in an instant. You do not know, you do not believe, perhaps, my brethren, that there is a veil over the minds of unchristian men, the sudden raising of which would reveal a world as new and lovely and inviting as that which the blind man, restored miraculously to sight, would behold in a summer's day on the fairest spot of earth. You do not see the world the child of faith sees—sees here, sees everywhere. It is not superior intelligence, acuter intellect, longer study, that opens this world. It is only simplicity, humility, lowliness of heart, that reveals it—these are angels that can behold the face of the Father in heaven ; and they become our angels, our guardians, inspirers and illuminators, from the moment we welcome them to our presence, or cease to shut them out from our souls.

FEB. 14, 1858.

II.

GOD AND HIS PROVIDENCE.

II.

GOD AND HIS PROVIDENCE.

SERMON IX

THE ABODE OF GOD AND CHRIST IN THE DISCIPLE'S HEART.

"If a man love me, he will keep my words: and my Father will love him, and we will come unto him, and make our abode with him."—John xiv. 23.

No one can have read attentively the few middle chapters of St. John's Gospel without a sense of the spiritual entanglement in which God and Christ, the Holy Spirit and the human soul, are there involved. You will notice, with surprise, that I add to the usual catalogue of divine persons, the human soul. Yet it is only custom that justifies your surprise, for the New Testament brings the soul into as close a union and oneness with Christ, or God, or the Holy Spirit, or all of them together, as it does either of the others with the rest. It is indeed strange, that among the variety of ingenious theological systems, there has not been one based not on a Trinity, but a Quaternity, the human soul forming the fourth person in the ineffable association. Perhaps as sound arguments could be adduced to prove the equality and oneness of the soul with God, as the equality and oneness of the alleged persons in the ecclesiastical trinity.

We are exhorted to be one with God, even as Christ is one with the Father. We are said to be *in* God, in the same terms in which God is said to be *in* us ; now, to have Christ *in* us, and then to be *in* Christ—and in short, are so inextricably mixed up in our spiritual relations, as to make it quite impossible to say which is which, and what is what, when we seek to distinguish the operations of the human and divine, the direct and the indirect influences of the Holy Spirit, the paternal and the filial elements in the Godhead, the motions of the Holy Ghost, and the motions of the God-created soul. "At that day"—meaning the day when his disciples should fully obey him—"ye shall know," said Jesus, "that I am in my Father, and ye in me, and I in you ;" and again, in the text, "If a man love me, he will keep my words : and my Father will love him, and we will come unto him, and make our abode with him."

It is far from my present intention (and may it be far from any and all the religious meditations of this place) to attempt any navigation of the ice-bound, wreck-strewn sea of metaphysics, in search of the passages that connect the great oceans of that spiritual globe we call the Godhead. It may be as curious an inquiry as that which has carried so many baffled expeditions to the Arctic seas ; but if rewarded with success, (which it never has been,) it is difficult to see how it could be any more practically useful to the moral navigator in his voyage to heaven, than a North-west passage would be, when found, to the commerce of the world.

A close attention to this subject—and any other would be useless to the hearer—will serve, I think, to dispersè, or, at any rate, to set in their true character, many of the discouraging and perplexing irrationalities of religious statement, now current in the Christian world.

I suppose the sort of moral complexity, or, to speak more correctly, the kind of indefinite fusion, not to say confusion, among the persons and relations of the divine and the human, found in the New Testament, gives us a most useful and instructive hint as to the actual constitution of the moral and spiritual world ; of the fluid relations, the inter-dependence, the hearty sympathy, the perfect co-operation and communion of God, and Christ, and good men. God, and Christ, and the Holy Spirit, and faithful human souls, are related in so many ways—are so much one in thought, and feeling, and conduct—interchange so naturally and easily their mutual influences, that it becomes quite as impossible to distinguish their separate beings and define the boundaries of each, as to mark the precise lines which divide its gulfs and bays from the ocean, or to say whether it is the rivers that feed the sea, or the sea, with its mighty exhalations falling in rains and snows, that feeds the rivers. When Christ says, "Believe me, I am in the Father and the Father in me," he describes an interpenetration of being, a completeness of mutual possession, which ought not to be wholly unintelligible to any two human hearts that have so given and received,

received and given, as not to know which is the container and which the contained. And when, in like manner, he speaks of his disciples, "I in you, and you in me," he describes a similar community of feeling, in which the relations are too subtle and thorough to be the subjects of exact measurement, or of any more specific description.

The spiritual world, my brethren, of which, by the possession of spiritual natures we are now inhabitants, and to which God, and Christ, and angels belong, is, doubtless, in its unity and closeness of relations, copied and illustrated in the unity and mutual dependencies of the material world. It does not seem strange to us that the elements should know each other and conspire with friendly sympathy to one result. Let the mountains heave their heads ever so high, the sea knows how to overtop them with the plighted clouds, and through her mighty syphons, to pour the ocean back upon the hills from whence it came. The earth feels the wants of every tiny fibre that strikes into her soil, and from her great laboratory, feeds and medicines the root with an exquisite chemistry that learned science reverently adores. Or is it the plant which knows her own errand, and in the dark selects her own peculiar property from the mother's swarthy breast?

The air is, in its agitation, the locomotive power of nature; in its constitution, her food. How impossible is it to overstate, or even to state, the completeness of the relations among the powers of outward nature? or to arrange in any scale of relative importance, elements which are alike indispensable, and for the want of either of which all the rest would be useless? Is it the oceans that surround the earth, or the earth that divides the oceans? Is it the air that nourishes vegetation, or vegetation that purges the air? Where is the beginning, what the order, of the constitution of physical nature? As well might we seek the beginning of a circle, or the starting point on a globe. Each part of nature runs into and is lost in the other parts. The earth flows into the sea in the diluvium of her rivers, the sea mounts by her vapors into the air, the air descends by her clouds into the earth, and thus the eternal circuit, not without constant difference and improvement, is forever going on. In like manner, the mineral elements of the earth are taking shape in plants and animals, all by necessary decay, destined to give back their constitents to the globe, though not without such changes of place and circumstance as by their perpetual revolution must help on a career of progress to its consummation. If we imagine the circuits of the material world to have no end but their own repetition, we misread geological and chemical science, which show a beautiful work of improvement, not a mere process of change, to be going on in nature.

Moreover, in this community and co-operation of nature's forces and faculties, a union, in which it is impossible to trace the lines where the elements or kingdoms join, or leave, each other—there is, nevertheless, no imperilling, no confounding, of distinctions. Things are not the less separate and characteristic, because they have relations the intimacy of which it is impossible to interrupt. Birds, fishes, beasts, plants, stones, are none the less distinguished and specific, because there are fishes that are hardly distinguishable from beasts, and plants that fall within the definition of minerals. The union, sympathy, and roundness of nature, does not exclude or endanger her beautiful variety or manifold individualities. Now, doubtless, the spiritual world is really the basis and cause of the visible world. At any rate, our minds instinctively trust to the analogies between them, as if, by the highest law, they corresponded as substance and shadow. The sympathy, the modes and degrees of community in the material world, hint, then, at the nature and laws of the sympathy and community in the spiritual world. If so, the spiritual world is a whole. Its component parts sustain settled, organic, and necessary relations with each other, and these relations are involved in the very nature of the different elements that compose it.

Thus, the communion and intercourse of the soul with its Maker and Saviour is not accidental, contrary to analogy, and to be regarded as unreal, because it is confessedly mysterious.

We may wonder how it is possible for the human soul to sustain relations with God and Christ, and wonder the more, if we cannot very distinctly trace the nature and form of these relations. It may appear to our rude apprehension of such mysteries, a very indefinite form of statement, to affirm that obedience to conscience, aspiration, truth, gratitude, wonder, veneration —all of them certainly human acts—are just as really points of contact with God, interpenetrations of his spirit, possession of him and by him, as though we laid our very hand upon him, and had his everlasting arms palpably about us. Yet this is the testimony of the spirit. It is not obvious to sense, it is true, for the soul has its own senses ; they are not bodily senses ; its own language ; it is not a scientific one. For the spiritual world, in which the soul is always living, is a world having its own laws. Its intercourse, friendships, sympathies, are different from, because higher and nobler than, those of flesh and sense. But let us not suppose them less real. No candid mind will deny that the communion or intercourse with God, which the soul has in prayer, is a vastly less describable and definite kind of intercourse than that we have with an absent friend. And the difference is not merely one of degree : it is a difference in kind. The most spiritual and devout minds, provided they possess an intelligence competent to observe and discriminate their own inward acts, will feel this difference most. But they also will be the best satisfied that this difference should exist, will soonest discover that it is founded in the very nature of spiritual things, and is a higher and more satisfying, not a lower and less sustaining, kind of intercourse, than a more definite and palpable one. In like manner, the communion with Christ, which a spiritual disciple comes to know and enjoy, is a communion which is attained by a gradual experience of the Christian life. Living in this world with the moral and spiritual ends commended to us in the Gospel, struggling with our own hearts and with outward circumstances, and at the same time reading and reflecting upon our Saviour's career, until his conflicts, trials, victories, his words and ways, sink into our memories, and grow familiar to our thoughts and affections, we gradually come to blend his life and our own together. Sometimes we go back and live over with him his sorrows and joys ; sometimes he comes forward and lives over with us our trials and successes ; until our several beings grow into one, and it is difficult to say whether we are in Christ, or whether Christ is in us. Continuing on in this way, we live into Christ and Christ lives into us. We understand him more and more, love and venerate him more and more, and he yields us more and sweeter influences. Does any one say that this is an intercourse of fancy, of imagination, of feeling ? I reply, that under these names you describe the law of spiritual intercourse ; and that fancy, imagination, and feeling, are the senses by which the soul holds its relations and communion with the unseen ; and that you have done nothing to prove this intercourse unreal by thoughtlessly disparaging the instruments by which it is carried on, having only shown, what is not denied, that it is different from ordinary intercourse.

If we revert a moment to the possible communion of the soul with God, we shall see this, perhaps, more clearly. What is the history of a religious mind's intercourse with God ? It has its various stages and processes. It begins, in a religious childhood, with comparatively gross and external ideas. God is in the sky, seated on a throne, a venerable Being in human form. It is enough for childhood. By degrees, as we begin to know ourselves by our minds, and not by our bodies, we find the external image of the Deity growing more dim to our thoughts. We shrink from a conception which limits and humanizes an infinite and perfect God. As we contemplate the divine attributes and character more and more, the Deity gradually moves from his throne in the skies, or rather expands his presence, until his works seem everywhere pervaded by his Being. Then we partly, though perhaps never entirely, lose the instinctive tendency to look *up* for God, rather than *about*. Finally, with the development of our own souls, God, whom we have been seeing in nature, now begins to appear more distinctly in our own hearts and consciences. For, with spiritual development, we are moved, by we know not what commanding quality, to reverence and fear ourselves, and slowly we discover that the ground of this reverence and fear, is God in us. From this time our communion and intercourse with God is more intimate, though perhaps not more definite. For it is not the law of the spiritual nature to require an increasing definiteness. Indeed, the contemplation of God in nature, and especially in human nature, in our own soul, so increases our knowledge and love of his character, so moralizes and exalts our notions and our faith, that we cease to wish to walk by sight—that is, supported by those definite and describable conceptions which the timid, unknowing, unspiritual mind requires. We heartily and cheerfully acquiesce in the manner and degree in which God chooses to be known and to be seen. A spiritual instinct teaches us that the character of our intercourse with him is of a higher and nobler sort, a more inspiring and nourishing communion, than one of a more definite kind. We adore and love what is obscure and unrevealed in God as well as what is plain and seen. And thus, without having made the least progress in breaking down the barriers which hide God's personality from our senses, without having attained any miraculous or describable vision of God, we do attain, if we strive for such a blessing with the obedient efforts which it so infinitely rewards—we do attain to a kind of intercourse or communion with God, which is inexpressibly sweet, sustaining, glorious, and real. If any man tells me this is dreamy, intangible, imaginative, I answer him, that his very soul is dreamy, intangible, imaginative. Let him show me his soul; bound it, prove its existence! The relations and intercourse of the soul with its Maker must partake of the soul's own nature and indefiniteness. If God be as real as our own souls—if our intercourse with him has all the reality belonging to thought and affection—what more can we expect or wish? And this is the actual truth: that those who seek God and Christ, find them in a way, and to a degree which satisfies the wants of the soul, in precise proportion to its faithfulness and spirituality. "If any man love me, he will keep my words: and my Father will love him, and we will come unto him and make our abode with him."

The abode of God and Christ in the loving and obedient human heart! Oh! my beloved brethren, I wish it were in my power to satisfy you how real and true this language is, spiritually and believingly received. Remember that the soul is made by God and for God; that he is always in it, though we see and feel him not. Remember that Jesus Christ, our Saviour, is our Saviour from the foundation of the world; that our moral and spiritual salvation has from eternity laid in the knowledge and adoption of his temper and spirit, and in a life substantially conformed to his. Perceive, then, that to dwell with God and Christ is not to dwell with strangers; and that for them to take up their abode in us, is not for them to enter into a stranger's door. God and Christ are always seeking us, and our blind souls, in the groanings and dissatisfactions of their life-long wants, are always, if unconsciously, seeking them. Nature, with all its inarticulate voices, with all its symbols, and whispers, and beckoning hands, is but God's shadowy form, his veiled figure, his choked, paternal voice, seeking his child, like blind Isaac, struggling to lay his dying hands on Esau's head. Society, with all its divine order and teachings, its nursing care, its schooling apparatus, its developments of love, and mercy, and protection—what is it but God, trying to put his attributes into such simple sentences that the dullest soul may spell him out! What is history, but God's presence, reflected on the walls of sense, and passing in shadow, magnified and prolonged for the slow, inapt perception of mankind? The Church—why, what is it but Christ's body? the pierced feet in its persecuted progress, the bleeding hands in its repulsed embraces; Christ's body, still warm with his spirit, still near to his disciples' touch, willing still to be crucified, always dying, always rising and ascending; Christ with us, preaching, loving, warning, beseeching, still making disciples, taking new Johns to his bosom, telling other denying Peters, with thrice-repeated forgiveness, to feed his sheep; feeling the treachery of new Judases, lifting fresh Magdalens from the ground, and raising many another widow's son from the grave.

In every way, my brethren, by constitution, by circumstances, by inheritance; as the offspring and heirs of God's earth and the outward universe; as rational, moral, and spiritual beings ; as the heirs of past history ; as the subjects of a mysterious and sacred providence ; as the possessors of the Christian Church ; as the owners of the Bible—in every way we are bound up with God and Christ, and cannot escape our blessed imprisonment. If we but knew the things that belong unto our peace ! Whether we will or not, *they* love us, bless us, possess us ! But we can only consciously know and feel this possession and blessing, by giving them our obedience and service. "If a man love me, he will keep my words : and my Father will love him, and we will come unto him and make our abode with him."

The harmony and union of nature, the relations and co-operations of her forces, have no hindrance from self-will, from folly and vice ! Her snows resist not the returning sun, her springs refuse not to flow, her buds to burst, her birds to sing, her grasses to grow green, when Spring leads back the year, grown young in his winter grave, and calls on all the youth in nature's sympathetic breast to give him fitting welcome ! There is no obduracy, no discord, no disunion in these ! But into the spiritual world, in which even now our souls are living, enters this Satan among the sons of God. Sin ! this wilful, capricious, discord-breathing, obdurate, and selfish private heart, that will not join the chorus of divine praise, that will not be at peace with God, that will not let Christ bless and save it ; that madly, blindly—and oh ! how ignorantly and pitiably ! —thinks it knows its own way, its own peace and interest, better than its gentle and holy Master, who pleads in its secret bosom ; better than its God that entreats it and yearns for it, and bears and forbears, and ceases not to whisper, and beckon, and entreat its obdurate egotism and suicidal alienation from the truth!

Oh, my brethren, what shall make us willing to give our houseless Saviour a shelter in our bosoms—our spurned God a temple in our hearts? Are we not old enough to have learned the hopelessness and despair of unbelief, and of unloving, untrusting hearts? Is it not a dark and wretched hell enough that we have already reached, in our selfishness and sins, in our unrestrained lusts and passions, that we seek a lower and more dreadful depth! Are we not alone and solitary, and forsaken enough in our present irreligion, inhumanity, worldliness, and frivolity, that we would isolate and chain ourselves down in a narrower dungeon, by new hardness of heart and longer contempt of God's law! Turn ye, then, turn ye, for why will ye die? Ye know not the company ye are disowning, the harmony ye break, the glorious guests ye bar out! God and Christ are waiting to make their abode with you! Could you look into some hearts that are gathered here to-day, you would soon know the tender secret, the sacred, blissful reality of this society! You think God is far away in the heavens—Christ at his side. Oh! much more are they now here in the souls that have given a hearty, trusting welcome to their approach. They have come and joined the blessed circle in which the humble, loving, believing human soul forever sits—sits in a half-unconscious, because in so familiar and natural a companionship with God and with Christ. For do not suppose, ye faithful, pious souls, that feel in your humility that these words do not describe you—that dare not, will not permit yourselves to claim that you are the witnesses of God's presence and Christ's communion—do not suppose that your misgivings, your disclaimers, your unconscious piety, baffles the penetration or confounds the doctrine of him who speaks to you. To the simplest, deepest piety, such as yours, religion has become so natural, that it loses its strangeness; life, so universally sacred, that its altar disappears; God, so loved and known, that his presence pervades without notice; Christ, so accepted and formed in you, that his personality is dissolved in yours. You know not God and Christ and your own soul apart, so interfused and blended has obedience, and love, and faith, gradually made them. You wait not the withdrawing of any veil to reveal heaven. It is here. Nature, society, providence, life, humanity, all have become divine! God and Christ dwell in you and you in them so fully, that they seem yourself; and it is mainly in the reverence, the humility, the humanity, the love, the truth, the goodness you know and feel, which you exercise and show forth, that it is apparent to all that you have been with Jesus, and that God is dwelling in your heart. Thus does the ripeness of piety return to the simplicity of childhood, and religion mature into the blessed unconsciousness in which it begins. Lost in God, identified with Christ, the noblest and sweetest faith is half ready to doubt its own reality, because the chains of duty have lost all their weight, and the faces of the blessed ones all their strangeness! Comfort yourselves, ye lowly children of love, with these words. Let us, who are not of them, aspire to a piety which thus saturates the soul, and remember who it was that said, "If a man love me, he will keep my words: and my Father will love him, and we will come unto him and make our abode with him."

MARCH 4, 1854.

SERMON X.

"THE KINGDOM OF GOD."

"Whereunto shall I liken the kingdom of God? It is like leaven, which a woman took and hid in three measures of meal, till the whole was leavened."—LUKE xiii. 20, 21.

THE influence of that kingdom of God, of which the risen Saviour was the corner-stone, upon the kingdoms of the world—the influence of Christianity upon the history of man since the first Easter—could not be more aptly described, than in the words of the text. The slowly transforming power of the Gospel upon society and civilization, has been that of leaven upon the lump, raising up and sweetening the whole mass. Our Saviour had previously compared the kingdom of God to a grain of mustard seed, which a man took and cast into his garden, and it grew and waxed a great tree, and the fowls of the air lodged in the branches. We have, then, a double clue to the meaning our Lord intended to convey. It was clearly this: that his truth and power, though feeble and unpromising then—a little leaven, a grain of mustard seed—was destined in its consequences to be mighty and universal—to leaven the whole lump—to wax a great tree ; that this influence was to be gradual and unobserved in its processes—steady and patient in its work—but thorough and general in its effects.

I do not propose to prove and illustrate this more general proposition now, but to advance to a more personal theme.

What is true of the relation of the Church to history and civilization, is true, also, of the relation of Christianity to the private soul. The truth which the Gospel has for the individual man, is a truth which is designed to bear the same relation to the natural and congenital truths he already possesses—the influence the Gospel wishes to exert upon him, bears the same relation to his original faculties and affections—that the leaven does to the meal. Religion—and we mean the religion which Christ teaches, and illustrates, and communicates—sustains to human nature and human character the relation of the leaven to the meal ; and *vice versa*, human nature and human character are to religion, what the meal is to the leaven. I know the danger and the dishonesty of pressing scriptural analogies beyond the intention of their original employer—and I do not wish so much to found what I have to say upon the authority of our Lord's comparison, as to use it for the illustration of a truth evident enough and quite demonstrable from general considerations.

In the progress of this discourse—designed to correct and refute prevailing errors of religious opinion, not by contending with them, but by illuminating the region whence they spring and where they reside—I shall aim, under the guidance of the text, to show three things:

1. That religion is for man—not man for religion; the leaven for the meal—not the meal for the leaven.

2. That religion is to be known and valued for its effects—not for itself; the leaven hid in the meal—seen in the loaf, and not in itself.

3. That religion is for our complete humanity and whole life—not for any separate or partial experience, faculty or end; the leaven hid in the *three* measures of meal till the *whole* was leavened.

1. In the first place, religion is for man—not man for religion. The meal is greater than the leaven, and the leaven is for the sake of the meal—not the meal for the sake of the leaven. Man's soul, man's nature, is his great gift from God. The original affections, the powers of understanding, willing, feeling, which the Creator bestowed upon his child, are his great and permanent possession, the ground and essence of his immortality. By these, he sustains from the very outset, relations to nature, to humanity, and to God, which, in importance, can never be paralleled by any fresh acquisitions. These powers may need waking, but waking is not creating; they may need regulating, but regulating is not bestowing; they may need development, but development is not origination. When God creates the seed-corn—whose abundant fruit is bruised into meal—he does a work which sun and rain cannot perform; though without their aid, the seed-corn can never send up "first the blade, then the ear, then the full corn in the ear." And, comparing the influences which God's spirit may exert upon the soul he has

created, to the influence of sun and rain upon the seed, we are still left with the incontrovertible truth, that the spirit performs a work inferior to the work of creation; that it gives opportunity and occasion, furnishes aids and inducements, inspirations and facilities—but not faculties, powers, affections—mind, will, heart,—the original bestowment of the Creator.

Precisely what our Lord said of the Sabbath, therefore, is to be said of the Gospel; the Gospel is made for man—not man for the Gospel; religion is made for man—not man for religion. For, supposing man, or a being like man, to be wanting, religion would have no occasion, and could have no existence. God has no religion. He worships no one; obeys no one. Religion is a relation—between man and his Maker. Man does not exist, and is not created, for the purpose of having this relation; but he has this relation that he may exist and flourish, and find his existence and faculties a blessing to himself. There is no religion, and there can be no religion, therefore, except as there are human faculties, affections and powers, to come into right relations with God—any more than there could be navigation, though an ocean and the winds existed, if there were no ships. Navigation implies ocean, winds, and ships, and is the art growing out of the relation of the ship to the ocean. So religion is the relation, and the adjustment of the relation, between the soul and its Maker.

You can readily appreciate this distinction by comparing the leaven to the meal. Who would ever have thought of leaven, or discovered its properties, but for the sake of the meal? It is of no use or value in itself.

It cannot be eaten or drunken. Meal is good even without leaven, flour without yeast; as life is good even without the revealed knowledge of God. But leaven is useless, except for what it does for the meal. There is one great difference between leaven and religion, in favor of leaven—namely, that leaven exists independently of the meal, and can be seen and handled, though useless in its proper self; whereas, religion, being a relation, has no existence except in operation. Nobody ever saw it, felt it, recognized it, except as an affection of the soul, a posture of the faculties. We thoughtlessly talk of it, precisely as if it had a possible existence, independently of our faculties. We might as well talk of sight, as having an existence independently of the eye, or hearing, independently of the ear. Religion is a state—a state of the soul—and it has no possible existence out of the soul, and no residence any where but in the soul. When you have thought without a thinker; love, without a lover; sensibility, without a sentient agent; you may have religion without a human heart. Because God is the source of our souls, and of all the influences that bless and save us, the world is in the vain habit of talking of religion, as if it were up with God in heaven, in the charge of the Holy Spirit—like some precious ointment or panacea, in the keeping of the angels—for which we ought willingly to give all we have to obtain just enough to save us. But we might as soon expect the sun to come down from heaven, and enter into the plants he nourishes, in sparks of solar fire, as the Holy Spirit to come down from heaven and enter into our souls in some mysterious shape called religious experience. The Holy Spirit is the name for the enlightening, uplifting, blessed influence, which God, the Creator and Father of the soul, is ever exerting upon the moral and rational offspring of his hand. It is never more nor less in itself—but only more or less as we receive and use it. I do not mean to deny that we are more in the way of feeling and recognizing it at some than at other times—for our whole moral, intellectual, and spiritual training are very dependent on opportunities and circumstances beyond our own control. But what I would guard your minds against, is the impression that God is ever any more or less graciously disposed—any more or less loving and kind, merciful and helpful; or that there is any place where the Holy Spirit is any more really present than in every human soul. As of religion, so of the Holy Spirit, I say, man is not made for the Holy Spirit; but the Holy Spirit for man. It is the name for the gracious influence exerted by God over human affections; and it has no existence except in human affections, being just as much a relation of God to us, as religion is a relation of our souls to God. Relations, you know, have no existence in themselves—they are names for the attitude or posture of things or persons towards each other. You cannot have friendship without friends; nor love, without lovers; nor religion, without human wills; nor a holy spirit, without human hearts.

Thus it is that the leaven is for the lump, not the lump for the leaven. Religion is for the soul, not the soul for religion. Religion is for man, not man for religion.

2. It is hid in the soul, as leaven is hid in the three measures of meal. We do not see the leaven when we

cut into the loaf; we do not taste it when we eat of the bread. The loaf is not good, the bread is not wholesome, in which the leaven has a distinguishable appearance and flavor. It performs its office when it communicates its effects, transfers its properties, and merges itself in the meal. You see the influence of the leaven on the loaf; you find the meal changed, improved, and made far more palatable and wholesome. And this is precisely the office of religion upon the will, the heart, the understanding. It develops and ripens qualities latent in humanity, brings them into new and beautiful relations to each other, and so effects an indispensable service. But it has no distinct and separate existence in the soul apart from the faculties and affections. It is hid in, not fastened upon, the soul. It suffuses our nature with a tone, and color, and atmosphere, instead of occupying it with a special and precise sentiment. It penetrates it like a savor, instead of puncturing it like a knife. The sword of the spirit does not leave its mark in a wound, but in a spiritual rank and knighthood. It communicates to him on whom it is laid, a character, not a scar. Therefore said our Master, speaking of the Holy Spirit, "The wind bloweth where it listeth, and thou hearest the sound thereof, but canst not tell whence it cometh or whither it goeth. So is every one that is born of the Spirit." As the viewless air communicates an indispensable vitality to the blood, which, oxygenated in the lungs, carries its new life to the heart, which again distributes it to every member, joint, and limb, until the whole body is fed upon the heavenly food of the all-surrounding atmosphere, so that circumambient and all-penetrating spirit of God finds its way, by the appropriate organs of the soul, into the complete spiritual circulation, and builds up the immortal body of our inner life. As we breathe, not for the sake of the lungs, but for the sake of the whole body, so we believe in God, not for the sake of religion, but for the sake of life; we pray, not to exercise our prayerful sensibilities, but to supply the wants of our whole system; we are conscientious, not because conscientiousness is a good thing in itself, any more than the multiplication-table is a good thing in itself; but because conscientiousness is the arithmetic and geometry of the soul—the scales, measuring-rod, guage, and road-guide of the total man—just as the multiplication table is the instrument of our commercial and economic transactions.

Now, my brethren, I do not mean, for the sake of withstanding an opposite error, to forget or deny that religion, as an instrumentality, deserves special attention. On the contrary, I would earnestly insist upon this, and make it the basis of a more urgent application of the general principle I am expounding. My proposition is, that religion is to be chiefly sought for and valued in its effects; but not exclusively. Instruments are not ends, but they deserve attention as instruments. If the bread is not good, among other investigations, we inquire into the state of the leaven; and it may be necessary to give a special and deliberate attention to the increase and improvement of its quality. If the practical character in an individual case is not what it ought to be—if a human soul is manifestly disordered, and life goes irregularly and unsatisfactorily, it is a very fitting and necessary question to ask, Is there religion in this soul, or is the religion of a right kind, genuine and pure? "By their fruits ye shall know them." If the fruit is meagre, sour, and blighted, we begin to examine the root and the soil. And those who know the character of soils and the secrets of horticulture, are very necessary in helping us to cure our sick orchards. So it is with religion. It is a special study; and the way in which it works is a profoundly interesting inquiry. From the fact that it is to the whole human soul what the air is to the blood and the blood to the body, we must not infer that it is not capable of being considered by itself, analyzed, purified from taint, carefully measured, and characterized. There is good air and bad air, stimulating and debilitating air. The air can be weighed, strained, medicated, rarified, densified. We move our sick from moist to dry air, from fresh to salt, from cold to hot, from dense to rare. Yet we expect the air, under all circumstances, to produce its effects, only as it enters into the whole tissues and organism of the body. So it is with religion. Its work lies in its hidden influence and circulation. But it is itself capable of examination as a theory, a creed, a discipline, an influence. It may be examined by the intellect as a system of opinions; it may be examined by the affections as a mode of feeling; it may be examined by the will as a kind of motive. And there are times and seasons when it deserves the same attention as the carpenter's or farmer's tools, the surveyor's instruments, the sailor's art of navigation, the painter's colors and brushes. According as these are in order or in disorder, good or bad, correct or false, will the products created by their aid usually be. We attend to the quality of our bodily food; why not of our spiritual? Oftentimes, therefore, it is observed that those who insist that religion is a life, forget that it is also the food of life, which must be regularly provided, carefully chosen, and systematically taken.

I insist that we need times and seasons to think specially of our relations to God; opportunities and occasions to increase our acquaintance with Christ; habits of prayer and meditation, to secure our full recognition of our duty and destiny; times of self-examination and careful inquisition into our moral and spiritual state. And it seems natural to me that our purely and specifically religious apparatus, our theological opinions, modes of worship, habits of self-discipline, should, at particular dates and crises, have an engrossing interest and care.. But we must not allow this necessity for a moment to mislead us as to the nature of the relation which religion, considered as an instrument, a tool, a discipline, bears to life itself, considered as the real interest. The tool is for the work, the food is for the body, and religion, however important, is the leaven, not the meal. Society at this time seems to be divided between those on the one hand disposed to mistake the leaven for the meal, the sign for the thing signified, the tools for the architecture and house; and those, on the other hand, disposed to say that the meal is all in all; loaf and leaven too; that the sign is of no use, the tools of no account; the thing signified—namely, character—being the only and all-engrossing object. But why rush into extremes? Why decry or neglect either signs, or things signified? The workman is known by his tools, as well as by his fabric. The religious man may be known by his religious opinions, methods, and observances, as well as by his good works, his balanced character, his stable and reliable virtue, his humane and self-sacrificing dispositions. And I confess, with all my preference for fruit, I expect little where no attention is paid to seed and culture. Why neglect the purity, the freshness, and the active character of the leaven, because it is not the meal? Why neglect prayer, meditation, self-searching, the reading of holy books, the assiduous attendance on religious instruction, because these are not the ends, but only the means of a true life—the seed and culture, not the soil, the tree, nor the fruit?

No doubt this unfortunate tendency is due to a strong sense of the evil of the other and more common extreme, the evil of mistaking religious apparatus, for the religious life; religious usages and methods, for religious results; the sensibilities and practices of a directly religious occupation, for the influence and application of these emotions and usages to the ordinary and complete life. The world has been for ages under the delusion that in religion the means are the ends; that there is a virtue in believing certain propositions, without any regard to the bearing of those propositions on life; a virtue in a certain class of moods and emotions, without any regard to their influence on all the other moods and emotions of the soul; that religion has a value independent of character, separate from goodness, distinct from morality, apart from ordinary life. And the results of this old and obstinate superstition are still seen in the popular religious opinions of our own day. The leaven is kept apart from the loaf, and valued for itself, and not for its use. People still talk of getting religion, as though it were a peculiar kind of coin, alone receivable at the heavenly toll-gate ; of experiencing religion, as though it were experiencing an electric shock ; of an interest in Christ, as a shareholder does of his stock in some prosperous venture. The kingdom of heaven, which Christ declared to be within us, is banished to the skies. God, whom our Lord pronounced everywhere present, and especially in the soul of man, his chosen temple, is driven away, up beyond the stars. Christ, present wherever two or three are gathered in his name, is exiled to a great white throne. The use of religion is not, according to this childish and shallow faith, that we may acquire, by its means, a noble, disinterested, loving character, and lead a useful, generous, and pure life, showing forth God's glory in the soul, and forming Christ within, but that through it we may escape some impending wrath, and secure some promised bliss ; keep out of hell, and get into heaven—heaven and hell being not frames of mind and states of being, but a pit and a palace, mere external places. The greatest pains is taken to distinguish between noble, generous, and exalted deeds, springing from motives not distinctly felt to be religious, and the peculiar frames of feeling recognized by some pious free-masonry, as the special fruits of the Spirit.

A popular preacher, recently addressing a vast assembly, said, after describing the noble self-forgetfulness of a fireman, who saved the life of a child by an act of glorious daring, "But that man, who virtually gave his life—mark, gentlemen, noble, glorious, almost Godlike as was his deed—had he been lost, (in his effort,) would have been banished from God and from the glory of his power forever: he was without religion."

Now, I do not object to this statement, which must have been instinctively and shudderingly repelled by all who heard it, because it failed to accept this heroic act as a proof of piety, but because of the implications of this style of thought. I do not say that this heroic act proved this noble fireman to be religious, and I even think it takes less religion to do grand acts of impulse than to live a life of patient duty. But would not this rash teacher have said of a life of steady worth and sober integrity, governed passions, mild, chastened affections, expansive feelings, and spotless moral excellency, provided its subject had been unable to utter the shibboleth of a creed, to avow a faith in the efficacy of a Saviour's atoning blood, and to assert a special religious experience, precisely what he said of the generous fireman: that dying, "he would be banished from God and the glory of his power forever, for he was without religion"? What, then, is religion, if the noblest deeds can be done without it, and the lowliest and most constant duties can be performed in its complete absence? It must be something against which generous and just natures will revolt. It must be something which men must be heated in crowds, and put beyond the control of reason and common sense, before they will believe or receive it. It must be a subject of inflammatory appeal and contagious excitement, and occasional impassioned attention; not "our reasonable service," not our sober, intelligible, every-day duty. This is not the religion which Christ described, when he said, The kingdom of God is like leaven, which a woman took and *hid* in three measures of meal! Alas! there has perhaps been least of true religion when religious apparatus and religious profession, and religious ostentation and noise, have been most rife. When the aim is to build up the Church, not the order, truth, and purity of society, to carry men into the Church instead of carrying the Church into them, to give great and special prominence to religious usages, and forms, and acts—instead of making the ordinary acts and motives of life, pure, and loyal, and pious, then there is nothing vital, because there is nothing *hidden* about religion. Religion is not doing its best work, when it attracts attention in its own character, but only when it is felt in its general effects on the life and conversation; as a well is not fulfilling its appointed duty when we are building a showy well-house over it, but when it is lending its almost unrecognized aid to every requirement of thirst, cleanliness, health and comfort, in the household.

3. The kingdom of God is like leaven, which a woman took and hid in *three* measures of meal, till the *whole* was leavened.

Religion, I have said, 1, is for the soul, not the soul for religion. It is the leaven, not the lump. 2. Religion is an influence, not a result; dew and sunshine, not fruit. It is hid in the meal, not seen in the loaf. 3. Religion, I now add, has universal, not limited and partial ends. It is like leaven, which a woman took and hid in *three* measures of meal, till the *whole* was leavened. Why *three* and not one, but to intimate the manifold character of the operation? The sense of God's presence, the aid of his Spirit, the example and inspiration of his Son, the obligations of conscience, the attractions of immortality, these are designed to exert a universal influence upon the body, soul and spirit; the mind, heart, and will; the private, the social, and the public man; upon man in his relations to the external, the internal, and the eternal—in short, on every strand in the three-fold cord that binds his various being. There is a perpetual tendency to separate man's interests and concerns into secular and sacred; religious and unreligious, mortal and immortal, temporary and eternal. And, for certain ends, the discrimination is allowable and important. But only as a method—as one might distinguish between the arteries and veins; the nerves and muscles; the bones and ligaments; the right and left ventricles in the heart; all parts of the one inseparable living body. It is only dead bodies in which any real division can be made. And it is only in dead creeds and dead bodies of divinity, only on paper and parchment, that any division can be made between secular and sacred, religious and unreligious interests. The soul is never secular; life is never temporal. There are no duties which are not religious duties; as there are no interests which are not religious interests. The human body, for instance, is just as much God's work as the human soul. It has a religion—certain laws and conditions of health and usefulness—which will not be observed except under the direction and control of reason and conscience supported and inspired by allegiance to God and Christ. There has been a vast deal of superstition in regard to the body. It has been treated with something of the same mistaken abuse that is still poured upon the soul. To lash, and starve, and macerate and afflict the body, has been deemed useful to the soul, and acceptable to God ; and every form of mortification has been practised to expel its evil lusts, and through its tortures, to bless and save the soul. Why has it not been understood, that to develop and perfect the human frame and make it strong, beautiful, supple, enduring—to teach it the obedience of an intelligent, helpful, ready servant, was the true way to honor its maker and serve the body's master, the soul ? Good masters do not abuse their servants. Besides, a true care of the body, is, in the end, even a severer discipline, whether of body or soul, than a periodical severity. Strict temperance and due exercise are greater draughts on moral resolution and self-discipline than spiked girdles and sackcloth—than long fasts and many stripes.

And as of the body, so of the soul ; the intellect is as much a part of the soul as the heart. To think, is as much a religious duty as to love. That is to say, thought itself has a religion. Candor, patience, coherency, modesty, aspiration, belong to the exercises of reason as much as to the exercises of charity. How vain, then, is the prejudice which would drive reason out of the temple of the soul, as a profane intruder into God's presence ? And so the tastes, the pleasure-seeking propensities, the natural appetites and passions—these are just as divine in their origin, just as sacred in their place, as the motions of the conscience or the affections of the heart. There is a religion of beauty and taste, as well as a religion of duty and charity. That is to say, we can and we must exercise our feelings of beauty and our aptitudes and capacities for pleasure, under a sense of their origin in God's nature and God's beneficence, and recognize their allegiance to the same plan and the same authority, which works in and reigns over the more obviously moral part of our Nature.

And so of external Nature, the material universe, the world we live in. It is not properly to be opposed to the world we are going to, or to the inner world of the spiritual senses. Matter is not the opposite, or the foe of spirit; it is rather its shadow and echo. The life that now is, is not the antagonist and contrast of the life that is to be; but its infancy and boyhood, the beginning of what shall never end.

And so, our ordinary pursuits, our business, our pleasure, our politics, our literature, our buying and selling, and visiting, and eating, and dressing, are not the base and low necessities of our mortal state, against which the noble and exalting aspirations of our immortal state are steadily protesting and striving; but rather the divinely-given opportunities and occasions, in which our various powers, tastes and aptitudes find their culture and growth—and the real channels into which our religious feelings and duty to God and Christ and ourselves, should send their sanctifying, chastening, and elevating tides.

God means us to be religious through and through. Religious in our thoughts, affections, pleasures, business, tastes. And no one who does not hope and strive to bring his whole nature into a divine loyalty and Christian subjection, has fitly conceived his vocation as a Christian. It is not that we are to be equally serious, much less equally devout, at all times. Serious and devout feelings are as much out of place in times of relaxation and social gayety, as laughter and jest are in the house of prayer, or in the closet of self-examination. The loyalty to religion to be shown in pleasure—is in recognizing the faculties and tastes for pleasure as being divine in their origin, and designed to bring parts of God's character and government, and of our own wonderful and divinely-framed constitution, into view and exercise; is, in keeping pleasure within the bounds of health, strength and usefulness; is, in insisting that it shall observe the profoundest deference to right, purity and goodness, in its form and spirit. Nor is the religion to be shown in business, to consist in talking religion over the counter; nor in running from the office to the prayer-meeting; nor in carrying religious tracts within the leaves of the ledger, or in the folds of the pocket-book; but in dealing with scrupulous integrity, exact justice and thorough kindness with our fellow-men, in moderating the desire of gain, in consecrating success to God's glory and man's welfare, and in seeing the divine significance of trade and commerce, so grand and worthy of God in their laws, and in connection with the education of humanity and the triumph of liberty, peace and charity.

My brethren, what can be so much needed at this time as the proper understanding of the broad, and deep, and high ground covered by the kingdom of God? There is in the late religious excitement—of which much good, and more hope of good is to be predicated —an unmistakable evidence of a profound popular ignorance in regard to the very nature of religion. Its relation to human nature, to human life and to human prospects—all, all need the most pains-taking and detailed explanation.

What can fill one with a more saddening sense of the state of religious prejudice and darkness among even educated minds, than to be met by an accomplished, acute and worthy man, who stops to thank you, as for a new truth, on having somewhere read a report of your saying that the proper sphere for the display of religious principle and religious feeling, is in the ordinary duties and ordinary intercourse of life! or to see a man, like the admirable Arthur Helps—the author of some of the best and wisest books in our language, cautiously suggesting, that the intellect may possibly be a part of the soul, and that our intellectual acquirements may even possibly be of some value in another state of existence? And this is quoted into a literary journal of the day, as a new and grand suggestion—a little eccentric, perhaps, but startling and important! What must be the state of popular feeling in regard to the nature and character of the soul and its destiny, the relation of the intellectual and moral powers, the meaning of life, the significance of nature, the bearing of religion as an institution upon religion as a state of character, or of religion as an emotion upon religion as a universal allegiance of the powers of body and soul—tastes, appetites, affections, thoughts—to their Maker, God, and to their first friend—their pattern, guide and Saviour—Christ? The implications of false and shallow reasoning, partial observation, intellectual groping, moral obliquity, spiritual ignorance—in short, of puerility and superstition—involved in a large part of the appeals, the preaching, the cant terms, the popular dogmas, the current conversation of Christendom—are discouraging evidences, how backward is the religious thought of our day, as compared with its general thought; how little harmony there is between our schools and our churches ; our thinkers and our religious guides ; our political and national institutions and our popular theology. It is not Christianity—the rational, thorough, all-embracing Gospel of Christ—which throws its blessed sanctities over and around our whole humanity—which owns and consecrates our whole nature and our whole life—which is thus taught. It is a system which is narrower than Judaism—and compared with which Romanism is a princely and magnificent theology. I say advisedly, that if Protestantism endorses the vulgar notions of a God-cursed world—a fallen race—a commercial atonement—a doomed and hell-devoted humanity—a mysterious conversion—a church, which is a sort of life-boat, hanging round a wreck, that may carry off a few women and selfishly-affrighted men—leaving the bolder, braver, larger proportion to go down with the ship ; if this be the sum and substance of religion—if these notions be the grounds of the late religious excitement and the doctrines which gave it power—then, it is not so true to human nature, its wants and woes, its various and manifold tastes, talents and faculties—as the old Catholic system—and that, instead of trembling at the growth and prospects of Romanism in this country, we should more reasonably rejoice in its triumphs, as the worthier occupant of the confidence and affections of the people. But this narrow system, with all its arrogant claims to be the only Evangelical faith, is not Protestantism ; or, rather, it is mere Protestantism. It has been from its origin too busy in protesting against Romanism, to affirm the grander and more practical truths of a positive religion, and we have imitated it too well in spending our time in protesting against this mere Protestantism. Let us all arouse ourselves to the duty of asserting the noble grandeur and sublime simplicity of the Gospel of Christ—the friend of free thought, the exalter of human nature, the interpreter and consecrator of common life—the emancipator of the soul from mere dogmas, and the inaugurator of a divine morality and heaven-inspired order and harmony, in the practical character and in the daily life of men.

Thus alone, will Christ's kingdom come. For then it will be like the leaven, which a woman took and hid in three measures of meal, till the *whole* was leavened.

MAY 9, 1858.

SERMON XI.

RELIGION CONSIDERED AS A REFUGE FROM THE MYSTERY OF EVIL.

"I—beseech you, by the meekness and gentleness of Christ."—2 Cor. x. 1.

It is a great argument! the one mighty motive by which God seeks to convince and convert the world, "the meekness and gentleness of Christ." Christ's character—is God's beseeching message to humanity. Instead of threats and bribes, of warnings and reproaches, of a code of laws written in blood, or a table of commandments thundered from the burning mount, the Almighty goodness sets his Son in the midst of men—the Son of Omnipotence, of infinite sovereignty, but clothed in meekness and gentleness—and waits to see the effect of such goodness, the influence of such loveliness, upon the hearts of mankind.

It was no new experiment in principle, my brethren! How could it be? For is not the unchangeable God the author of the Gospel, and was not the same character, behind all the Almighty's dealings, which more evidently appeared in his express likeness, our Saviour?

It is the glorious work of Christ's meekness and

gentleness, that it is the image and shadow of God's own merciful and gentle character. It would be worth little to us, if it did not imply and establish that blessed truth. And, if without a vain intention of glorifying later manifestations of the divine character by disparaging earlier ones, we study the spirit and temper of the old dispensations, we shall find that the loving-kindness and tender mercy of the Lord, his patience and forgivingness, are the characteristic qualities of all his direct dealings and communications with men, and have always been the arguments by which he has sought to win the world.

"But surely, you do not mean to say," I hear some one interpose, "that the moral government of the world, the constitution of things of which God is author and upholder, reveal him exclusively as a gentle and tender being, unwilling to give pain, reluctant to punish, trusting only to goodness and forbearance for his influence over us?"

Certainly, I do not mean to deny, or to underrate, the solemn issues of right and wrong, the great equipoise of pleasure and pain, the vast sum of suffering and evil in the universe. Surely, I cannot forget the awfulness of constitution which belongs to the human soul—its exposure to temptation, the power of its passions, its sensibility to sorrow and capacity of wrong, with all the dreadful force of circumstances so often preying upon it! Who can conceal, or wishes to conceal, the dark and dreadful history of our race—its public wars, its private crimes, its selfishness and sins? or who will undertake to cover its present half-barbarous and half-wicked state! Can we listen with patience to the sophistry that would extenuate, or the smoothness that would hide, the darkness of History's great problem, or to the harpings of the pleasant instrument that would persuade us that humanity is characteristically attuned to virtue and purity. Alas! my brethren! there can be no exaggeration in the statement of the difficulty which hangs over this great fact of evil in God's universe, and in our own nature which God has made. The evil in the world has always been, and continues to be, immense; the evil in *us* has always been, and continues to be, immeasurable. The constitution of things, the nature God has given us, the circumstances in which he has placed us, are things which we must accept as facts—and facts which it is beyond our present faculties to reconcile and account for. If any man think he has solved the problem of evil, and reconciled its beginning or its continuance in the universe, with the supposition of the Divine Omnipotence and Infinite Benevolence, he has nothing left to learn, and may, indeed, boast of understanding the Almighty to perfection. But what theory, boasting such a success, does any thing but give us a juggle of words!

No! my brethren, the actual condition of things, this world of mingled good and evil, vice and virtue, temptation and support—is a profound and insoluble mystery—which philosophy and religion make no approaches to dissipate. No wisdom can say why a season of moral discipline was requisite for us, more than for the spiritual beings whom we suppose never to have sinned. Seeing God is omnipotent, why were we not all created with angelic affections, a strength of will which could not be tempted, a native purity that nothing could soil? Our only relief is to reflect that created beings must always somewhere come to what is unknown and inexplicable—and we find support in the reasonable conviction, that what *we* cannot fathom, is not necessarily unfathomable, what we cannot understand and reconcile is not inherently irreconcilable—but has its interpreter in the Infinite mind.

My brethren, you will not misunderstand me when I am really trying to help you. The world, in its very constitution, affords innumerable proofs of the benevolence of the Creator. But do you not see that a benevolence which has to be substantiated by evidence, confesses difficulty and acknowledges evil? This evil I do not choose to deny or conceal; for it is the very thing which makes religion necessary. I will not be so presumptuous as to say I see the reason why human nature is so weak, and temptation so strong, and wickedness so common, and man's moral being so often degraded. But these facts are the very basis of all we know of religion. If human nature were strong, and temptation powerless, and virtue universal, and man erect and pure, what occasion should we have to know God, or to think about God? We should be all we could be and have all we wanted, and religion, which is dependence, and a cry for mercy and help, and a guidance and support under difficulty, and an aspiration and struggle upwards, would have no place, and need no existence! And do I propose this as our solution of the problem? that we were made weak that we might lean on God, and sinful that we might be forgiven, and ignorant that we might learn the joy of faith? No! plausible as it might sound, I will not suppose defects created only that they might be corrected, and wants originated that they might be supplied. Far rather let us, in the simplicity and modesty that becomes our limited faculties, acknowledge and bow ourselves before the immense and unsounded mystery of our condition, as tempted, and morally imperfect, and exposed, and often wretched beings! Why we should have been made or left so, defies explanation from human powers. But this is the fact, and it is a fact which is the basis of religion; for man's call on God has sprung from his sense of sin and his experience of evil. He has appealed from his condition and from himself to One greater than himself, free from his perplexities, and deemed able to help him. It is the sorrow of the world that has built its altars, the wail of woe that has made its liturgies. Weakness, want, guilt, sorrow, doubt, and despair, have turned from earth to heaven, from the human to the divine, and have implored strength, consolation, light, deliverance, in the midst of darkness and calamity, sinfulness and shame.

And how has this cry been answered? Allowing—nay, how can we but allow?—that man and life are full of difficulty and doubt, weakness and wrong, so far as the working of the moral and spiritual life is concerned, must we not say, that whatever obscurity may hang around the benevolence of God viewed as our original Creator, however equivocal his will may there appear to be in respect to our happiness and moral excellency—however we may have gotten into this difficulty of moral and physical evil—God as our present Father, God as he is revealed, is revealed wholly and exclusively as our friend and helper—as one who is doing the utmost, within the limits of our nature and circumstances, to lift us out of our difficulties, to repair our misfortunes, to recover us, and make up, in the best and most tender manner, for our sorrows and struggles. You may ask why Infinite power, which controlled the whole, should have *any* difficulties to contend with in us or in our history or nature, that we should require patience, or he show mercy. But this, I remind you, is the insoluble question, which our faculties are too limited to answer. It is enough that difficulties *do* exist; that we *are* within and without imperilled, beset, in need of help, mercy, consideration. And I repeat, that God gives us that help, mercy, and consideration; and that all we know of God directly—God in his relations to us as imperfect, erring, and suffering creatures—is what is worthy of an infinitely good Being: a Father and helper, a merciful, considerate, and ever-patient and forgiving God.

The great argument of God in his Gospel, as I began with saying, is that which forms the words of our text: "I beseech you by the meekness and gentleness of Christ." God's *love* to man, despite his erring and imperfect nature, despite his gross and numerous sins, is the source and the import of all religion. Whatever there is hard or sorrowful, dark or desperate in ourselves, or our circumstances, or our lot, comes not from any thing in God's disposition towards us. There is hardship, there is difficulty, there is seeming injustice—nay, there are terrible and awful issues hanging over us. They come from a mysterious source; a fatal necessity; they grow out of what we do not and cannot understand. Call it fate, call it mystery, call it Satan ; but do not call it God. At any rate, call it not God's character, if you ascribe it to God's nature. God's nature may involve tremendous necessities—may be grounded in inflexible justice—may require a hard, retributive code—may have something, or much, or all, of the pitiless mechanism of nature, sounding on its solemn and fearful way through the moral universe, without respect of persons. But we know little or nothing, and can understand little or nothing, of this. God's character we *do* know and can understand. And that character has nothing of the harshness, or cold severity, or inflexible justice which may be ascribed to God's nature. It is all motherly, tender, striving to help, ready to bind up our wounds, and breaking out only in efforts and promises of love and mercy. The two great revelations may be said to have grown out of God's longing to be understood and loved, and to be distinguished, in his personal character, from the source of human woes and sinfulness. He presents himself in his voluntary and personal character, as the friend of man in his struggle with himself and the world ; as his merciful and gracious helper and consoler. Will you still insist that he *made* the very nature, and the very world, that so much needs his help and consolation ? Will you say, that what is sad, and threatening, and evil in nature, and the soul, and man's history, tell against the tenderness of God, as much as his Word and his revelations of himself tell in its favor ? that to be placed in a condition to *need* this mercy is as cruel, as to have it extended, is kind ? I acknowledge the logical form and force of the argument. But I remind you, that in judging God's nature, you judge what it is manifestly beyond the reach of your faculties to judge decisively; but that in judging the positive declarations of himself in his Word, in estimating his character as it appears in his direct dealings with us by his prophets and his Son, you have a subject within the range of your powers, and on the plane of your present experience.

I press this point, because I wish to present religion to you as the unmixed benefaction of Heaven; I wish you to think of it solely as the gentle and helpful friend of your souls. Too often and too long have we dwelt upon it, as if it were answerable for all the dark problems in our lot; as if every question the metaphysician and philosopher could ask, religion must either answer, or hold itself responsible for not answering. I tell you that religion has nothing to do with the evil in the world, or the evil in your nature, or the evil over your destiny, except to save you from them and avert them. It finds you blind, sick, sad, forlorn, and wishes only to give you light, health, cheerfulness, and gracious communion. Admitting all of human error, weakness and misfortune, all that is alarming and trying in our moral state, it sets to work, like the good Samaritan, to heal the wounded man it finds by the wayside. It does not say, "How came you here thus buffeted and bruised, and what business had you in this dangerous road—or what use will you make of the healing I offer you, supposing I administer it!" It does not stop to give an account of the reasons why the sufferer has been permitted to fall among thieves, and be robbed and beaten. Nothing of this. But it goes straight to work pouring oil and wine into the wounds, and binding up the broken limbs, and bearing the unfortunate to shelter and tender care.

Alas, my brethren, how many are there declining God's blessed consolation, guidance and help, until they can settle a hundred metaphysical questions about their origin and destiny! They must have a rational and exhaustive system of religious philosophy, before they will lean on the arm that is offered them, or accept the deliverance which is extended. They must know how they got into this dilemma, before they will allow themselves to be got out of it. They must first discover what made them sick, before they will permit the good physician to heal them! as if these were not secondary questions, which, if never settled at all, do not affect the primary one. Man's weakness, sorrow, sinfulness, are facts, dreadful facts, of immediate and pressing urgency. You may not think it fair that an Infinite Being should have given you a precarious and exposed existence. But the fact remains; you *have* a precarious and exposed existence. You may not understand the justice of hereditary weakness and constitutional tendencies to moral obliquity, but it does not change the fact. You may not see how a perfect God could have made an imperfect world. But it *is* an imperfect world, and you have an imperfect nature. And your metaphysical or moral difficulty will never alter that fact a hair. Moreover, does it give you the least comfort to think God *im*perfect; or will it help your philosophy at all to imagine him, or even to prove him, imperfect? What then can be greater folly than to postpone the use and enjoyment of what is so real as religion—which is a beautiful ministry to our weakness and sorrow and doubt—until we have obtained, what never yet was found, an harmonious, perfectly coherent and logical system of the universe, with the problem of evil fairly solved !

Do not think that I am arguing with an imaginary class of objectors. Society is full of intelligent minds, that are keenly alive to the knotty difficulties involved in the science of human origin and destiny, and who imagine that practical religion, religion as a faith, a consolation, a life, is involved in the obscurity, or waits the answer, of their metaphysical problems. Some of the most powerful and generous minds and hearts are in this suspense, thinking it quite inconsistent and illogical, quite weak and unmanly, to profess piety, or adopt Christianity, or bow before God, while these difficulties remain unsettled. And so their logic and their good sense seem to bar them out of God's kingdom. I tell such men fairly, that they are quarrelling with a mystery which is mightier than the mightiest—waiting for a light that never yet has blest the eye of sage or philosopher. It is not by that door of a satisfied intellect that any man enters the kingdom of God. A child can ask questions which an apostle cannot answer, and the feeblest intellect feel and propose difficulties which the strongest cannot remove. It is precisely because sight fails us that we need faith. It is just because we are so baffled as thinkers, that we are driven to living rightly in place of thinking satisfactorily, driven to worship instead of to philosophy. The Church has called *religion* a mystery. Never was a more ill-deserved name attached to it. It is *life* which is the mystery—man, the soul, human circumstances and prospects. Religion, on the contrary, is the light which Heaven throws across this mystery; the door it opens out of this darkness. Surely it is not mysterious that God offers us help, consolation, pity, and promises us strength in our efforts at goodness, and acceptance in our penitence. The mystery is that we should require this help and pity, not that it should come to us. Religion is the very opposite of mystery, of which nature and man and life are full.

I wish, my brethren, without the use of paradoxical language, I could show you how ill-fitted to guide us through life, or to help us out of our real moral difficulties and darkness, this boasted understanding is, on which we rely so exclusively. I suppose there is no part of our immortal nature—fearfully and wonderfully made as it is—full of grandeur and awe, but undeveloped and unarranged as yet—I suppose there is no part of that nature so little competent to deal with unseen things, as our reasoning powers so called. We touch God with any of our other faculties, and compass him with any of our other powers, more readily and adequately than with our understanding. Our hearts, our consciences, our imaginations, our instincts, are far more fully developed, far nearer on a level with God, than our logical faculty. It is precisely between God and us as between other superiors and inferiors, the educated and the ignorant, or the adult and the child. In all these cases, the affections, the imagination, the instincts, establish ready and even equal relations, but the intellect is only a barrier and division wall. The moment I begin to reason with my child, or with my servant, I feel the distance we are apart. But when we are only exchanging affections, or relying on the instincts of our common nature, we are mutually near, and perfectly intelligible. My child understands me fully with his heart, let my government, let my occupations and ways, be ever so obscure and mysterious to him. And he is perfectly justified in trusting his heart and leaning wholly and unreservedly upon my protection. Lord Bacon has said that man is the God of the dog,[1] who worships and obeys him, and feels the dignity and happiness of being his servant; and in the total lack of reason, how touching and instructive is the affectionate brute's communion with and devotion to his master! Can we not, without irreverence, say that we know less of God intellectually, than the dog knows of his master's mind, and are less competent to fathom him? but if we can know God *as* the dog knows his master—know him to love him and to glory in his protection, and to develop beautiful qualities and enjoy a heightened existence in his service, do we not know him to a glorious and satisfactory purpose—know him really, and by moral instincts and affections,

[1] Lord Bacon's precise words are: "They that deny a God destroy man's nobility; for certainly man is of kin to the beasts by his body, and if he be not of kin to God by his spirit, he is a base and ignoble creature. It destroys, likewise, magnanimity, and the raising of human nature: for take an example of a dog, and mark what a generosity and courage he will put on, when he finds himself maintained by a man who, to him, is in place of a God, or *melior natura;* which courage is manifestly such as that creature, without confidence of a better nature than his own, could never attain. So man, when he resteth and assureth himself upon divine protection and favor, gathereth a force and faith which human nature in itself could not obtain: therefore, as atheism in in all respects hateful, so in this, that it depriveth human nature of the means to exalt itself above human frailty."—*Bacon's Essays*, vol. i. p. 274.

which are the beauty, aye, and the strength of our nature? The greatest intellects, my brethren, have been those which have felt most humbly their own utter incompetency to wrestle with the mystery of the universe, and have, with the readiest homage, bowed themselves in worship and faith, where sight failed them. Do you think it a triumph of consistency, a proof of intellectual power, to stand up unawed, and, with a bold stare and curious questioning, before religion, determined not to wink before its glory, or to bow one inch in the presence of its beauty, until it justifies itself exactly to your reason? Ah! my vain fellow-creature; it is not that your reason is too great, or too searching, or too sharp, that religion cannot satisfy you; but too small, and too inapt, and too dull. Reflect that you are not asked to do God any service, but that he is waiting to do you one; that religion does not want you, but that you want religion. Suppose you are *not* satisfied with the government of the universe, or with your nature, or God's providence; will that hurt anybody but yourself? You are the only one to be hurt, or helped. You are not a strong man, whose enlistment in the ranks of religion is anxiously solicited for the service you may supply; but a sick man, whose acceptance of religious care and cure is affectionately asked for your own sake. By the meekness and gentleness of Christ, I beseech you to accept the offer of guidance and consolation which it tenders to your heart.

Come, then, in the spirit of needy and erring men, who feel your blindness and your wants, who know your sins and follies—your openness to temptation, your urgent want of aim and object, of inspiration and divine communion ; come to the altar of God, to the Church of Christ, and render up your hearts to your Father and your Saviour ! Do you not long to bow down before your Maker—to rest those strained and weary muscles that have held out so long against the impulse that would throw you prostrate at his feet ? Do you not desire to flood those eyes, that ache with their dry, fixed lids of proud intelligence, with the gracious tears of penitence and trust ? Is there not a hidden, long-repressed yearning in your souls, to give up to God and to Christ the care and charge of your troublous being, and to find in trust and in worship the rest and the peace nothing else is able to give ? I beseech you, by the meekness and gentleness of Christ, do not resist these holy impulses. They come from heaven. Obeyed, they will give you the meekness and gentleness of the Master ! And when you have received any considerable measure of that, you will no longer question the sacredness and blessedness of the fountain whence such refreshment has come. *A character*, a Christian character, is the immense benefaction of the Gospel ! To be like Christ ! if any thing can give you that, will you not bless it, and honor it, and trust it ? Is that not what you would give all else in the world for ? Yes ; and that will descend upon you, steal in upon your affections, take possession of your conscience, fix and empower your will, renew and transform you, beginning its work from the moment you heartily close with the Gospel of Christ—adopt and take home as a bride, for better and for worse, through good report and through evil report, in sickness and in health, the religion of the holy Son of God. I beseech you, by the meekness and gentleness of Christ, and by the mercies and goodness of God, to take up with this offer! Commit yourselves, by the bravest and most open confession, to the service of God. If it be unpopular to avow a religious faith, let that be a fresh appeal to your moral courage to do it. If it cost an effort to encounter the surmises and glances of the world in a religious profession, thank God there is some stigma still left by which to honor him who was buffeted for our sins. If consistency and rationality hinder you, cast them behind you as the temptations of Satan. If the Gospel of Christ be not what it seems; if the communion of Christ's suffering be not a holy and beautiful memorial of divine excellences; if the religion which has clothed the noblest humanity of nineteen centuries with graces and charities, be a delusion; if the sweetness of a trust in God, the comfort of prayer, the sanctities of an obedient spirit, the hopes and confidences of a religious heart; if the Church of the Lamb, and the worship of the Father, and the communion of saints, and the fellowship of the Holy Spirit—if, my brethren, these be all dreams, superstitions, delusions, they are blessed dreams. Oh! may I never wake from them. I do not wish to live, if I cannot live in their light, and upon their comfort. I care not what death is, nor when it comes, nor where it carries me, if the religion of Jesus Christ be not true. I take it as it is, and on it I cast my all. I will live and die in it. All scruples, doubts, misgivings, I fling to the winds. "For I am persuaded that neither death, nor life, nor angels, nor principalities, nor powers, nor things present, nor things to come, nor height, nor depth, nor any other creature, shall be able to separate us from the love of God, which is in Christ Jesus our Lord."[1]

November 4, 1855.

[1] Rom. viii. 39.

SERMON XII.

GENERAL LAWS AND A SPECIAL PROVIDENCE RECONCILED.

OCCASIONED BY THE BURNING OF THE "AUSTRIA" AT SEA.

"Master, carest thou not that we perish?"—MARK iv. 38.

IT was in the midst of a sudden storm on the little sea of Galilee, that the disciples in charge of the vessel, waking Jesus from his trustful repose in the hinder part of the boat, addressed this natural appeal to his protection. Suppose he had confessed his inability to calm the sea, and as the danger grew more and more imminent, had only given himself up to a deeper sleep, until the vessel, with its living freight, sunk into the waves! What would have been the confidence of the few possible survivors of the wreck, in his power or goodness? what that of the friends of the perished crew? No such occasion was given. "Jesus arose and rebuked the wind, and said unto the sea, Peace, be still; and the wind ceased, and there was a great calm." That calm was a miracle; that rescue, a special interposition. Jesus represented in that vessel, as he did on the earth, the immediate presence of God. It was fit that his authority should be asserted, his office proclaimed and illustrated by marvels ; that his spiritual work, a Gospel for all time, should be attested by miracles—i. e., special departures from the ordinary course of God's providence. And, therefore, on all proper occasions, Jesus worked miracles : feeding crowds with bread, that at his command grew beneath the hands of them that broke the seven loaves, into food for thousands ; healing the sick with a touch, calming the winds and the sea, making the water solid beneath the sinking Peter, the air firm as the ground under his own weight, when they led him to the brow of the hill whereon Nazareth was built, that they might cast him down headlong ; stone walls and wooden doors yielding as the atmosphere, when he chose to pass through them. By miracles he averted danger from his friends, raised their dead, and secured the confidence of his timid disciples and the foundation of his religion in the world. But now, mark the contrast !

When lately, in much more urgent and distressing circumstances, another imperilled crew—not in a little lake, in sight of land, but on the vast, unbounded ocean —not a handful of fishermen, used to the water, but six hundred souls, collected from all quarters, and all pursuits—husbands and wives, parents and children—men of all professions and callings, merchants, missionaries, mechanics, artists, rich and poor—prosperous visitors to their old home returning to their new and adopted country, bringing their wives and children to taste their own dear-bought success—emigrants, after great struggles to achieve the opportunity, seeking with hope a better career in an uncrowded continent—representatives of all nationalities, as of all grades and callings—when this other crew, the population of a town, as it were, compressed within one ship, beset, not by a single element, usually regarded as the most pitiless, but now found kinder than another; whom fire and water together vie with their opposite terrors to destroy—when, I say, such a wretched crew, on the 13th of September, cried, with shrieks and prayers, that must ring for ever in the ears of the saved, "Lord Jesus, help! Dost thou not care that we perish! God have mercy! Spare us, our wives, our little ones!" No benignant Saviour then descended to rescue this most helpless, in part most innocent, this wholly surprised and frightfully beleaguered freight of precious souls! The panic-stricken, dastardly officers, seem not more careless of the fate of six hundred lives than Divine Providence itself! Had the Almighty been asleep, and slept through those awful groans and shrieks demanding his pity and protection, fire and water could not have had a more unimpeded way, a more merciless and cruel victory. Where was Jesus, that he who said "peace" to that ancient sea, did not calm this modern ocean, and that more terrible sea of fire? Where was God, that his impartial and paternal heart did not hasten to allay those flames, to save those innocent children, to bless those tender pairs whose love burned brighter than the fires that drove them, locked in each other's arms, into the sea? How could heavenly mercy see that noble Hungarian father fling his children, one by one, after their mother, into the gulf of death, and then, with his baby on his breast, himself the greatest sufferer of all, leap after them into the watery grave! Can we spare such brave, heroic souls? Can God allow the mean and cowardly officers of such a ship to carry off their branded and worthless lives, and those precious, tender, manly hearts—those lovely women, those loving men, those innocent children—to perish ?

These, my brethren, are natural, if awful, questions. In forms more or less distinct, in ways more or less direct, they do, they must come, when calamities like this occur, into all minds that dare to think. Is it not well to meet them fairly, honestly, and in the courageous spirit in which some of the victims of the Austrian wreck met their appalling fate ? Convinced as I am, from the very depths of my soul, that God was present in his most paternal character in that very disaster, as he is on all battle-fields, in pestilences, murders, calamities, no matter how promiscuous, or terrible their circumstances ; that each and every prayer, groan, tear, pang of quivering flesh, and gasp of choking lungs, was then and is always noted and pitied in heaven, even when unrelieved—that Jesus is as really present, and as really saving to his disciples, though they are left to perish in the storm, as though they were plucked from its fury—I cannot fail to desire to communicate this faith to you, and to lead you to perfect repose and confidence, in view of so overwhelming a public calamity as that which lately arrested and tortured public attention.

I begin with calling your attention to an important preliminary consideration :

The circumstances that try our Christian faith and introduce distressing doubts of God's special providence, as of his justice and kindness, in all events like this, are not essentially different from those which task our intelligence and try our hearts in the ordinary course of human affairs. To see the good and the bad, the important and the insignificant, the faithful and the unbelieving, whelmed in a common fate—the victims of a sudden stroke of misfortune, a petty accident, itself without necessity or excuse, and yet so mighty and awful in its instant consequences—doubtless tends to suggest a sense of the reign of chance,—the dominion of pitiless, indiscriminate law or blind force—terribly shocking to filial confidence, to belief in a personal superintendent and direct and punctilious Governor of the universe. This event, however, I repeat, differs from a thousand others, nay, from the general character of human experience, not in principle, but only in being more bold and arresting in its features. What happened here, in a way to shock, as it must, the awe-stricken sensibility of the civilized world, is happening, so far as the principles mooted in it are concerned, every day, and is the rule, indeed, of all human experience. The good and bad, the young and the old, irrespective of merit, are constantly made forcible and equal partners both in prosperity and in adversity. As a general rule, not in evil alone, you notice, but also in good, we share the blessings and misfortunes of those contiguous to us, and, outwardly viewed, are not permitted, except to a very limited degree, to separate ourselves from a certain promiscuous experience, whether of good or of evil. Thus no man, good or bad, escapes the tendencies of his age, the spirit of his neighborhood, the fortunes of his nation, the experiences of his community, the influence of his family. General calamities, like general blessings, fall on whole eras, whole cities, whole races, whole neighborhoods, whole families. War, peace, famine, plenty, pestilence, health, make no distinction in favor of individuals, when they come to wither, or come to bless, the seasons and the nations. If you undertake to run any guage of merit, or even fitness, through the dealings of death, or pestilence, or war, you must know that you will find no satisfaction in your inquiry. It is not the bad who die early, nor is it the good! It is not the worthless, nor is it the exalted whom pestilence smites. They seem impartial and indiscriminate. Whoever is found on their ground, no matter what his character or claims may be, how insignificant or how important, falls before them. There seems to be neither an eye to merit, nor to what we think importance, in the allotments of external misfortunes. Lightning, just as naturally and pitilessly, strikes down a king as his meanest subject; shipwreck visits a vessel freighted with a thousand souls with as little compunction as a pilot-boat. Death destroys more infants than old men; nor is there the least apparent discrimination or tenderness shown to human worth. The good mother is taken from her orphans; the only child from his virtuous parents. The bad often live on to torment their protectors and supporters. The drunkard survives the faithful wife he has beaten into her grave, after having broken her heart. Yet there is no rule even for this. The good, the deserving, the excellent, are often visited with long life, experience great outward prosperity, are unexpectedly spared in danger. The only thing that the Providence of God would seem determined to impress upon us, is the utter folly of attempting to read its counsels, or of taking any methodical account of its dealings in individual instances. It baffles all our penetration, upsets all our calculations, and denies us the possession of any means of anticipating or of accounting for its modes of action in particular cases.

I suppose, however, that the benignity, wisdom and power of God are confessed and obvious, spite of exceptional cases, in the general government of the world ; and that as we acknowledge the kindness of Nature, in full view of her volcanoes, storms and poisons, so we are ready, in our philosophic and comprehensive moods, and when not pressed by special experiences of misfortune, to own the goodness of God in the general ordering of his Providence towards men. In short, we acknowledge the wisdom and benevolence of general laws —in a general way.

It is evident that the real difficulty presented by every case like the present is this : how to reconcile the action of general laws and secondary causes, admitted to be good and necessary in their ordinary tendencies, with what the heart so much craves for its support under distress and sorrow—the idea of a present, an interested, and a particular Providence. All considerate observers of the workings of the general plan, confess that its rules are plainly good rules, that it proceeds upon wise, kind, and even necessary principles, if the divine government must be carried on thus generally ; but what tries their faith, is that an omnipotent Being, by theory everywhere present, should be shut up to general laws, should not desire to interpose, should not actually interpose in any case of special hardship and injustice, to correct the cruel operation of pitiless rules. How can a living, personal, omnipresent God and Father submit to have his own heart, his own love and mercy, hampered and hindered by such rigid and indiscriminate regulations?

Now, in order to understand how such a rigid and often terrible state of things consists with the theory of a moral Governor of the universe, and a paternal, personal Deity, directing all affairs, I beg your attention to one leading thought. It respects the method of the divine activity. God's *natural* mode of action would be by miracle, by constant interposition, or rather by a perpetual and direct exercise of his will, applied to every specific occasion. A Being everywhere present, all-wise, omnipotent, can find no difficulty in such universal directness and immediacy of action! Why, then, is the world in which we live and the universe we are acquainted with, so undeniably *not* governed by miracle, so obviously *not* governed by interpositions, and special appliances, and accommodations on the part of the Deity? Not, I ask you to notice, not for God's convenience, not to save him trouble and time, and to economize his government and facilitate his affairs—not to permit him to absent himself while his agents do his work—but plainly, for our sake, to allow us to get away from the feeling of his immediate control, away from the direct beams of his burning and overwhelming presence, that we may have some little chance to find ourselves, to establish our free will, to act an independent part, and thus achieve a moral existence! God benevolently puts the seeming restraint of what we call law, that is, a regular method of acting, upon himself—for *our* sakes—to create a domain of liberty for us to move in—certain opportunities of foresight, calculation, reliance, on which we can depend, and which form the only possible basis of a human, rational and moral existence. All the so-called laws of Nature are of this character—though in appearance only—self-acting, rigid, uncompromising, and maintained in their general, impartial, and therefore often promiscuous and sweeping, operation—for the sake of man's education, which is found in struggling with and understanding them, using them, avoiding the penalties of their infraction, enjoying the advantages of obedience to them. God's paternal heart is all the while, under "this garment we see him by," beating fast with pity and sympathy for those who temporarily suffer by the exceptional evils involved in this method adopted for the general good ; and not only for the general good, but the good of every individual who belongs to this common humanity. But, being chosen, because it is for the general good, it would be an act of unkindness, on the part of the Deity, to interrupt its operation when it presses cruelly upon the exceptional cases. Nor, indeed, would these laws, which are as yet only partially known, ever be discovered in all their benignant tendencies, were not the violations of them attended with frightful consequences, which create earnest and profound investigations, that carry on and up the human intellect and advance the interests of society. And when I speak of disobedience to those laws, I do not mean only wilful and conscious neglect or breakage, but also innocent and unconscious ; for we learn from both. When the innocent suffer, as Christ's own case sufficiently illustrates, they suffer for the guilty, and are the means of doing immense services for society. Suppose only the worthless, and the vile, and the ignorant, were subject to shipwreck and pestilence—who would care to investigate their causes, or to allay their consequences? And this explains another difficulty, which perplexes most, namely, that the general laws of Nature operate not only without any allowance for exceptional cases, but quite independently of moral desert! I hold it to be one of the greatest proofs of God's universal love for man, that he mixes up the good and the bad in a common external fortune, and refuses to treat them, so far as outward circumstances are concerned, in separate departments. He thus rebukes that self-complacency and selfishness which would otherwise corrupt even the better portion of the race. He says to the intelligent, the good, the orderly, the cautious and the wise, you shall not only suffer the consequences of your own faults, but you shall even be involved in the external consequences of the faults and mistakes and follies of the unwise, the weak, the precipitate and the wicked, that you may understand that you are members one of another, bound to be hands and feet, heart and brain, prudence and goodness, not only for yourselves, but for all other men less fortunate than yourselves. I behold a special tenderness, wisdom and love in God, nay, a special justice, too, in thus mixing up all conditions, classes, ages and degrees of moral desert, in a common calamity to-day, in a common benefaction to-morrow, that he may bind us together, and perfect that fusion and unity which Christ came from heaven to establish, and whose recognition involves the present and final happiness of our race.

You see, then, that the operation of general laws, producing painful consequences, in frequent and particular cases, is maintained by God, for high public reasons, is indeed the only conceivable plan upon which a world, designed for human education and the common good of a whole race, could go on. But you also see, I trust, that these general laws are not powers, at any time, independent of God's will—a machinery originally set a-going by his hand, and now moving on in his absence, without his direct knowledge and consent, crushing and tearing whatever comes in its way. Laws have no power to execute themselves, and as physical science is proving every day, they are but names for our observations of the regularity and order with which God chooses—in his imperturbable and changeless, because all-wise and holy, will—to govern the world.

God, then, is as personally, directly present, in all actions that fall under rule or law, as in miracle itself. Because the apple of this autumn falls to the ground, as certainly as it did from the first tree that bore that oldest fruit, we are not to suppose that the law of gravitation acts by itself to-day, any more than it did the first instant it manifested itself. Strictly speaking, there is no law of gravitation ; it is our name for one of the ways in which God every instant compels material bodies to stand related to each other. And so of all general laws. God is *in* them, *behind* them, is *all* the force they have. They are our observations of the uniform way in which he acts under given circumstances, and he acts thus uniformly, because, if he did not, there could be no such thing as nature, no such thing as observation, experience, human existence. In short, when we quarrel with the operation of exact and rigid method in God, we quarrel with the first and indispensable condition of our very being. God himself could exist and act by miracle always. It were, if I may use such an expression, easier for him to do so. But man can only exist where God puts upon himself certain seeming restraints—for all laws and rules have that aspect—for man's sake; that is, to give him liberty of will, opportunities of experience and education—*i. e.*, only when God acts after a general plan, made intelligible to his creatures, reckoned upon by them, and found always reliable and constant.

Do not for one instant, then, imagine, that because general laws, and what we call Nature, the forces of the elements, the laws of matter, remove us from God, hide *Him* from *our* view, and seem to take us from his immediate and direct protection—do not imagine that they remove God from us, hide *us* from *his* view, or really deprive us of his immediate, direct, and perfect care and love. It is only on one side that the veil is opaque; only at one end that the action is indirect and general. God knows no such thing as general laws, secondary forces, material powers, physical agents; these are our names for his ways of action, which to himself are always direct, immediate, personal. There is not the least difference to him between a general and a special providence. The difference exists only to us. That part of God's good providence which we can reduce to rule, we call general; that part we cannot, special. But it is all special and particular to him, and it is literally true, that "the hairs of our head are all numbered," and that "not a sparrow falleth to the ground without our Father."

But what, I hear you ask, becomes of God's justice,

what of moral distinctions, what of a wise discrimination, if God, being actually present, and enforcing his own will, can whelm in common misfortunes hundreds of human beings unequal in desert, opposite in character, vastly dissimilar in wants and in responsibilities? "Master, carest thou not that we perish?" Is it not a natural cry for the good, the wise, the responsible, to raise, when they see themselves exposed to common ruin with the careless, the worn out, the useless, or the wicked? Could chance itself act with more disregard of particular claims, with less consideration for special cases, than God himself acts upon the theory now advanced, in a case, for instance, like that of the Austria?

My brethren, moral distinctions, exact justice, the most delicate and minute discriminations, reign eternally, universally, and with undisturbed accuracy, throughout God's government on earth and in heaven —reign in the moment when pestilence, fire, war, ocean, seem most successfully obliterating their lines and confusing their voices. Only we are foolish and blind enough to look for their operation in places and modes in which they never act, and where they are not made to act, while we fail to seek them in places and modes in which they ceaselessly act, and without the least exception, are always to be observed. The distinction lies here. Matter, by God's will, obeys material laws; spirit, spiritual laws. God's government in the physical world is regulated by physical principles; in the spiritual world, by spiritual principles. Now, man, being body and soul, belongs to both these kingdoms: the kingdom of matter, the kingdom of mind or spirit. As a part of the kingdom of matter, he falls, so far as his body is concerned, under regulations that do not have, and *must* not have, any obvious reference to his spiritual state. Fire burns the body of the holy martyr, precisely as if it were a lump of bullock's fat; water drowns a crew of five hundred precious lives as if it were a litter of kittens. The infant's innocent hand, caressing the pretty flame of the candle, is just as quickly and pitilessly scorched, as though it were that of a villain, kindling a fire beneath the floor of a house, that he might avenge some injury, or commit some further crime. Why does justice, pity, love, permit this gross confounding of good and bad, of innocent and guilty? But what have justice, pity, and love to do in the sphere of what is, for the highest and kindest ends, meant to be brute force, rigid, immoral, unconscious matter? *That* is a part of creation that God has not made, and could not make, without defeating its very purpose, otherwise than blind and deaf to all moral distinctions. Shall a good man expect his teeth not to ache, or only his *conscience* not to ache? Shall a wise man expect his body to be any stronger, less exposed to injury from heat and cold, than a foolish man? or only his mind to be stronger and less exposed to ignorance and superstition? In short, we must look for moral discriminations, moral equity, moral rewards and penalties in the moral sphere; in the fortunes of the mind, and heart, and conscience, not in the fortunes of the body and limbs. It is true that the mind takes care of the body, and the prudent and good man is not liable to all the risks and accidents that overtake the reckless. But no care can obviate all the casualties to which the bodies of the best are exposed, and when they fall, as to their bodies, into the general wreck that visits alike good and bad, we are not to look for the moral discrimination exercised towards them, in physical quarters, but in spiritual quarters. Sagacity, prudence, calmness, self-discipline, give the wise and good an advantage even in respect of physical perils; but God cannot, and does not, seem any more anxious to save the body of a tender woman than of a strong man; of a young child, than of a worn-out life; of a missionary, than of a heathen. But are you on this account to suppose that he makes no *moral* distinction between them? Are you to suppose that they are really undergoing the same inward experience, because their outward fortune is the same, or that the attitude of their minds, hearts, consciences, are alike, because they are equally at the mercy of sea and fire? Oh, no. The solid, happy, safe earth, did not present, the very hour the poor Austria was wrapped in indiscriminate flames, greater contrasts of feelings, greater varieties of moral condition, greater differences of relation to spiritual things, to truth, honor, virtue, to Christ, God, immortality, than the sufferers by that common fate, on the decks of that weltering vessel. Justice, a special providence, the rewards of virtue, the penalties of vice, were all in the inner world of conscience, vindicating and illustrating themselves, then and there, with just as much variety and distinctness, both to God's eye and probably to the soul's own experience, as though the victims had all, at the distance of years, been dying in their different beds. Good men did not become bad men then and there, nor bad men good men. The innocent did not lose their purity, nor the guilty acquire innocency. The believing did not abandon their faith, nor the unbelieving enjoy its support. No good and pious Christian regretted he had led a holy life, because it was suddenly to end, and no wicked man thought his past folly and crime likely to be washed out by the sea, or burnt up in the fire ! There were as many grades of character, as many sorts of heart and conscience, as many indicated triumphs of faith, submission, moral courage, and patience—as many defalcations of principle, of disinterestedness, of duty and honor, illustrated in the conduct of that single hour, as though the lives of those sufferers had been continued to their natural close. God's spirit, Christ's religion, vindicated themselves in that dreadful hour, in the triumphant, believing souls, though in the smitten and dying bodies, of the pious and the pure. The spirit of the world, the flesh and the devil, vindicated themselves in the panic, the cowardice, the selfishness, the folly and agony of the impious, the base, and the abandoned. God's spiritual laws, his holy will, his promises of love, pity, and protection, were all fulfilled towards the souls of his children in that trying moment, and we are not left to any rightful murmur, or even proper wonder, that his pity, his special providence, his fatherly care, were not exerted. They *were* exerted ; perfectly, accurately, completely. God was there in all his omniscience, in all his fatherhood, in all his sovereignty. Fire and sea obtained no triumph over him, baffled none of his desires, defeated none of his plans, seized nothing from his grasp. The inward peace, the spiritual safety, the moral salvation of his saints, was far beyond the reach of accident, and could be mixed up in no promiscuous fate. And it is so everywhere and always. General laws do not forbid or hinder a special providence ; there is no difference between them.

One other reflection. God does not think of *death* as we think of it. Indeed, it does not exist to him. What we see as men dropping out of existence, he sees as men springing into new and higher life ; the fire that parts their vital thread to us, does to him but melt their chain of imprisonment. What call for interference is there to God, who sees five hundred souls making a short passage to another state of existence, where we see only five hundred precious lives extinguished ?

Let me add two or three special thoughts more immediately connected with this particular calamity. In the recent triumphs of man over matter, time, space and sea, there has been, perhaps, too much spiritual pride ; it may be that God's providence has kindly rebuked a general peril for our souls, in this sudden disaster upon the very element where our victories were lately won.

Again, the sufferers by this calamity were not Americans, but foreigners. It was not American recklessness that occasioned the disaster ; and this may serve as a useful rebuke to the other side of the world, too fond of charging us with sins that, to say the least, are not peculiar to us. But, more especially, the sympathies drawn forth from our own people towards the noble and heroic sufferers by this event, the display many of them made, of brave and gentle humanity, may have a beneficent tendency to unite us more cordially with our foreign population, so valuable, so large, often so misunderstood a portion of our people. God grant, that their homes, full of wailing and sorrow, may call forth towards the whole German race in America, a heartier sympathy, and a more cordial fraternity !

Finally, brethren, on shore and at home, God's laws are now silently operating in the same temper and spirit in which they worked on board that fated vessel. A sea of destruction surrounds us ; the flames of temptation are lapping our garments ; the very tabernacles we dwell in, are on fire with our appetites. What matters a few days, months, or years, in which we are still to live—seeing that our death-doom is already pronounced, our mortal ruin fixed and inevitable? Sixty-seven escaped from the Austria ; not one shall escape from this ocean-bound, fire-hearted, doomed world we inhabit. "Master, carest thou not that we perish?" we may just as reasonably cry as those who saw death at their very side. Invisibly he is at ours ; only a moment for God, separates us from our fate ! But God does care, cares most anxiously, paternally, tenderly—cares every day and hour, that we perish not. So far as we neglect our duty, darken our consciences, harden our hearts, reject our Saviour, break our Maker's laws, stain our bodies, abuse our earthly home, squander our time, bury our talents, we are now perishing. The wildest ocean could not quench, the fiercest fire could not burn, as sin now quenches the soul's light, as sin now shrivels the soul's life. God is, meanwhile, imploring us by his Son, by our own consciences, by his written and by his unwritten word, not to perish—to clothe ourselves in the adamantine garments of righteousness that cannot burn, when hay and stubble shall turn to ashes—to put on that robe of faith our Lord gave Peter, which shall buoy us up beyond the power of any waves. Behold, Christ, no longer asleep in the hinder part of the boat, but here awake—standing behind the thin veil of these elements, that are his body and his blood, and saying to the storms of the world, "Peace, be still"; saying, in answer to your prayers, "Master, carest thou not that we perish?"—"He that believeth in me, though he were dead, yet shall he live; and whosoever liveth and believeth in me, shall never die."

OCTOBER 1, 1858.

III.

MAN.

III.

MAN.

SERMON XIII.

HUMAN NATURE—ITS DIGNITY.

"For what man knoweth the things of a man, save the spirit of man which is in him?"—1 Cor. ii. 11.

Different questions demand different tribunals and different witnesses. Some are to be tried by the Scriptures, others by universal reason; others, still, by positive experts. If we carry a question of law to a court of equity, or a question of fact to a court of law, a question of physics to a spiritual tribunal, or a question of religious experience before a bench of mathematicians, we shall make no progress towards a just decision. In like manner, questions strictly of our own day cannot be settled by appeal to the past; questions of statesmanship, by abstract principles; nor questions of absolute morals, by expediency. Thus, questions touching human nature, are not to be debated exegetically, and by appeals to Scripture—but psychologically, and by appeals to consciousness; for, as our text well says, "What man knoweth the things of a man, but the spirit of man that is in him?"

But is not the question of human nature a theological question, and therefore to be determined by the arbiter of all theological disputes—the Scriptures? Let us consider this point a moment.

The settlement of any of our modern questions in theology by an appeal to the Scriptures, is a much less easy method of adjudication than might at first appear. The fairer, the more sagacious and learned, the investigator is, the more conscious will he be of the enormous difficulty of arriving at the actual teachings of the New Testament in regard to opinions that have first become important long since the Scriptures were written, and upon which, accordingly, they express no formal and direct decision. Notwithstanding this, there is a half-dishonest and half-superstitious way of forcing texts that sound decisive, into the service of sectarian prejudice, which, though very much in vogue, every frank and truth-loving spirit must despise and condemn.

Any thing can be proved out of the Scriptures by word-mongers to the satisfaction of those who already agree with them. What can be more astonishing than that the advocates of Trinitarianism and Unitarianism, of Calvinism and Arminianism, of eternal punishment and universal salvation, of Episcopacy and Congregationalism, should all appeal with equal confidence to the Scriptures as being unqualifiedly on their own side? The views of these disputants are directly contradictory and exclusive of each other; and yet, with absolute boldness, they not only assert that their own opinions are the clear and express teaching of the New Testament, but that the study of the Bible alone has brought them to these several opposite conclusions! Possibly they think so, for it is not easy to know whence we derive our opinions. But, I am confident that no man living gets, or can get, his theological opinions exclusively, or even mainly, from the Scriptures. The judgment is forestalled; the mind early taken possession of by prevailing views, the expectations shaped, the belief settled, long before we come to read the Scriptures with critical attention. The whole experience of ages, the light of science, the influence of political ideas, the conclusions of practical wisdom—as well as the authority of traditions, established churches and sacred usages—combine to prepossess us in this age with certain opinions, antecedent to scriptural investigations, which color and communicate their own perspective to the sacred records; and, on examining them, we find there what we look for—arguments for conclusions already adopted. The Trinitarian finds his pre-assumed Trinity; the Unitarian his pre-assumed Unity; the Calvinist his predetermined total depravity; the Arminian his predetermined free-will. It is quite impossible that a collection of writings of any description, sacred or profane, written two thousand years ago, should throw a direct light upon questions of our own day. The spirit and temper, the drift and tenor of the New Testament may be indirectly decisive of all such questions, and it is this which candid minds and single-eyed lovers of truth will look to; but so long as the letter of the Scriptures is appealed to, to settle questions which were never before the minds of their authors—so long we shall have fruitless controversies, and bitter strifes of opinion.

I do not hesitate to say that *our* questions, the theological disputes of this, or of any recent age, were never in, or before, the minds of the scriptural writers. They never agitated, or anticipated, our question of unity and trinity ; of original sin and innate rectitude ; of eternal punishment and final restoration. They had questions that looked like these, or which may be tortured into a resemblance to these, but they were not the same, nor any thing near the same ; and we can honestly expect little positive and direct help from the Scriptures in adjudicating these modern disputes. I do not say that they are not very important—just as important as the scriptural disputes—or that the general tenor of Scripture does not sustain one or the other side, but only that they are not fairly to be settled by textual authority, and cannot honestly be referred to that tribunal, as if it had distinctly anticipated and adjudged them.

The proper use of the Scriptures is this : to fill ourselves with the spirit of them ; their pure morality and exalted piety, their great and undisputed facts and principles, their general drift and aim ; and then, thus furnished, to allow our minds, in the formation of specific opinions, the freest play, which our total general culture, knowledge of human nature, experience of life, acquaintance with philosophy and the general illumination of the age, demand or inspire. Indeed, this is a method followed by all, and necessarily so, to some degree : timidly, inconsistently, and with theoretical protest, by most ; courageously, consistently, and openly—with full conviction of its propriety—by a few. It is not to be inferred from this view that the New Testament teaches nothing definite; that it has no doctrines; that its truth is not inspired, or its authority not decisive; that its spirit is the only thing that binds us. I freely confess my rational allegiance to the letter of Christ's teachings, as well as the spirit of them, although I cannot extend this deference to the letter of his disciples' teachings. But what I maintain is that the letter is silent upon *our* disputes, and that it is only inferentially and in the help of his spirit that we can settle our later controversies by the New Testament.

This conclusion is very strongly forced upon me, when I look into the Bible for its doctrine of human nature. Considering the obstinacy of assertion on both sides, it is really extraordinary how little is said there about human nature, and how contradictory of itself that little is, supposing our triangular question of total depravity, hereditary depravity, or original rectitude, to be the question referred to. I presume there is not the least real incongruity, and that the inconsistency all proceeds from our insisting that the writers are intending to settle our questions, when they are speaking of quite other matters. Imagine two persons of dignity, B and C, equally acquainted with another man, A, to be earnestly conversing about him. B says indignantly, in view of some recent misbehavior on his part, "Well, what a *bad* fellow A is!" "Yes," replies C, "still he has a *good* heart!" to which B reluctantly assents. Is there any real inconsistency here? But now imagine two overhearers of this short colloquy to assume that B and C were carrying on a metaphysical discussion as to the original character of human nature; one maintaining that B, when he called A a *bad* fellow, characterized his nature, and consequently human nature, as utterly depraved; while the other maintained that when C declared A to have a *good* heart, he pronounced a general eulogy on the rectitude of human nature. Suppose this, and you have a fair example of the way in which the scattered sayings, found in the Scriptures, for and against men, their characters and state, have been abused by theologians. Man is said, in the first chapter of Genesis, to have been made in the image of God—referring, doubtless, to his gifts of reason and conscience; but a very unfair and unreasonable use is made of this passage, when the whole doctrine of the dignity of human nature, as opposed to the doctrine of the fall, is built up upon it. In the same book, God is said to have cursed the ground, on account of Adam's sin; but what a monstrous inference is it, that he cursed him and his race, and allowed our whole nature to be changed, on this account? Again, Christ calls certain men children of God; and certain other men children of the devil! Are we to presume that he was, in either case, expressing any opinion upon the metaphysical question of native depravity or original goodness? How eagerly have we snatched at the text in Ecclesiastes, "Lo! this only have I found, that God hath made man upright; but they have sought out many inventions,"—as a distinct and positive decision of this question. When, any one who will honestly examine the context, will see that Solomon had a very low idea of mankind, and a worse one of womankind, expressed in the very previous verse, with a bitterness never exceeded: "One man among a thousand have I found; but a woman among all these have I not found."

On the other hand, the famous phrase in Ephesians ii. 3, "And were by nature (or naturally) children of wrath, even as others,"—which was, as any ordinary candor will see, no expression of Paul's opinion touching the constitutional state of human nature, but only a passing criticism of the actual immorality of the Gentiles—has been made a very corner-stone of a theory that "all men are born under God's wrath and curse, and so made liable to all the miseries of this life and the pains of hell for ever."

I confess that I must take the same kind of exception to the sweeping inferences drawn by Dr. Channing and other noble minds, from Peter's famous sentence, "Honor all men." He adds, you remember, "Honor the king." Might we not as reasonably imagine him to be expressing an opinion in favor of monarchical institutions in that phrase, as in defence of human nature in the other?

The simple truth is, that our question touching human nature is not a scriptural question; but a question of philosophy, of experience, of natural religion, of history, of metaphysics and psychology. The Scriptures, indeed, throw light upon it, in their whole tenor, object and spirit. Christ's character and mission illuminates it. The influences and spirit of Christianity are indispensable to its solution; but it is, after all, not a textual question, nor mainly a scriptural question, and so long as we hope to settle it with concordance, lexicon and grammar, we shall only belittle ourselves and the subject, and help to perpetuate the narrowness, superstition and literality, which are the chief hindrances to truth's progress. The question belongs to another court. "For what man knoweth the things of a man, but the spirit of man that is in him?"

What, then, is the real, practical question touching human nature, as it lies in the mind, and affects the civilization of our own day? It is not the question of the Scriptures, which was purely an inquiry about human *character*. Men are spoken of as good and bad, as sinners and saints, as children of God and of the devil there, purely with reference to their *character*, and without the least reference to their *nature*. The difference is easily shown. You do not discuss the nature of the horse, his admirable adaptation by strength and docility, by speed and weight, by beauty and use, to human wants—when you are criticizing this or that horse, as good or bad. If the question were to come up whether camels were not better than horses, or machines than either, for all locomotive or draught purposes, then it would be directly in order, to consider the *nature* of the horse, his capacity for improvement in breed, his essential and relative merits as compared with other animals, or instruments—with a view to decide whether true economy should not abandon his use and exterminate his species. There is an obvious distinction, then, between nature and character. Ordinarily, the question of human character is a much more practical and important question, than that of human nature. But there are times and occasions, when the question of human nature is far more important and more practical than the other. Because, the treatment, correction and improvement of human character and of society, by means of it, may, and often does, depend vastly upon the accuracy, justness and truth of our knowledge and estimate of human nature.

As to the question of human character, there cannot well be any essential difference of opinion among people who mingle freely in the world. Different people have different ways of talking about it, according to temperament, discrimination and habit; but they cannot think very differently about it, more than they can differ about the climate, or the weather, or other staring facts. Men are good and bad, mixed creatures all. In that part of themselves in which spontaneousness prevails, they are more or less good—with a decided leaning to what we admire or like; in that part in which *will* and *responsibility* reign, they are more or less good and bad, with a decided leaning to what is not approvable and right. But as the spontaneous, irresponsible portion of man is far larger than the voluntary and moral portion, there is—I do not say, more merit than demerit, but—more good than bad in all, or, at any rate, in most men, that is to say, in man generally considered. Thus the affections, sympathies, motives, apprehensions —all that part of man which acts spontaneously—are generous, kind, prompt and reliable. We universally trust them. Where self-interest is not aroused, we expect men to be kind, courteous, pitiful. Why, then, has humanity so evil a reputation? For this reason. The good part of human character (if we ought not rather to say human nature; and yet, as we speak of men and women, and not of man or humanity, character is the more accurate phrase)—we have less occasion to praise, than we have to blame the bad part, just as we note our ill days and not our well ones ; and make conspicuous public buildings of our courts, and jails and hospitals—while our happy private homes, unnoticed, cover ten thousand times over their area of ground. This is the reason why, judging by ordinary talk, you might think men practically had a low opinion of their race ; that ordinarily they have occasion to talk only of that part of man in which he is confessedly weak.

There was lately a weekly newspaper published in New York, probably by English capitalists, whose object I presume to have been, though it was not confessed, to divert emigration from the United States into the Canadas. Into this paper, most ably conducted, were transferred reliable accounts, copied out of all the newspapers from all quarters of the country, of the murders, robberies, slave-insurrections, planters' cruelties, election-riots, party-frauds, defalcations, sufferings of emigrants, crash of banks, insecurity of property—in short, every thing that could give an unfavorable, discouraging and disgusting view of American life and society. So far as I have studied this mortifying periodical—which, it is really creditable to our toleration, enjoyed a free existence—it stated nothing that was not true. But, it absolutely, and of purpose, excluded from its columns every thing that painted the prosperity, order, freedom, industry, progress, humanity, good morals or piety of the land. Now let a German or an Englishman take this newspaper, containing nothing false, but devoted exclusively to the collection of what is disgusting, criminal and dangerous in our political and economic condition, and form his estimate of American institutions and American character from it, and he would do precisely what theorists do when they accept the ordinary confession and criticism of human faults and weaknesses, as man's complete and reliable account of his whole self. The confession and criticism may be ever so true ; but it is not the whole truth, nor half the truth, and, in the full light of what is good, amiable and encouraging in human character, the bad sinks into a very hopeful disproportion. And this is not my judgment, but yours and everybody's, when we take time to think about it, as we seldom do.

But dropping here the question of human character, the very different one of human nature remains. This is comparatively a new question, considered practically. True, in the Eastern nations, it was early and greatly discussed by philosophers. That eternal problem of the origin of evil always demands solution, and the hypothesis of a good and an evil principle struggling for mastery in the universe, represented by spirit and matter—one a blessed, and the other a cursed thing—furnished at least an adroit evasion of the difficulty. Doubtless this speculation of the Hindoos, and of the Oriental nations generally, growing out of their soft and meditative temperament, confirmed their fatalistic tendencies, and in some degree accounts for the unprogressive and monotonous state of their society. But in our day, when matter has come to occupy a thousand times the attention it ever did before, and if bad, ought to be a thousand times more mischievous, we have been compelled to acknowledge its beneficent influence on human character and prospects. Its development, use, and transformation, is a chief occasion and cause of the education, advancement, and happiness of man. In like manner, other things, once deemed evil in the constitution of the globe—its wide and stormy oceans, vast deserts, rugged soils, volcanoes, and earthquakes—physical geography, in the light of a better economic and political science, has discovered to be blessings in disguise, and wonderfully fitted to the wants and felicitation of the race. In a parallel way, the appetites, passions and properties, even the jealousies, suspicions, and apprehensions of humanity, are gradually getting to be understood as indispensable elements of our nature, and in their proper place, and under control quite possible to us, altogether good, and not at all evil ; not one of them to be wished out of the marvellous compound ; not one of them, otherwise than fundamentally important and essential. That some of these powers are subject to excess and liable to explosion, is no more decisive of their evil origin or bad character, than the prevailing ophthalmia of Egypt is a proof of the poor design of the human eye ; or the consumption of New England, of the bad planning of the human lungs ; or the occasional devastation by fire, of its hellish origin ; or the now and then destructive copiousness of rain, of its malevolent source. Human nature has enormous elements of danger in it, as the sea has storms, wrecks, ruin, in its mighty and beneficent depths. The passions of man, glorious and divine endowments as they are, are betraying, perilous, and forever requiring watch and ward. But the vessel of war might as well sail without its powder-magazine, or adduce the incessant care demanded in its use and guardianship, as a proof of the necessity of abandoning it, as human nature allege the excesses of human weakness, folly and crime, as evidences of its diabolic, disordered, and imperfect constitution. Its constitution is good and only good, divine and only divine ; but it is in the hands of a growing, progressive, and inexperienced creature, who neither at once understands it, nor could be expected to understand it ; who uses it, much as a child uses his tool-box, to cut his fingers, tear his clothes, and bruise the furniture, but who presently learns to hammer, saw, and plane, in a way that proves his tools not of a malignant or superfluous origin.

The alleged depravity, or the constitutionally disordered state, by some theologians attributed to human nature, has led to practical results of a very sad and disastrous sort. You can easily see what different policies, education, government, police, society would pursue, according as it adopted the theory that human passions, appetites, and instincts, were to be withstood and suppressed, as malignant and devilish in their origin, or directed and controlled as merely blind and excessive, while flowing from a pure and divine source. You see, for instance, a will in your child, which tends to obstinacy. You may either call the *will* evil, or you may only call the *obstinacy* evil. If you call the *will* evil, you will proceed to break it ; and in this process you will either fail, besides arousing all the possible hatefulness which injustice and ignorance can evoke, or by a mightier force, you will succeed, and crush, not only the will, but the whole nature you dealt with. You meant to tear off a crooked branch, and you pulled over the whole tree. If, on the contrary, you merely call the *obstinacy* evil, you will spare and respect the will, and endeavor, by aid of the intellect and conscience, to teach it self-control, and direct it where all its vigor and determination will be useful. Thus, obstinacy is converted into firmness, and the ungoverned boy becomes the self-controlled hero! In like manner, anger is the excess of indignation at injustice and wrong—jealousy, excess of love. There are no qualities of a bad origin in human nature, any more than in physical nature; and for the same reason, that God made them both.

The growing perception of this truth is changing the temper of the physical sciences, and will ultimately change moral and theological science. How reverent and watchful of law has science become! how believing in the beneficence and divinity of nature! Adoring worshippers sit before the microscope, the photographic mirror, the geologic strata. There is nothing common or unclean. "Dirt," as was well said, "is matter in the wrong place." There is no dirt, when matter is kept in its proper place. There is only order, beauty, beneficence, in physical nature or human nature, when considered in their design. How tenderly and patiently has medicine, once so bold, aggressive, and alert, learned to wait on nature, following her hints, assisting her efforts, and relying chiefly on her own healing and recuperative powers? And how has politics grown generous and favorable to human rights and human improvement, in precise proportion as it has learned to trust man, to educate, encourage, and bless him, instead of standing over him with sword and bayonet, addressing his fears, and repressing his hopes and his faculties?

Modern civilization, so far as it is new, encouraging, and successful, is based on faith in human nature, as God's work, and not as Satan's botch. And this faith is at the root of all reforms, as want of it is at the bottom of all resistance to light, freedom, happiness, and is the perpetuation of conventional wrongs and prejudices.

Let us not suppose, that to maintain this great and glorious doctrine in all its integrity and encouragement, it is necessary to keep any facts out of view, or to maintain any one-sided and uncandid opinion.

Who, for instance, will wish to conceal, or to deny the hereditary descent of dangerous propensities, any more than of good and beautiful dispositions? We do not deny that goitre, consumption, gout, are hereditary, but we do not allow that this shows the human body to be depraved in its origin or constitution. When we take away the subjects of these diseases from the circumstances that produced them, they recover, and in a generation or two their diseases are extinguished. There is a resistance to them in the body, which, assisted, may overcome them. Obedient to this analogy, I would not deny hereditary tendencies to rage, to jealousy, to insanity. The mind may be diseased, and through its connection with the body may be propagated in a diseased condition. But this proves nothing against the worth, or rectitude, or wholesomeness of human nature, more than a murrain among sheep establishes the general defeat of that creature's final cause to produce wool and food for man. We recognize these hereditary defects as diseases, excrescences, perversions of human nature, and treat them as such ; not as its normal, ordinary, and wholesome condition. The real question is, how deep and how common is this alleged disease ? Is it total, or vast, or general ? Has it not been immensely exaggerated ? Has not the disposition to treat the soul as sick, been at least as common an error as to treat the body as sick—and have not both of them been over-dosed and over-watched ? It is the want of food, and not of medicine, which has impoverished whole races and tribes. Hereditary diseases, virulent as they are, are not the common causes of physical degeneracy, but bad habits, self-indulgence, poor diet, or hardship and toil. And so of the soul. Its hereditary disorders, not to be denied, are not its chief difficulties, but its present want of light, education, encouragement, confidence, sympathy, and help. We have heard Christ called the Physician of souls, until we have forgotten that his more common office is that of the shepherd of the sheep. To give our daily food, not to cure our occasional hurts, is his great and constant office. The bread that came down from heaven, the well of water, the light of the world—these are his most appropriate symbols ; not the vinegar and the gall, which he drank that we might be spared them ; not the nails and the spear, that he felt that we might not feel them !

Nor let us, in our sense of the greatness of human nature, forget that what is sometimes said to disparage and abase it, may be said, with equal earnestness, to exalt and honor it ; namely, that it is an entire dependent on the grace of God ; that all it has of good, or hopes of good, or can do of good, is from above, and in the inspiration and strength of the divine mercy, love, and assistance. By itself it is indeed most weak, impotent, and blind. Leave the eye, and strike away the sun; the ear, and destroy the vibrating air; the palate, and deny it food; and what has become of the glory of the senses? Or imagine the earth, with all its roots, and plants, and herbs, waiting for spring rains that never come, and a tardy sun that will not climb the sky?

Is it to the shame, the sorrow, the mortification of human nature, that it needs God's presence, blessing, support, assistance, to give it strength, wisdom, and happiness? Is not this its glory, and beauty, and joy? That it needs God, and that God loves its need, and will supply it? I insist, with the fullest conviction, that our nature is far more hopeful, considered in its capacities, than in its faculties, if such a distinction may be allowed. But just this is human nature: its openness to God, its power to entertain the heavenly guest, and to become the temple and residence of the Most High.

But God's coming, in and by his Christ or his Spirit, changes human nature, as the rain from heaven changes the channels of the brooks and rivers, the look of the trees and grasses. It creates, by developing and completing. The ocean out of the bay, leaves us an ugly basin of flats and mud; but how does the returning tide beautify the place!

It becomes us to remember, however, that we have power, such as nature does not possess, to resist and shut out the divine influence! God will not intrude. Christ is never an uninvited guest. The heavenly powers respect our freedom, and it is essential to our dignity, as moral beings, that our loyalty should be voluntary and our obedience professed. This, our dignity, is also our peril. Glorious as our nature is, it is fraught with enormous perils—none, perhaps, that are fatal, but many of terrible significance and dreadfulness.

Any account of humanity that leaves out its crimes, its frightful sorrows, its self-cruelties, its enormous mistakes and capacities for evil and punishment, is a false and a deluding, a partial and a childish, view of it. But any view of its sorrows, crimes, and sins, which hides its glory, denies its sacred origin, hinders its liberty, or introduces a policy of discouragement and despair, is infinitely more false, puerile, and unjust.

Reverence your nature! reverence your race! honor humanity! study your own soul, and all souls, with tender awe, and pity, and love! welcome Christ as your example, guide, and helper—your food and your medicine! receive the Holy Spirit as the residue of that of which you have the earnest in your hearts! For God comes to His own as Christ came to his own; and our nature is equally sacred in its origin and its constitution, in its need and supply of divine grace, its law of progress, and its immortal destiny!

FEB. 14, 1858.

SERMON XIV.

THE ORIGIN AND QUALITY OF SIN.

"Have they stumbled, that they should fall? God forbid: but rather through their fall salvation is come unto the Gentiles, for to provoke them unto jealousy. Now, if the fall of them be the riches of the world, and the diminishing of them the riches of the Gentiles; how much more their fulness?"—ROMANS xi. 11, 12.

THE fall or unfaithfulness of the Jews was, according to these words, to be converted by God into the elevation of the Gentiles; and their fall was only a stumble, not an overthrow, which was to teach even them, in future, a more careful walk. I do not quote this passage, which many other texts support, but which many others also conflict with, as decisive of the doctrine which I am about to lay down—which is better argued on general than on merely scriptural grounds—but as an evidence that whatever else may be taught in the New Testament at other times, the doctrine of moral good coming out of moral evil, of sin being overruled to the salvation even of its authors and victims, is also taught there.

In addressing you in my last discourse, on the subject of human nature, its constitution and worth, I purposely omitted one great department of the theme, as being too important for any but a separate and exclusive discussion—i. e., the origin, nature, and effects of sin. I showed you at that time, that human nature was divine in its origin and constitution ; that its powers and faculties were all good ; that its injurious and unhappy fruits proceeded from the abuse of attributes and qualities whose use was lawful and beneficent ; and that the errors, follies, and wickedness of the world, were not traceable to any depravity of human nature, which is God's perfect work, but to the ignorance, wilfulness, and folly of those who possess this nature, without understanding or respecting it.

Now, it may fairly enough be asked, whether this wilfulness, ignorance, and folly, are not a part of human nature ; and how the contempt and reprobation we feel for them are to be averted from human nature itself? If we confess that men are everywhere weak, erring, passionate, sinful, what avails it to say that their nature is not so? How have universal laxity, disobedience and wrong, crept into a race, whose nature is divine and pure ; made for goodness and happiness alone? Does a sweet fountain well out bitter waters, or a fig-tree bring forth thorns? Let me answer with an illustration.

If you look into any work of natural history for an account of the lion, you will find him described as a powerful, ferocious animal, capable of destroying the most fierce and dangerous beasts of the forest ; his height four feet, his length six or eight, his mane shaggy and copious, his roar deafening, his claws of enormous size, sharpness, and power. But suppose the hunter, coming upon the lion's den, in the absence of the dam, finds the new-born whelps, hunts them with his hounds, and carries them home as his trophies. They are young lions! But how do they correspond with the naturalist's description? Yet they certainly have the nature of the lion, and the naturalist has described the lion truly. It is evident that the naturalist would have done no justice to the lion's nature, if he had given the whelp as a sample of it.

Does it not at once come home to us, that the nature of a thing is described only when the perfection of which it is capable, and to which it ultimately attains, is depicted; that the whelp is not the lion; that the oaken sapling is not the oak; that the infant is not the man; that the growing, undeveloped, unregulated human creature, is not the representative of human nature?

All lions do not come to their majestic growth; all oaks are not spreading and long-lived; but this does not make the lion less than the king of beasts, the oak less than the monarch of the woods. It may, however, properly be asked, whether, if only here and there a lion, or an oak were found of noble proportions, we should still hold on to our lofty description of these products. I answer, perhaps not; for the ordinary and permanent circumstances in which things are placed, must be accepted as a part of their description or nature.

If an orange-tree in a glass-house were capable of being grown to the size of an oak, we should not call this forced and unnatural product a representative of the nature of the orange-tree. But in truth such artificial circumstances are *not* capable of producing the perfection of any fruit.

It must be conceded, then, that human nature is not to be contemplated independently of human circumstances; that what men ordinarily come to, has a proper place in our estimate of their nature; that we have no right to select a few specimens of great men and exalted characters, and present them as the representatives of our common nature.

It must, however, on the other hand, be remembered that unlike the lion or the oak, man does not, in any case, according to Scripture teachings and our admitted theory, attain his growth in this world; that his whole terrestrial existence, if we seriously and thoughtfully accept the doctrine of his immortality, is an inconceivably small part of his complete life, comparing with his endless existence in a ratio infinitely less than his earthly infancy compares with his earthly manhood. If it be his nature to live forever, his nature can show itself only in its rudimentary forms in his brief lifetime. All that we can fitly demand of his nature, to constitute a claim for it on our respect and awe, is that it should exhibit a design and plan, with original faculties and dispositions corresponding to it, of a divine beauty, skill and excellence; that we should see a general tendency in his providential circumstances to develop this plan; that the failures in it should be explicable on principles not inconsistent with its alleged worth, or the divine love for it; and that the general idea of humanity, with all its errors, weaknesses and follies, left upon the honest, thoughtful student of his nature, should be that of reverence, tenderness, hope and sympathy. Such a position we claim for it.

If the errors, sins, follies, mistakes of humanity

are such as were to have been expected from the infancy of an immortal creature, made in the image of God; if they have a tendency to correct themselves; if they diminish as the race grows older; if the providence of God, natural and supernatural, is successfully directed to the education, and adapted, by ever improving methods, to the theory of his gradual and progressive emancipation; then there is nothing in the admitted blunders, failures or sins of the race, to discourage our hopes of it, or abate our respect for its design. If it is of the nature of humanity to grow, and to grow in alternate moral sunshine and storm; to grow amid winds that sometimes uproot it, or break its boughs, but oftener under rains that feed its roots and skies that warm its sap—then we must not adduce its ruined specimens, or its bruised and battered branches, as evidences of its worthlessness or of the divine indignation, but acknowledge that its general trials and obstacles, and even individual overthrows, are not inconsistent with its characteristic success. Man advances, though men fall. The army conquers, though many dead are left on the field. The campaign is glorious, though this skirmish was unfortunate; that company defeated; and many promising officers were lost in the war. Its object was gained; its flag waved in triumph over the capitol and citadel of its foe.

Few, I suppose, will be disposed to deny, that, since Adam left Paradise, humanity has ever been, and continues in, an educational and progressive state, or that such a state has been recognized and responded to by God's Providence! How else can we account for the slow supplantation of less by more elevated codes of morality and religion, in the successive dispensations, Noachic, Abrahamic, Mosaic and Christian? God recognizes, that is, expects and provides for, progress. In other words, he does not demand of humanity to produce its perfect fruits at its planting. It is a slow growth, and requires a different kind of culture at different stages; now transplantation, then pruning; here rain; there sunshine; its shoots precede its blossoms; its blossoms its fruit; "first the blade, then the ear, then the full corn in the ear."

But, according to popular theories, all this progress has been made necessary by an unexpected falling away from perfection in our first ancestor. Had he not sinned, our race would have continued perfect and happy without the necessity for progress, or the need of any of those educational and recuperative processes to which Providence has resorted. Let those who can, believe this! Let those also who can, call the unfallen Adam and Eve, satisfactory patterns and types of our complete humanity! Imagine a world of Adams and Eves, living in a garden, on spontaneous fruits, ignorant of the distinction between good and evil, and without any capacity of moral change or improvement! Can any amount of credulity enable an enlightened and candid mind of the present day to think this world originally made to be occupied by such a race; that unfallen Adams and Eves could ever have developed its resources, or their own powers and capacities of moral and spiritual happiness? Can any subtlety perceive a true distinction between their condition and that of the innocent but feeble islanders of some few spots in the Pacific? Can any degree of superstition regard a state of unfallen holiness, which allowed our first parents to succumb in the midst of perfect bliss, and under God's own direct care, and instructions, before the first temptation, as superior to our present moral condition?

If Adam fell, the race rose by his fall; he fell up, and nothing happier for our final fortunes ever occurred than when the innocents of the garden learned their shame, and fled into the hardships and experiences of a disciplinary and growing humanity. Nor think me bold in saying as much as this; for the whole Christian scheme proceeds upon the popular hypothesis that "sin abounded, that grace might more abound." Would the Church consent to give up its Christ, to regain its unfallen Adam? But for the fallen Adam, according to its theory, we could not have had the risen Christ. As our text says of the Jews, it may be said also of our first parents—"Have they stumbled that they should fall? God forbid; but rather through their fall, salvation is come unto the Gentiles." Has not God himself then made Adam's fall a blessing to the race? and if so, why do we inconsistently continue to call it a curse? The truth is, God's curses are only blessings in disguise, and his punishments, the strokes of his mercy and love.

The radical vice of the popular way of thinking about moral evil, lies in the supposition that God did not originally design or anticipate our earthly experiences as a race; that Adam and Eve's condition was one of possible and desirable continuance; that a state of spotless innocency is better than a state of moral exposure and moral struggle; and that all our humanity is not entitled to use, development and play, in its grand career of being. On the other hand, the true theory of humanity presents us with a race brought into this world for its education, starting with moral and intellectual infancy, and liable to all the mistakes, weaknesses and follies, which an ungrown and inexperienced nature begets.

But this is evidently not a full account of the origin and nature of what we call *sin*, though it might be of evil. If we stopped here, we should certainly leave some of the most characteristic experiences, and most universal and profound instincts of our nature and life, entirely unexplained.

If all the evil in the world is the result of inexperience, mistake, youthful blundering and weakness, whence arises the general sense of the difference between faults and misfortunes, the right and the expedient, the mistaken and the criminal? How shall we account for the phenomena of conscience, its approving and disapproving voice, its remorse, its apprehensions? If sin be only weakness, error, mistake, inexperience, it can hardly be regarded as voluntary, or wilful, as worthy of blame, or of punishment; and the universal consciousness of wrong and unworthiness would be proved to be a gigantic delusion, and an enormous superstition.

Now, an answer to this objection is found in the statement that our condition, as a race, is that of the education and development of *moral* beings; and that moral beings are—by the very force of the term moral—free, accountable, responsible, and therefore liable to become sinful. The difference between sins and mistakes is, that a voluntary or moral element enters into that transgression of the law, which is properly styled a sin; while a mistake has no such quality.

But why should this element of free will, this moral power, which distinguishes us from the beasts, be so solemn and awful a faculty? The beasts have will, and some measure of freedom, but they have no moral nature. What is it that constitutes a moral nature? This question throws us back upon the nature of God, who is a moral being. And his morality lies in his love and unswerving practice of justice, truth, goodness. These qualities are not merely expedient, productive of happiness, in accordance with law; but they are intrinsically sacred, holy, lovely and awful, and they constitute the glory, sanctity, and blessedness of the divine nature. Man's moral nature consists in his constitutional power to perceive these attributes of right, of goodness, of sanctity in God, and to recognize their authority over his own soul and life. He approves himself when he obeys this authority. He disapproves himself when he disobeys it; and this is what he means by, and feels as, sin. It is not merely a mistake to do that which is contrary to justice, truth, and goodness—a weakness, an impolitic and unwise step; it is a sin, a cause for self-reproach, remorse, repentance. It is not that one's happiness is impaired, but one's being wronged, and God's holiness insulted or grieved. For a moral nature makes its owner a partner in all other moral natures, and gives him an awful power to involve other moral natures by his offences. In wronging his own soul, he wrongs universal justice, truth, and goodness; just as a social nature gives its possessor a partnership in all society, and enables him to wrong society in general, by his offences against order and law. Thus the possessor of a moral nature has an enormous and glorious responsibility, and one attended with the gravest perils, as well as the most exalted privileges! Mistakes, blunders, errors, may be repaired, but sins have a quality of irreparableness about them, which gives a certain awful and infinite quality to wrong. You can repent of sin; you can repair your wrong as far as others have directly suffered by it; but how can you heal the wound your sin has made in the principle of justice—how prevent your disobedience from encouraging rebellion, and infecting other moral natures as weak as your own? It is the profound sense of this awful element in sin which has led to the extravagant notion that Adam's sin shook the throne of God, was punished with the curse of death upon the race, and only repaired by the sacrifice of Christ—God's other self—upon the cross!

But surely, to keep up an honest and profitable view of the enormous evil and hatefulness of sin, we are not to rush into absurdities like this! There is evidently in the divine mind one thing worse than sin, and that is the absence *of all opportunities of moral life and spiritual goodness.* God proves to us, by his having, in full foreknowledge of its history, created our race, that he loves life more than he hates death, loves virtue and holiness more than he hates vice and unrighteousness; that is to say, that for the sake of producing a race capable of knowing, loving, and serving him, and which should be put under circumstances ultimately leading to that result, he would endure the moral evil, the sin, which their moral education would certainly involve. How easy had it been for infinite power to abstain from creating moral beings, and thus avoid the possibility of sin in his universe! But the whole order of nature shows that the production of *good* is a more fundamental principle with God than the suppression of evil; that to make much happiness he will—be it spoken reverently—risk some unhappiness; much good, some evil; much virtue, some vice. There is no moral allowance for wrong in God's universe, no sympathy with evil, no countenance for sin. God is never the author of either; but he permits wrong, evil and sin, so far as they grow out of the exigencies of moral beings, and doubtless considers them as spots upon the sun, when compared with the freedom, aspiration, tendencies to truth and virtue, which his providential care is gradually preparing for our race. It is not, then, that sin has been too seriously, but only too exclusively, regarded by theologians; not that its nature has been too darkly painted, but that man's brighter characteristics, his cheering manifestations, the general bent of his moral powers and affections, have not been enough considered in connection with it—that a negative instead of a positive view has prevailed, in which the difficulty of sin, instead of the problem of moral being, has been made the whole hinge of morality, religion, and human destiny. Man's nature and existence, as a child of God, a moral and intellectual being, receiving his education here, is the primary fact, to which the other fact, that he has sinned, is subsidiary, and of secondary importance. A true view of God's plan and man's destiny must date from man's nature, not Adam's sin; from God's love, not man's weakness; from all the facts of human experience, not from a single fact. The world has been too long and too horribly darkened by the monstrously magnified shadow of the first sin. It has hid God's love, it has blighted humanity, it has made religion a bugbear and a superstition.

We shall understand the nature of sin, and the operation of conscience, better, if we keep in mind one other fact. Right and wrong are not relative, but absolute terms, answering to eternal distinctions in the divine character and nature. Our knowledge of right and wrong, on the other hand, is not entirely, perhaps not prevailingly, intuitive, but a result of educated attention, experience, and illumination from revelation and life. We have some instinctive sense of absolute right and wrong, but our nature is even more distinguished for its power to grow up into an ever higher and more complete knowledge of right and wrong. Now, it is evident that, with this condition of moral growth, there is involved an experience of moral weakness and error, which is not sin, but which *is* alienation from the law of God. Paul, before his illumination on the way to Damascus, "verily thought it right to do many things contrary to the name of Jesus of Nazareth." *Was* it right in itself? No. Was it right for him? Yes! but not safe. And consequently, when he got his moral and spiritual eyes open, he condemned himself seriously. This retrospective power of conscience is constantly confounded with its directing and guiding power. We may and must justly lament and sorrow for sins which have only become sins long after they were committed as errors, mistakes, and blunders. For it is an inevitable part of our progress, as moral beings, to apply the highest light we possess to the judgment of what is past, as well as to what is immediate. And this immaturity, infancy, and weakness of the moral nature, which temporarily allows so much that a better conscience afterwards shows to be sin, theologians have ventured to call our wicked heart, our depraved nature, our hereditary sinfulness. But what would be a pure heart, a regenerate nature, a native holiness? Would they have men born with perfect moral illumination, with complete and absolute views of duty, with all the nicety of conscience and wisdom of heart, which, at present, long discipline under the Gospel alone communicates? But would not this require an equal perfection and adultness of intellect and experience? In short, is not the demand this: that moral beings ought not to be put into this world at all for education or discipline, but only for enjoyment of their already perfected state? But this experiment was tried, according to the prevailing theory, in the original Paradise, with Adam and Eve! Was the success such as to make us desirous of its repetition?

To the *retro*spective action of conscience, which, without any dishonor to human nature, or even to human character, accounts largely for the sense of sin, we must add, as an equal cause, the *pro*spective action of conscience. As the memory of our moral mistakes is converted into remorse when our ignorance passes away, so the pursuit of a moral ideal afflicts the soul with pangs of guilt, in view of an obedience it emulates, but is not now able to pay. This self-dissatisfaction is the condition of progress—is an inevitable attendant on humanity, and must not be confounded with the frown of God, or the reproach of a sinful nature. Christ himself recoiled from the ascription of *good*, in his own humble consciousness of heights of excellence yet to be won.

According to the view now presented, sin, though not the great fact in the universe, overshadowing the glory of our nature and the power and love of God, is no light thing, nay, is no negative thing—like the lost lessons, misused opportunities and unimproved talents of our school-days—leaving a mere vacancy in our education. It is rather like the bad habits, wrong tastes and depraved dispositions, which self-indulgence, disobedience and folly in our youth, fasten upon the soul, and give a fixed root there. It is positive and self-propagating. Sin is a different thing from sins, as the bitter fruit of a corrupt tree, is a different thing from the tree itself. A criminal, or vicious disposition, a wicked heart, in short, is a positive thing, with a tendency by its own action to become worse. Because our nature is made for virtue and goodness, it does not follow that it may not be corrupted even in its very springs. You may poison a well—you may poison a human soul. Nay, it may poison itself; and thus, that which God made for purity, peace and joy, be converted into a curse to its possessor and the world.

Let us not flatter ourselves that there is not a great deal of wickedness and depravity, of absolute and positive sin, in the world. A true theory of the dignity, glory, and divine perfection, of human nature, demands no such assumption. The liability of our nature to corruption in our own hands, and to injury from our companions and friends, is a part of its delicacy, its wondrous sensibility, sympathetic power and moral freedom. Its exposure is incidental to its extraordinary and perfect constitution. We may account it a perilous thing to have such a nature; nay, we may find this call to moral and intellectual life, a summons which we shudder to answer. But we have no choice. God made us for his own glory and service, and we must accept our arduous, imperilled and glorious post as moral beings, with submission and gratitude. Positively considered, sin may be no less an evil, wickedness no less common a fact, the perversity of human beings and their depraving influence over each other, no smaller, than the Westminster Catechism in its darkest passages represents; but Calvinism can give no account of the origin, nature and cure of sin, which is not shocking to the heart, conscience and hope. It makes sin as desperate, final, and overwhelming an evil in the sight of God, as it is terrible, trying, and hazardous to us. It involves the universe in this earth-born snarl. It ties up God's hands and heaven's gate with our disordered heart-strings. It blots out the spiritual sun with this terrestrial cloud. Sin, and sin only, possesses the human heart, and all its natural motions are sinful! Its affections, its thoughts, its purposes, before they know themselves, are sinful and only sinful. We are altogether born in sin—and life is a mere ocean of depravity, in which, with mill-stones already tied round our necks, we swim, with a bare chance, by desperate exertions, of loosening the cord and escaping to the life-boat, that picks up here and there a fortunate or elected soul.

Against this blasting, discouraging, depraving view of sin, and of God its author, and Christ its victim, we place our own view of it, as being equally solemn, serious, earnest, and a thousand times more rational, scriptural and credible—as fitted to warn and encourage; to make sin hateful and leave God lovely, man's wickedness dreaded and dreadful, while his nature is conceded to be divine and beautiful, and Christ's mission one of universal mercy and helpfulness, instead of being a proclamation of blessedness to a few and of despair to the mass of our race.

With our theory of life as a vast educational scheme and system, in which God uses for great ends, great risks and exposures, with plans extending indefinitely into the future; and which, without the least abuse of human freedom, or the smallest departure from a moral ground, his Infinite Providence is slowly shaping to the possible recovery of all his offspring, and the possible salvation of all men in some ulterior state of being—we can afford to look sin distinctly in the face; to acknowledge all its baseness, blackness and ruin; to feel our own accountability for it, and to own that its nature and fruits are evil only. We are not driven artfully to evade our responsibility—either by laying its origin to the first Adam, or shifting off its consequences upon the second. Calvinism, despite its rigid aspect, is a terribly lax system of theology in practice. It weakens the native conscience by its horrid metaphysics touching the origin of sin, and completes its perversion by its unnatural philosophy touching the cure of it. How comfortable to lay off our moral obligations upon a depraved nature, and shift the burden of self-heed on to an infinite atonement! What has this doctrine led to, but a practical Universalism of the coarsest kind—not that which bravely takes the name—but that which is seen in the ordinary confidence which every one feels about the security and immediate salvation of his own kindred, family and friends? The popular theology diminishes the sanctions of the moral law. It is an infinitely easier, more popular and conscience-soothing system than our own, because it puts justice and mercy at war with each other, God and Christ on different sides, and encourages the soul to think duty a hardship, law a curse, virtue an impossibility, and salvation an adroit evasion. What does the world need so much as to return to, or rather to go on towards, a faith, which pronounces *law* holy, just and merciful; human nature, sacred and perfect in design; our earthly condition wondrously and thoroughly adapted to our development as moral beings; sin, a personal matter, lying at every man's own door, and to be escaped only by repentance and reformation—and then not without scars and penalties inherent in every offence.

The almost universal account of life as a probationary state, is a false and narrow account of it, if it means any thing more, than that every preceding state is probationary to that which follows it. To moral beings of immortal destinies, every stage of existence involves more or less, and for good and evil, that which succeeds it. And thus the life that now is, is probationary to that which is to come; as youth is to manhood, and manhood to old age. But the truer term for it is a disciplinary and educational state—in the result of which all abused, neglected or perverted talents and opportunities, will give a retributive account of themselves at the bar of God, which is the eternal law of our moral constitution.

Compare this account of sin with the more popular one, and decide honestly, with Bible in hand, conscience in lively action, experience and observation all broadly rendering in their testimony—which is most worthy of God's character, of Christ's Gospel, of man's soul? which is most candid, credible, true, affecting, and able to bear the light of futurity?

May 23, 1857.

SERMON XV.

HUMAN NATURE—ITS EXPOSURE TO SIN.

"I am the Lord, and there is none else. I form the light and create darkness. I make peace, and create evil. I the Lord, do all these things." —ISAIAH xlv. 6, 7.

THE prophets and apostles were much bolder in their assertions than their degenerate followers dare to be. The evil that is in the world they ascribe, without hesitation, not to the perversion which the divine order has received from man, but to the position and direct creation of God, whom they represent, in the text, as saying, "I make peace, and create evil." An honorable unwillingness to conceive of God, as creating evil, has vitiated very much all the discussions touching the origin of evil, whether in nature or in humanity ; and is at the bottom of the abiding antagonism between the assertors of the original rectitude and perfection of human nature, and the assertors of a universal corruption and total depravity. That God may create evil, and yet be a perfectly good and holy Being, may possibly appear less self-contradictory, after considering anew the original constitution of our nature, and the nature and rise of sin in a being created by omnipotent wisdom and goodness. Full satisfaction is not to be had on this subject; but some relief may be secured from its perplexities.

There is a permanent dispute in the world and the Church respecting human nature, some affirming it to be constitutionally and originally good and well-disposed; others, naturally evil and ill-disposed. It is really, I suppose, mainly a dispute about words; that is, the parties to it are not talking about the same thing. One side looks at man, as a mass of materials and with reference to the design of his Creator, and finding nothing in his appetites, passions, or total faculties, which is not adapted to the ultimate perfection of the plan—nothing which it could desire to get rid of, or to change, it pronounces human nature sound, good, and every way approvable. The other side looks at man, with reference to his present order and completeness—as a creature to be judged of in his actual state—and seeing the manifest deficiencies, the great confusion, the total unsatisfactoriness of this being, when compared with a perfect standard, it pronounces human nature corrupt, depraved, fallen. It is as if two travellers of intelligence, learning and elevated sentiment, had at the same moment arrived from different foreign countries, at a place where a proposed temple, of such splendor as to arouse the curiosity of the whole world, was in process of building. They, of course, find the ground strewn with materials in utter confusion, the plan of the architect only just emerging from heaps of stone and mortar, columns and slabs—while dust, dirt and disorder everywhere prevail. Both acquaint themselves with the general design, and admire it equally. But the attention of one is, by constitution, habit or theory, fastened upon the disorder ; the contrast between the plan and the present condition of the works ; the slowness of the progress, the want of a satisfactory concert among the workmen, the disproportioned way in which the building rises—two stories finished in one part, before the foundations are fairly laid in another part ; ornamentation done here, while use is neglected there—evident waste, and fraud, and jobbing, revealing themselves to him in the contractors and workmen. The attention of the other, on the contrary, is, by constitution, habit and theory, fastened upon the wonderful fitness of the materials collected, their vast amount and excellence, and the admirable result to which their arrangement is tending. In his imaginative eye, he sees the parts and pieces already in their places ; he wonders at the industry, patience and skill which has achieved so much ; even now, he praises the architect, as if he had finished his work ; the structure, as if it were completed. One of these travellers accordingly goes home, and gives an account of the extreme confusion, the unsatisfactory condition, the hopeless state, of the temple he has visited ; the other goes home and describes the fine progress, the rich preparations, the admirable design. Both have seen the same thing. Yet one describes the temple as a ruin, a mortification, a disappointment ; the other declares it a perfect work, a glorious object, a grand success. But have not both equally admired the design? and have not both, probably, equally perceived its present incompleteness, and been equally conscious of the confusion and rubbish about the works ? Are they, then, as much disagreed in fact, as they are in language ? When one speaks of the building, he refers to the design, and the fitness of the materials, and the progress of the works towards the consummation of the plan ; when the other speaks of it, he refers to the works, and their present incomplete state, and disappointing condition as compared with the plan itself. So it is with human nature ; some men, seeing the glorious design in its materials, fasten their attention upon its capacities, its powers, its destiny, and will allow none of its temporary flaws, weaknesses and crudities, to detract from their sense of its proper glory and perfection ; others, noticing its actual distance from its goal, its immature and struggling state, its discouragements and obstacles within and without, and, comparing it with the divine standard of character, pronounce it fallen, depraved and lost. But they are evidently not talking about the same thing. The phrase human nature does not mean the same to both parties. The word *man* is applied differently by them. One means by it the possible, the designed, the ideal being ; the other, the actual, undeveloped, incomplete creature. One finds the glorious standard triumphantly indicated and pointed to in the materials ; the other sees the standard looking down upon and shaming the materials which are pointed *at* rather than pointing *to*. But I have long thought that the doctrine of Human Depravity was only an inverted praise and exaltation of human nature, as a schoolmaster, when he complains of the imperfect handwriting of his pupil, and points him with shame to his copy, confesses the boy's capacity to write better, and stimulates him to an excellence he has latent in his will.

This dispute about the materials of our nature, however, is not the whole of the dispute, and is, indeed, much the least difficult part of it. We have spoken of a half-finished structure, which might be called a ruin, or a rising edifice, according as it gave evidence or not of ever having been any thing better; or of there being now any building force at work upon it. Human nature, perfect in its design, it is asserted, has lost both the plan on which it was framed, and the architect alone capable of rearing it rightly. The plan was originally revealed in a clear and perfect conscience, the architect present in an unbroken and righteous will. The ample materials—their presence, their beauty and fitness, are not by this hypothesis denied. Man's passions, powers, emotions, apprehensions, confess their divine origin and their glorious paternity. But man, no longer, since the fall, sees what God made him for, and seeing imperfectly, is, for a double reason, incapable of doing what God demands of him, because his will is as weak as his conscience is blind. This, it is maintained, was his real fall—not the change of his faculties and powers, his natural affections, aspirations and qualities—his building materials, so to speak—but the change of his moral nature; of his conscience, which is now defiled, of his will, which is now broken and perverted—that is, the loss of plan and architect, of the knowledge how to use the materials he possesses for his proper edification, and of the energy and disposition to use them. Now, if a change like this were alleged to have occurred at some considerable time after man's creation, we might think it not incredible; for it would then look as if man, originally made with powers and faculties fitted for his own protection and growth, had, through wilfulness, abused and perverted his trust, and involved his successors in moral difficulty. But when we are asked to believe that the first man—who, though fresh from the Creator's hands, and with no companions to misuse or tempt him aside, on the first opportunity succumbed in his conscience and his will, before a frivolous temptation—had a better nature than we have, a keener and clearer conscience, a more erect and powerful will, we confess that reason refuses her assent. In what respect did he exhibit any moral faculties superior to ours? Of what advantage to him was his unfallen nature and his fresh and pure soul? Did not his fall prove that conscience and will are faculties in man which, by the very theory of his nature, are dependent on experience, culture and discipline for their development? How should an innocent being know any thing about temptation, or evil, or sin, before he had experienced either; and not knowing them, how should he know any thing about resistance, or goodness, or holiness? Adam's fall was the most natural thing in the world, and neither unforeseen by, nor discreditable to, his Maker; who knew that his child must learn to walk, by first stumbling; and the punishment so-called, which the first sin brought upon his head, was a blessing in disguise. The garden he was thrust from is that state of indolent innocence in which all children are born—where they are provided for by a domestic providence, which makes no demands upon them—but out of which they are thrust the moment they begin to feel the motions of an independent will; thrust into a state of exposure, of temptation and sin; but also of discipline, of virtue and progress. The race learned in the first man that it was framed for resistance, struggle, experience, growth

—for the knowledge of good and evil, and for the preference of good by the experience of evil; formed to sin and repent and reform, and achieve moral dignity and perfection, through tribulation, anguish and shame, subdued by ever-increasing light in the conscience, and growing vigor in the will.

Now, our orthodox brethren have a notion that all this temptation, trial and discipline might have been avoided; that sin need never have been a human experience; that if Adam had only obeyed God, his children would have obeyed him, too, and this world thus have been a perpetual Paradise; our nature everywhere reflecting perfectly its Maker's glory. But are there some honest people, who would like to exchange the world we live in, for the primeval paradise, and the people we live with, for Adams and Eves? Did Adam and Eve in their sinlessness reflect God's glory, as much as David and Peter, and St. Augustin and Cromwell, in their sinfulness? Is an idle life of innocence, preferred by God, to a busy and laborious life of mingled good and evil, resistance and submission to temptation? It is high time theologians dealt more honestly by their own convictions, and abandoned their theories for sober facts. If we are jealous for the glory of God, let us be a little jealous for his honor and character, as a creator; for his knowing what he was about when he made our race, and foresaw our history and planned our salvation. I know no indignity that can be put upon God, greater than the supposition, that the first human creature he made had power to thwart and defy his omnipotence, to change the whole plan of history, and to introduce into the world and the universe, an element, not desired, nor expected, nor controllable by him, called *sin*, the frightful cause of his eternal displeasure towards millions of his unborn creatures. *Sin* is, by the foreknowledge and permission, in plainer language, by the will of God, a characterestic element in the schooling of human nature. It is the friction of a vast machine, slowly finding its adjustment; it is the sweat and groaning of the soul's struggle with itself and its circumstances; it is the awful shadow of the moral nature; it is the frightful cost of our possible creation in the image of God; it is the blow the soul receives, when it passionately or ignorantly runs upon the bosses of God's buckler, the eternal law, and leaves gaping wounds upon itself, and blood upon the wall! I will do nothing to support the views of any who make light of sin, who name it error, mistake, negation—who think its sway superficial, and its effects temporary. I know too well its malignant nature and its bitter fruits—the pertinacity of its root, and the poison of its subtile sap. But vast, profound, tremendous as it is, lasting as its consequences, and frightful as its contagion, I hold it to be the necessary price and cost of human existence; that, without which, our being could not be projected, nor our discipline and creation in God's image, be undertaken. I do not think humanity a work of God's leisure; a creation of his infinite genius thrown from him in a mood of pleasure. Difficult as it may be to conceive of one thing as requiring aught more of effort than another, where infinite attributes are concerned, yet it is in a spirit of profound reverence and adoring awe, that I think of God as undertaking all that is most lasting and tremendous within his powers, in the conception and gradual creation of a race of moral and rational beings, destined finally to be his own companions, to dwell in his society and partake his own nature. The enormous and contradictory powers and processes involved in this undertaking—the union of free-will with utter dependence—the harmony of a creature set up on his own account, with subordination to the Creator who sets him up—the conflict of the powers necessary to make him strong, earnest, capable, with the restraints needful to keep him safe, upright and true—the necessity of temptation, with the dangers of it—the absolute requirement of the knowledge of evil, and the consequent origin of sin, with the necessity of God's not becoming the author of sin—what can exceed the tremendous difficulties involved in the very idea of humanity? It is not needful to look beyond the world we live in to perceive at what enormous cost the Almighty carries on his work of creation. If abortion, defect, failure, miscarriage in the parts, were objections involving so seriously his attributes and dignity, that he could fitly undertake nothing which did not succeed in all the particulars as well as in the general end, we should have neither fish, nor flowers, nor fruits, nor any of the products of soil or sea, of which the part that matures is always but a small proportion of the part that fails. Creation goes on in all its parts, with enormous waste and strain, at vast expense, and with a success in generals, in the preservation of orders and genera and species, purchased only by the loss and ruin of individuals and particulars. There is a certain obduracy and intractableness in matter itself, which seems to baffle the ever-striving soul of nature to perfect each and every work of her hand. And I repeat, were the perfections of the Deity compromised or disproved, by his permission or endurance of imperfection in the details of his material universe, that is, by the existence of physical evil, the pain of animals, the starvation of innocent flocks, the drying up of streams causing the death of myriads of fish, the blighting of flowers and fruits, we should be obliged to declare a Being not absolute in his attributes on the throne of the universe. But it is only because of our poor and superficial notions of what perfection is, that we reckon pain and evil and waste, as not possible under the government of an omnipotent God of infinite benevolence. Doubtless these very wastes are, in God's view, vast economies; this very pain, the occasion of greater pleasure; this very evil, the means of a preponderant good. A larger knowledge of the laws of matter, of the sensitive organization of insects and animals, of the relations between matter and mind; and of analogies of evil permitted, nay employed, in the material world, for the moral education of man, its possessor, would doubtless teach us that God sees proportion, where our partial vision finds deformity, and hears harmony where our dull ears, that lose most of the chords, catch only detached and broken notes.

"One part, one little part, we dimly scan
Through the dark medium of life's feverish dream;
Yet dare arraign the whole stupendous plan
If but that little part, incongruous seem.
Nor is that little part perhaps, what mortals dream;
Oft from apparent ill, our blessings rise."[1]

[1] Beattie's Minstrel, 50th stanza.

But the point lies here. If God encounter costly obstacles even in the material creation, and is willing to incur the appearance of defeat, the presence of evil, the failure of particulars, to accomplish certain grand results, why should we wonder, that in his mightier and holier aim, to create and rear children of his mind, and heart and conscience, he should incur moral risks, and the existence of moral evil, and the painful and frightful consequences which sin itself introduces into the universe?

Did he not anticipate and ordain physical evil in the material universe? or has it slipped in, in spite of him, without his consent and against his knowledge? Certainly, the last hypothesis is the more dishonorable to the Governor of the universe. Did he not, likewise, anticipate and permit sin? or has that surprised and disappointed and baffled his expectations and plans? Certainly this supposition is the more fatal to his honor and wisdom. It will not answer to say that God creates sin, or ordains sin; because, by its very definition, sin is the act of a free being—and it must always originate in perfect freedom. It belongs, therefore, to its perpetrator, and to nobody else. It may, indeed, be imputed, but it cannot be transferred. But God creates moral beings, and places them in circumstances where they will, and where he knows they will, *sin*. And if sin were so great and absolute an evil, that there is no good so good, as that evil is evil, God could not, with honor, create imperfect and tempted moral beings. That he has done so, proves that bad as sin is, goodness has a worth in God's eyes greater than his hatred of sin—that is, he will sooner have man with his sins, than not have man and get rid of all sin. He will sooner have moral beings, capable of likeness to himself, and take the risk of their defalcations and failures, than have a spotless, sinless universe, void and vacant of moral and rational life. The enormity, and hatefulness and indignity of sin, is the true measure of God's valuation of rectitude, and virtue and worth in man. But when we say that sin is not so great an evil as goodness is a blessing—and that sin abounds, that grace may more abound, let us remember that we are not taking away from sin its actual and intense evil—but only its power, to defeat the whole design of God's creation. Do not, then, make light of sin without you mean to make light of man, and light of God! No account of the horror, the malignity, the offensiveness of sin in God's eyes, or of its ruinous tendencies and consequences, can well be too darkly painted. We are not half aware how poisonous and permanent its virus is—how deep it reaches back, how far it stretches forward; how subtle, devilish and awful its works are! When I think of God—hating sin as a Holy Being must, with immeasurable hatred—seeing all its possible devastations, the disorder, guilt, confusion, misery, it must introduce into a fair and perfect and moral universe—hearing in advance its accumulated groans and anguish—seeing war and pestilence, murder and incest, sensuality and hatred, all dabbled in blood and reeking with pollution, yet blazoning their shame, and defying his throne, as they follow in the train of that cruel Queen of Hell; when I contemplate the pure and omniscient, the loving and omnipotent God, counting all this frightful sum of moral evil, as the certain cost of the creation of a race of moral beings—that is, beings with wills of their own, necessarily weak and exposed, left to struggle with temptations essential to their possible destiny as virtuous beings—that is, as children of God—I have a conception of the value which the Creator places on humanity, a sense of his intense and insatiable desire for true children, of his priceless estimate of human rectitude, and of the truth and love and goodness which come out of this fiery and slag-clogged crucible of human life, which I can get in no other way, and which fills me with an adoration and gratitude that no other reflections can excite!

Consider, then, my brethren, what an enormous responsibility you carry in your nature! God has trusted you, in the gift of a free and independent will, with the terrible power of making yourself a blot and a wreck upon the face of his universe—that you might possess the glorious power of making yourself a temple and an altar there! He has trusted you with a heavenly spark, with which you may kindle an undying flame of virtue, or may set off a magazine of wrong. He has given you the power to be a demon or an angel—to people the city of your God, or swell the ranks of ruin and despair. You have it in your own hands to become the child, the helper, the co-worker with God and Christ, or the slave of the devil and his angels. And yet, some of you are thinking how insignificant your influence, how unimportant your choice is! My brethren, nothing is insignificant, nothing unimportant, which a child of God, a moral and rational creature, does. All the folly, crime and sin, humanity has heaped upon itself, has not diminished its preciousness in God's sight;

nor did the leper, the harlot, and the murderer find themselves beyond the sympathy, the boundless interest and pitying love of Christ. He would have died as freely to have saved *one* of them as to save the race; for each of them had an immortal, priceless soul! And the depth of God's love is quickened by the very exposure, the possible ruin, of his children. We may, in our blindness, make light of sin—think of it as weakness, as error—as pardonable and superficial. Christ did not shed his holy blood for any such triviality. God did not send his only Son on any such indifferent message. The Bible was not written by any persons who thought so of sin; nor have saints and martyrs and apostles lived and died in any such faith. Conscience, that awful monitor, consents to no such verdict. Remorse gathers its blackness and paints its pictures from no such palette. The dignity and glory of virtue rejects the estimate which such views of vice and sin put upon her own struggling and scarred victories.

Think not of sin, then, as otherwise than infinitely hateful—as involving consequences of immeasurable misery—as utterly and forever the foe of God and man, the gate and the fire of hell. And that you may think rightly, and with an unquenchable aspiration of goodness—that you may know the glorious destiny of which your soul is capable—keep the nature and the dreadfulness of sin, and the possibilities of moral ruin and guilty degradation, to which you are constitutionally exposed, ever before you. Honor your nature—by thinking what your existence costs God! Hide not its exposures, its perils, its alternative doom of shame and ruin; for it is only by knowing, owning, measuring the depths of our possible guilt, that we can know and estimate the weight of that crown which obedience, virtue and holiness will place upon our heads.

Think not of evil, or of sin, as God's curse. But take up the language of the poet, and ask—

> "What golden fruit lies hidden in its husk.
> How shall it nurse my virtue, nerve my will,
> Chasten my passions, purify my love,
> And make me in some goodly sense, like Him
> Who bore the cross of evil, while he lived,
> Who hung and bled upon it when he died,
> And now in glory, wears the victor's crown." [1]

DEC. 12, 1858.

[1] Bitter-Sweet, by E. G. Holland.

SERMON XVI.

HUMAN NATURE—ITS NEED OF THE HOLY SPIRIT.

"For as in Adam all die, even so in Christ shall all be made alive."
"The first man, Adam, was made a living soul; the last Adam was made a quickening spirit."—1 COR. xv. 22, 45.

ADAM and Christ are here represented as the beginners of two different creations, man being the subject of both. Moreover, they are put forth as our representatives, so that what happened to them, in some very important sense, happened to us. I need not trouble you with the history of theological opinion in regard to the relations of humanity to Adam and to Christ. You are familiar with the great place which Adam's fall has had in the various systems of religion popular in the world, and with the peculiar efficacy attributed to Christ's sacrifice, in removing the curse which it is alleged to have brought upon the human race. It is not my purpose to controvert any opinions of others, but to explain and set forth the truth contained in these words of Scripture, for our own edification on this day of communion. So much of a believer am I in the gracious providence which has accompanied the history of the Christian Church, that I should have as great a reluctance as the most devoted Romanist to differ from, much more to deny, any article of faith which has ever received the stamp of Catholicity, i. e., which has been generally received by Christians as "the mind of the Spirit." I believe that the Church, meaning the great body of visible believers, has always had in its charge and in its consciousness, the essential doctrines and the saving spirit of the Gospel, and that the decrees of the great councils, and the statements of faith of the great fathers, have been made under the guidance of the Holy Ghost. I am persuaded that the very formularies in which the principles and spirit of the Gospel were enshrined—the now offensive and effete formulas of orthodoxy—were, at the time, the only forms which could have preserved, much more have set forth, the simple truths of our Christian faith, or brought them to bear upon society and humanity in a saving way. The significance and power which the creed of the Church possessed and emitted, was true, wholesome, saving; whether the propositions that enunciated it were logically and eternally true or not. For instance, it was far more important that Christ's authority should be recognized as divine, than that his person should not be confounded and identified with God's own; and if this temporary identification, honstly made, was necessary to the maintenance of his spiritual supremacy in the world, then the Athanasian creed was not false in spirit, or unwise and misguided in form, though it was only temporary in character. And so I might say of the doctrine of Adam's fall, or of the vicarious atonement, or of the sacramental character of the Christian ordinances. What the universal Church has taught on these subjects has been, in essence, the truth. What the people believed, was, in essence, the truth. We take these statements now, and examine them with cold, critical judgments, insisting upon making them mean all their words will hold, and then assuming that the grammatical meaning we can demonstrate them to have, is the sort of significance they possessed for those who formed, and those who received them. But I believe no such thing. I am yet to be persuaded that any of the dreadful contradictions and follies which we can show to exist in the *language* of these creeds, existed in the minds and hearts of those who made or first received them. Their framers did not use them for logical and metaphysical purposes, but as appeals to the imagination and the heart; and they evoked in the souls of their disciples, convictions and feelings which were not absurd and monstrous.

Thus the formal Trinitarianism of the ancient creeds was always interpreted by the essential Unitarianism of the more ancient human mind and heart. If you know perfectly, and feel in every member, joint, and limb, that the Creator of the universe is God, in a sense in which no other being can be God, then it is safe to call Christ, and the Holy Ghost, God, on account of their being essential to the true revelation of this only God. But if there were any real doubt about the sole and unshared unity of the Creator, then it would not be safe. Thus the Trinitarianism of the Church is to me only an additional argument for the Unitarianism of the soul. And I doubt not the deity of Christ (until these latter days of verbal criticism came) was held by the body of the Christian Church in a way not menacing to, or truly falsifying of, the proper, sole sovereignty of the Father. It was held (as the very phrase, the *second person*, intimated) in a way that recognized dependence and inferiority.

And so of the corruption of human nature, through its fall in Adam. I have never yet been able clearly to make out, after the proper explanations and modifications were admitted on both sides, much practical difference between those who affirm and those who deny the depravity of human nature. I am persuaded that among thinkers and experienced men of spiritual discernment, there cannot be now, and there never could have been, any real diversity of judgment concerning the character of human nature. Consider the absurdity of supposing men of sense to differ in regard to the most ancient, universal and cognizable of all subjects, to the extent of the difference implied in the terms the "total depravity," and "perfect rectitude" of man's nature! Do you suppose that on bringing together the most orthodox and the most liberal men of our day, assuming them to be equally intelligent and competent, and placing before them a new-born child—any real difference of opinion would exist between them, spite of all their antagonistic phraseology, in regard to the actual state of that child? Would not both of them admit the influence of hereditary traits and qualities; confess the connection which the child by his organization had with the infirmities and the virtues, the total qualities of its ancestry, its race and its age? Would not both believe in its freedom from actual sin, in its essential purity and innocency? Is it any thing more than a different way of saying the same thing, which these sectarian antagonists are about, when they seem to be at such sword-points of doctrine ?

There is then, doubtless, in accordance with this showing, a real and grand truth in the Catholic doctrine of the fall of man in Adam. Adam stood for and represented his race. Any other man in his circumstances would have acted as he acted, and every man since *has* acted as he acted. It was not, however, Adam's nature that fell, but merely he himself; that is to say, his nature was no other after his fall than before. It was no more weak than before. For if stronger before he fell than since, how did he yield so easily to temptation ? What advantage did his unfallen nature give him ? No ! Adam's nature was illustrated, not changed, by his fall. He was created liable to, and certain of, his fall. And his fall was simply an exhibition and evidence of his total inability to keep the commandments of God in his own independent strength ; that is to say, his intellect and conscience were made so much more powerful than his will, that he was constituted to see and feel the obligatoriness of duties which he had no adequate resolution and power of character to observe and perform. Do you think it a strange thing that God should have deliberately made man with a mind and conscience clearer and stronger than his heart and will ? I think I can make it probable to you, that God's apparent designs towards us could never have been completed upon any other plan ; that man must have been made an unbalanced, exposed, and self-ruining creature, to admit of his becoming in the end a divinely directed, heaven-controlled, and God-redeemed creature. And I have no difficulty in admitting that human nature, considered by itself, left to itself, tends, by its very and intentional constitution, to self-destruction. This indeed is precisely what is meant by Adam's fall, and by our all falling in him. Human nature is, by the act of creation, put upon its feet, and by its first step precipitates itself upon its head. It is a wondrous creation, full of power and beauty, and with evident capacities for doing noble acts and becoming a glorious thing ; but it is clear that the conditions of its success are yet wanting, and that it is a failure, if this is the best it can do. A fish upon the land, a bird in the sea, a beast in the quicksands, could not exhibit a more perfect defeat of its being than the first man, Adam, did of the glory of human nature. And yet he did, as we have said, only what any man would have done, and what every man does do : he yielded to temptation, he became a sinner, he put himself at enmity with God ! What the natural end of such a being and such a course of conduct must be, if not interfered with and prevented, is clear enough. You must know very well what a race tends to, whose very progenitor begins his career with deliberate transgression. Could it do any thing but fly from bad to worse ? Was not the first murderer the necessary offspring of such a parent, and a generation of incestuous and wicked people, worthy of being ingulfed in the original deluge, the inevitable successors of such an ancestry ? It was no unexpected result of human nature left to itself and acting out its own proclivities. All history shows us what man is and does ; what he tends to and becomes, when he follows out his own nature. His constitution is, in its original make, unbalanced. Its passions and desires are stronger than its power of self-control ; its perceptions of right, finer and firmer than its determinations of will. Thus man becomes a sinner naturally. You will, of course, ask, if this is not making his nature sinful, and so relieving him of all responsibility ? I reply, sin does not belong to natures, but to individuals. There is no such thing as a sinful nature, but only a sinful person ; and because our nature prompts, and even drives us into sin, you can no more free it from the sense of responsibility and of blame involved in it, than you can put the wolf, when, according to his nature, he tears the lamb, into the same category of compassionate interest and sympathy with the lamb itself. God does *not* commit *our* sins, and our ancestors do not commit them, and nobody can feel guilty for them but those who do commit them. That we have this nature is a ground of pity, which God himself admits and acts upon ; but it does not, and it never did, diminish any man's sense of sin, that all his race were sinners, and that his nature inevitably drove him into sin.

It is a theory of some that sin is educational ; that it springs from inexperience and ignorance ; is the first awkward movement of a nature that is gradually learning to move with grace ; that it tends to correct itself, and is to be regarded as the adolescence of the soul, not its manhood. Sin, doubtless, is educational ; but not in this sense. It educates, by teaching man his inability to live a successful life in his own strength and wisdom ; it educates, by communicating humility to the remorseful spirit ; it educates, by preparing the soul to seek for, and admit, the help which God is always waiting to communicate. But in all other respects, there is nothing strengthening or saving in the experience of sin. On the contrary, the more of it, the longer under its sway, the more debilitated and helpless the soul! It propagates itself like a poison in the individual; it spreads like a pestilence, and corrupts the whole community. Beginning with the animal part, it involves the affections, the intellectual nature and the more majestic powers, until every part of the soul is in its toils Tribes and neighborhoods, once under its dominion, tend, spite of the progress they make in arts and sciences, and of the greater degree of refinement which attends their vices, only to a maturer and more subtile iniquity. The prudential and selfish graces which an experienced community wraps around its depravity, only drapes the fatal sickness of the soul. Like the clear atmosphere, the delicious weather, which sometimes accompanies the reign of pestilence, like the rich flowers and beautiful fruits that glow beneath the dominion of the treacherous tropical sun—education, art, manners, softness and grace, not seldom mark a condition of society out of which faith, hope and charity have ebbed away, and where selfishness, deceit and treachery have taken up an undisputed possession. It is remarkable, indeed, how the senses and the soul were *both* united in the original temptation. It was not a vulgar bodily appetite that allured our first parents to their ruin. Never was a more respectable, a more intellectual temptation, held out to human creatures. It was the knowledge of good and evil, that grew upon the tree whose fruit they plucked; and what nobler form of spiritual weakness, what more fascinating and lofty kind of sin could you have than that which disobeys God for the sake of being more like him; possessing his own attributes and sharing his moral insight! But this independence of God, this unwillingness to owe our guidance and salvation to him; this reliance upon our own intellects and wills—is the very rebellion, which, in the most advanced stages of civilization, constantly returns. Adam's sin is the sin of our own day; because it is the very sin to which our nature prompts most those who possess it in its finest mould. The pride of intellect, the pride of knowledge, the pride of unbridled speculation, of self-idolatry, the worship of power, genius, art—of any thing other than, and sooner than, the Holy God—this is the form which the depravity of man takes in our day and amongst ourselves, and it is the cause of a large part of the moral weakness, the social difficulty, the domestic trouble, and the personal misery, of our generation.

And this brings us to the new creation in the second Adam, Christ. "For as in Adam all die, even so in Christ shall all be made alive." The natural man, left to himself, falls into ruin. His powers and faculties are incompetent to independence. They never were made for that; and in this defeat human nature does not change, it merely exhibits its quality, its original native inability to resist temptation and keep the law of God in its own unassisted strength! It was never meant to do it, and it does not do it. It is left to learn this peculiarity, or rather characteristic, of its constitution, by experience. It is necessary to its future destiny that it should have aspirations for independence, should have a certain confidence in itself, should have an eager desire for testing its own attributes and capacities; and so, as we leave our children to find out their need of us by thinking they can get along without us, and trying it, God leaves men to think they can live on their own wisdom, and be a law to themselves, and assert their own independent being, with safety. And as our disobedient children often end with seeking the authority they scorned, acknowledging the folly they deemed better than our wisdom, and thanking the painful discipline that brings them to their senses, so the race, God's children, from time to time, at their wit's end, stricken with a sense of orphanage, invite the face of the Father they have spurned, confess the insufficiency of the wisdom they have leaned upon, and cry aloud to God for intervention and salvation. It is the history of individuals and of nations, of men and of humanity. What happens to all men, with more or less decisive experiences, namely, periodical fits of humility, accompanied by a penitential sense of remorse, a consciousness of inadequacy to the wants of their own natures, happens at times to masses of men; seizes nations, eras, and the race. It is not that the want of God's spirit and guidance is any greater at one time than another; but only that the sense of this want is sometimes heightened. And, under this sense, it becomes evident what religion is; in short, that without this want, there would be no occasion of religion, and no sense of religion, and, indeed, no such thing as religion; that this is precisely what makes religion possible, or necessary, or desirable; namely, that man is framed and constituted to want God as much as a watch is made to want its key, and the intelligent mind that turns that key. The watch, supposing it conscious of itself, would not find this out till it *ran down,* and man does not find out that he needs God till, for the want of him, he runs down, or, in the language of theology, *falls.*

You may ask, if you will, why the Creator does not supply man with a self-sustaining power, and erect him into an independent sovereignty from the outset. I suppose it is for the same reason that the watchmaker does not give his watches the power of winding themselves up—namely, that this is beyond the possibilities of his art. I suppose that God *cannot* create beings to have spiritual life, independent of himself; that it is only in steadily communicating his life to them, and feeding them from the living fountain, that they can be filled with immortality. It is not to mend a defect, but to meet an eternal want in our nature, that God supplies his Holy Spirit through his Son. The work of religion is not an unexpected work of God's. Our need of him is not an accident, but a glorious constitutional necessity. The discovery of our incompetency to ourselves is not designed as a mortification, but a blessed revelation of our sufficiency in him. The orphanage we suffer sends us in search of a Father whom we find to be the King of kings; the weakness we experience drives us to a refuge that is omnipotent!

If, now, I am asked, whether the sense of God and the supply of the Spirit of God be not a perfectly free one, every man's nature opening, if he will, to God, as every bay in the coast opens to the ocean—if the vision of God be not universal, every man being opposite to God, as every eye is opposite to the sun, I answer, that while this is true, yet it is in accordance with all the analogies of nature and history, that every principle or truth connected with human welfare should embody itself in institutions, define itself in persons, and obey the laws of our social and historical position, before it can effectually operate, and yield its virtues to the race. Thus, while God is in us and holds perpetual access to our private souls, he is also out of us, and sustains a public relation to the race, which is only to be expressed by external revelations. In like manner, while religion is a secret need and cry of the individual soul, it must become a combined and organized want of society, and receive a combined and organized supply from above, before the social conditions are fulfilled by which it becomes practically saving to our race and ourselves. It is, in accordance with this obvious principle running through our whole condition, that God has accompanied the history of man by revelations, and embodied in positive laws, precepts, and sacraments, what we might imagine, prior to experience, he would have left to the immediate communications of his omnipresent Spirit in living contact with each private soul.

It is, I know, superficially objected to external revelation, that it confesses imperfection and defeat in the original creation. But it is only such imperfection as belongs to the watch without the key, the key being originally designed to accompany the watch. It is of a piece with the idea that God's presence in the soul is denied, or the sense of it impaired, by acknowledging his special presence in his Son; a thought equivalent to that which should assert that an elaborate public aqueduct, for the supply of a metropolis, denied the existence of water in the atmosphere, or water under the earth, or water in our very blood, of which it forms so large a part. Revelation does not deny God's spirit in the soul, or in the world, or in the age ; it only gives us a formal and fixed avenue to, and connection with, his Spirit. And the prophets, apostles, and inspired agents, who have connected the great truths of religion with times and places and persons, making them direct, historical, and affecting, capable of being embodied in records, institutions and symbols, and united with individualities, have met and satisfied wants in our religious affections and capacities that could not otherwise be supplied. Christ, the central figure among these inspired persons, who, in himself, contains and embodies all that the rest have labored to convey and illustrate—having, to our apprehension, exhausted the necessities of external revelation—matching nature itself in the breadth of his ministry, and, as experience has proved, supplying in his Church—the river that flowed out of his sublime and holy life—just what the world needed to finish the work of creation half done only in Adam—a ruin and a wreck, as it seemed, till completed in him—Christ is the second Adam, in that, while all men die in the first, they all live in him. In other words, Christianity supplies the motives, powers, attractions, hopes, inspirations, by which alone man is able to live the life of God in the soul, to live with God and for God, and in the successful keeping of his commandments. And the precise channel through which this vital current flows, through which God practically lends himself as a steady, utilizable force to men, is the Church, which, with its preached word, its common prayer, its sacraments and symbols, its holy days and instituted faith, is the chosen and only practical means for the continuous and systematic supply of man's great constitutional need of heavenly aid and succor, nurture and salvation. The importance of the Church does not depend upon any denial of God out of the Church; the authority of revelation does not imply any want of authority in reason or native conscience. Revealed truth is not opposed to natural or intuitive truth, nor institutional religion to natural religion. The Church is the externalization of man's perpetual need of organized and systematic relations with God, as the state is the expression and the form of man's need of instituted and external government. And the rhetoric which disparages the Church, or predicts its decay, or announces its demise, is a shallow apology for the true philosophy taught alike by the nature of man and the course of history.

In like manner, the reluctance which the minds of individual men in our day manifest towards the guidance, the help, and the fellowship of the Church, which thins the ranks of professed disciples, confines the use of the Gospel sacraments to the few, and leaves the administration of this great public interest to the hands of its professional supporters, is a reluctance not founded on large, or high, or profound views of the subject. The Church, considered in the light in which I have set it, is not an object for superstitious support or incredulous sneers; it is not a thing of the past. It has a deep foundation in the permanent nature and wants of man, the grandest place in the history of the race, and the most positive necessity in the existing wants of the world. In this light, its order, its ritual, its symbols, its times and seasons, acquire a dignity such, only a thousand times greater, as is communicated to the forms and technicalities of the law and the courts, by the awful principle of justice which they serve and enshrine. The petulant flippancy which can only smile or sneer at every technicality of the law, betraying its own ignorance and want of reflection, not the emptiness of the subject, may carry the same spirit into its skeptical indifference to religious forms and usages, opinions and doctrines. But every man who has reflection and intelligence enough to know how much the welfare and order of society depend upon the obstinacy of forms in commerce, in medicine, in law, in politics, in the mechanic arts—-for which no other reason can be given than that they protect precious interests—will understand that the Church stands, in every New Testament ordinance and usage, for vital things, which seek these embanking usages for the channel through which to enrich and bless and sanctify and save the world.

Uphold the Church, which upholds you! Join the Church, which joins you to Christ and God! Be not ashamed nor afraid to confess your urgent need of the shelter and protection of an external institution, a religious home, which perpetually reminds you of your obligations to God, of your dependence on the Holy Ghost, of your life in Christ, of your fellowship with the saints, and of your sonship to the Almighty Father!

June 4, 1859.

IV.

CHRIST.

IV.

CHRIST.

SERMON XVII.

EXPECTATION OF CHRIST.

(PREACHED CHRISTMAS EVE.)

"And the desire of all nations shall come."—HAGGAI ii. 7.

WE are upon the eve of the most important event in human history! To-morrow is our Saviour's birthday, and the Christian world is tuning its voice to join "the heavenly host, praising God, and saying, Glory to God in the highest, and on earth peace, good will toward men!" The proper service of to-day is not congratulation, but expectation. The Saviour is not yet born, but all men muse in their hearts of his coming. Let us, by an effort of the imagination, fling ourselves back of Christ's birth, and take our position among those who waited for the consolation of Israel. To-morrow we shall join those who welcome God's precious gift; to-night let us spend with those who long for it.

The concluding books of the Old Testament—short, convulsive sobs of a dying dispensation—contain, in their broken and pathetic eloquence, many gleams of glorious hope and splendid prediction, like the beautiful visions that cheer the death-bed of the sad and weary. "Faithful among the faithless," the prophets of a nation, wearied and discouraged with ages of baffled hope, still held on to the promise. The word that God had covenanted with the Israelites, when they came out of Egypt, they still expected him to fulfil; and Haggai, one of the last and most eloquent of them all, in the midst of the severest rebukes and the most anxious forebodings, is still true to his national convictions, and exclaims, "Fear ye not, for thus saith the Lord of hosts; Yet once, it is a little while, and I will shake the heavens, and the earth, and the sea, and the dry land. And I will shake all nations, and *the desire of all nations shall come.*" True, several hundred years elapsed, in which prophecy was dumb—years of long and sorrowful waiting—after Haggai, and later still, Zechariah and Malachi, had raised their expectant voices, and *the desire of all nations* was still an object of hope. That hope, however, had at length spread from the peculiar people to Gentile races. The interval between the conclusion of the prophecies of the Old Testament and the birth of Christ, is occupied by the best days of Greek and Roman history and literature, and it is not difficult to trace the influence of the Jewish superstitions, as they were then deemed, upon the richest and noblest minds of classic antiquity. Socrates and Plato, and still more as the actual era of our Saviour approached, Cicero and Virgil, begin to use almost inspired language in regard to the coming of a supernatural messenger to clear up the clouded and baffled intelligence of humanity. The nations, although only in the person of their highest and most gifted minds and hearts, unite in a common desire and expectation of light and deliverance from above.

But it is hardly necessary to look to supernatural prophecy, or even to the predictions of sensitive and prescient genius, for the origin of the hopes finally gratified in Christ's birth. Humanity contains in its very constitution a prediction of the Messiah. The first man, which is Adam, foreshadows the second man, which is the Lord from Heaven. Human nature is everywhere the same—a boundless, half-blind, half-seeing capacity, in pursuit of an ideal. It contains within itself a longing to rise above itself; an impatience of the material limits of its prison-house; a consciousness of powers which here have no adequate field; a sense of justice which is perpetually outraged by the actual condition of affairs; a love of consistency, of order, of beginning, middle and end, which is violated by this chaotic and defeated life of man.

What is the meaning of this grand exception to the whole analogy of nature? of this anomaly called man? Every other creature on the planet has its natural and perfect destiny. The bird has no wing which looks in vain for an element to move in; the beast no appetite that seeks unsuccessfully its food. Disorder and confusion do not shock the harmonious instincts of the animal creation. No superfluous powers baffle the naturalist as he surveys the structure of insect or plant. Each is adequate to its place, and its place is adequate to each. The flowers must die, but they do not tremble at the frost that cuts off their beauty; and though the hare flies from the tiger's whelp that makes him its prey, yet he flies from an instinct of self-preservation, not from the fear of death, of which he knows nothing. Man alone is burdened with faculties larger than his sphere ; hopes that transcend his opportunities ; thirsts that no river nor ocean can slake. Man alone asks questions that nature will not answer, shudders with fears against which he cannot provide, sees himself exposed to a fate that he contemplates with horror yet cannot escape.

Imagine, my brethren, this human heart of ours, emancipated as it now is by Christianity from its permanent alliance with the doomed flesh, from its short date of mortal life, and from its ignorance of its destiny —relieved of the magical, purposeless, obscure, and deformed conception of itself, gathered from nature's confused and uncertain teachings—imagine this fancy that now wanders through eternity, this conscience that expects for all defeats of justice a final and perfect tribunal, these affections that glory in their imperishable faithfulness—imagine man as Christianity has thus made him, remanded to his old estate of doubt and darkness, reinclosed in heathen or Jewish ignorance, sent back into the twilight of nature, and again beating at the bars of his prison-house, and longing for a keeper that would never appear ! Alas ! the horror of that change cannot be estimated ! And yet, in that destroying and inexplicable confinement, lay our race for four thousand years ! Does not what we know of ourselves tell us that cries of agony, anticipations full of yearning, prophecies that helped on their own fulfilment, desires that could not be repressed, convulsed the heart of our common humanity, in that long era when, with one exception, the nations were formally unowned of God, and without exception, were uncertain, or hopeless, of immortality? How often must the noble intellect, staggering under the dreadful problem of life, have turned its eye to heaven, with imploring but unanswered look? How many desperate hours must grief have spent in anticipating the havoc which the funeral pyre would make of its best beloved and dying kindred? Answer me, ye silent stars! speak out, dumb heavens! why do I live beneath your constant courses, to dread the day I shall see ye no more? Ye buried nations—generations that form the mould I tread—tell me what ye know, or if ye know nothing, in the graves ye fill! Ye winds that visit the distant boundaries of the earth, have ye nowhere seen a region where men live forever? Waves, is there no port ye ever make, where man can find his Maker, or know his being's aim and object? Ye lightnings, pierce me with your bolts, or else tell me, where is the hand that hurled ye down? Oh, cruel elements! Is there no prayer can soften your obdurate hearts, no tears that can melt your stony silence?

Such questions did not reach the ear of God in vain, though Nature had no answer for them.

But let us not suppose that longings like these were universal; else had they not been so long unsatisfied. In estimating the spiritual sensibility and conscious destitution of the race in ages prior to our Saviour's birth, an important distinction is to be observed and maintained between *men* and *man;* between the yearnings and aspirations of humanity in her sweetest and ripest specimens, and the apathy and carelessness which the great mass of human beings showed to the very questions so profoundly and sadly felt in great and bursting hearts. Had there been a universal desire for light from heaven, a conscious and urgent need of a Messenger from God, he would, we may be sure, have come ages before the Christian era. But human nature in the mass, though unchangeable in its elements and capacities, and pregnant with latent truth, is slow in its development, slow to find out its own wants, capable of resting long satisfied in its earthly estate, content to feed on its selfish instincts and to quench its higher affections. It was to allow it time to discover its own inherent faculties, to feel the pressure of its nobler wants, the necessities of reason, conscience and affection, that the gracious light of Revelation was withheld, and the Saviour reserved so long. For man is educated by want. That is the great method of Divine Providence. The supply is not furnished until it is sought, and earnestly sought; and it will not be sought until the want is seriously felt. Had man not been moved by hunger, he would have been as slothful as the grub that nestles in the heart of its winter's food. Want has built the world; raised its shelters, cultivated its fields, cleared its forests of wild beasts, bridged its rivers and oceans, fixed the place of its stars, and given civilization, luxury and peace to the world. Want alone it was that must break the silence of the mute heavens, and bring God's word to the ear of the hungering soul; that must unbar the grave, and let man's spirit forth on its immortal pathway. Four thousand years did not furnish too long a time to exhaust humanity's ways and means of contenting herself as a creature of time. She must needs try every experiment of living without a supernatural knowledge of God before she could ask that boon from heaven, must needs eke out her destitution with every earth-born resource—and her resources were many—must needs make a full and thorough use of all that human wit could invent, a careful and various trial of all the numerous theories and plans of wisdom and philosophy that her unaided genius could propose, before, with any general concurrence, she would begin to cry aloud for light from above! That hour arrived, was the fulness of the times—the times for which Divine mercy was waiting. The moment Christ should be the desire of all nations, he would come. We might be sure he lingered in the bosom of God for no other reason than because the world had no room for him in the heart he yearned to occupy and save.

Meanwhile, his withholding was the moral education of the world. Christ, *promised,* did for the Israelites what Christ, *given,* has done for us. "I would not ye should be ignorant," says Paul, in a most striking passage in the Corinthians,[1] "how that all our fathers were under the cloud and all passed through the sea; and were all baptized unto Moses in the cloud and in the sea; and did all eat the same spiritual meat and did all drink the same spiritual drink (*as we*); for they drank of that spiritual rock that followed them—and that rock was Christ." The promise of the Messiah—an indefinite, obscure, yet exciting hope—took hold of the imagination and heart of the Jewish people, more

[1] 1 Cor. x. 1.

than the actual bestowment of the Saviour would have done at any period preceding his actual appearing. For the expectation of him adapted itself, through the changing and growing conceptions of the Messiah which it allowed, to their successive wants. They would have rejected with universal disgust the very Messiah whose promise, clothed in their own fond ideas, they cherished so tenderly. Nay, when he did really come, with the exception of a glorious minority, they knew him not, but put him to a violent death ; and numerous descendants of theirs still wait, in a sublime though melancholy constancy, the birth of that Messiah whom for eighteen centuries and a half the world has recognized. Yet who can fail to see the dignity and culture which the expectation of Christ gave to the Hebrew race ? It led their thoughts forth into the future ; gave them a noble discontent with the present ; fed the sacred fires of poetry in their hearts ; wove a charm of sentiment, aspiration and longing into their national character, which makes their literature the glory of their age and the food of all time. Compared with the Jew, how cold and passionless, how wanting in true human tenderness and nearness to our hearts, is the Gentile of the most cultivated races—the Greek or the Roman !

Man becomes great, interesting, human, only as he is a hoper ; as he cherishes an ideal, longs for a future, pursues *the desire of all nations.* The world, satisfied with itself, engrossed in the present, content with its natural boundaries, is in its childhood. That is precisely the distinction of the child, that he has no future, that his longings and desires terminate in what is near, visible and attainable. And with all their culture, refinement and luxury, the great masses in the heathen and classic world—who entertained none of our modern and Christian conceptions of progress, lived for no future, and left the coming generations to provide for themselves—were in a childhood. The rude Goths and Vandals, with their wild northern superstitions, their dark prophecies and poetry, their crude predictions of a better future, were infinitely more human, mightier and more pregnant with promise to the destinies of the race, than those refined, self-satisfied, earth-born and time-worshipping races in the Roman Empire, which finally fell before their fierce but earnest superstitions.

There was no nation on the earth to whom Christ could have been sent, with any advantage, at the remote period of his actual coming, except the Jews. They indeed, crucified him—but not until they had heard his message and received it deep into hearts fully competent to communicate it. The longings, prophecies, predictions of ages, had not been all in vain. A few hearts in Judea were prepared, by that long discipline of centuries, to feel the greatness and preciousness of the gift God was bestowing; enough to begin the glorious circle which has now spread so fast and so far as to include our then unknown continent, our then unforeseen generations. Murderous and cruel as the Jews were, there was no country in the world but Palestine where Jesus could then have found even twelve disciples—no city but Jerusalem that would have allowed him to teach a year in its streets. God did not withhold his Son one moment from a world that would welcome him. He barely got a hearing, after ages of expectation had been preparing for him. He came the first moment his coming could have been recognized.

And my brethren, just what delayed his first coming, just what confined his mission to the Jews, when splendid and cultivated Gentile nations lay all around them, delays his progress and postpones his triumphs now that he is in the world. It took ages to prepare for his appearing ; it has taken ages to prepare for his installation. He came only to the nation that, through providential helps, had cherished a secret longing and desire for him—and alas ! He found in them only a faint, indefinite idea of what they wanted. Yet happily it was enough to plant his foot upon. He gained the Apostles at least. While the enthusiasm of his chosen disciples survived, the latent want in man of spiritual truth, the want of a mediator with God, and a guide to heaven, of an assurance of forgiveness on repentance and newness of life, of a life-plan and eternal goal, was developed with extraordinary zeal and success. The Missionary labors of the Apostles were abundantly prospered. Christ's Gospel was welcomed in its newness of spirit and wonderful works, with astonishing rapidity. But in a few centuries it exhausted the latent longing, the secret expectation and desire which had slowly accumulated in the world—and began to make its way, more by authority and force than by adaptation, or supply for an existing and painful want. At length it has become a familiar and uninteresting story. The general truths with which it was laden, man's immortality, God's fatherhood, have become the possession of the common intellect and affections of the world—and while their influence is vast, considered only as intellectual principles, in extending and clearing up the general horizon of human thought, solving the riddle and lightening the burden of the mystery of life, yet they act on the people of this generation much as the great truths of the Copernican system do upon the geography and commerce of the world, with immense practical effect, yet without calling forth much direct attention, or asking individual and conscious acceptance.

And this is a state of things in which Christ's birth in its spiritual sense is constantly hindered and postponed ; for it ever waits upon expectation and desire ; his coming follows upon the longing for him. We think perhaps that Christ is wholly come ! Oh, no ! my brethren, his revelation, his spirit, his message to the world, comes not yet fully to the birth. Born indeed in the flesh, he is not yet born into the world in the spirit. The deepest, richest part of his Gospel is still hid ! To what intent is he in the world, if the world knows him not ? Is he not much as though he had never been, to those who do not seek him and learn of him ? Is not Christ as much a mystery, a name, a superstition, to thousands dwelling in the very heart of Christendom, as though he were hid 1800 years deep in the future, instead of being 1800 years old in the knowledge of the past ? How do we, who continue indifferent to his guidance, materially differ from those who had no Saviour to turn to ?

We perhaps flatter ourselves that if this were the eve of Christ's birth, if to-morrow were the identical day in which Christ was to be born in Bethlehem, we should be among those eagerly expecting him ; among those preparing to carry gifts to his manger ; certainly not among those who denied his weary mother a place in the inn, and who afterward fell into Herod's employ and sought the young child's life ! Yet to-day is as truly the eve of Christ's birth as though eighteen centuries rolled back and placed us on the hills of Judea, among the shepherds tending their flocks by night, to whom the angels sang the first Christmas carol. The spiritual Christ is waiting to be born into the heart of the world, and there is no room for him there. Humanity does not yet long for him ; does not yet expect him, would not yet know him. For them, he still sleeps in his mother's bosom, an unborn babe ; and she, an unknown traveller, is turned from the door. Christ still lacks a birth-place, and Joseph and Mary in vain appeal for a becoming shelter !

We wonder that Christ was withheld so long from the world ; why do we not wonder rather that he is still withheld ? What matters it that his sacred feet have pressed our soil, his holy visage fallen on the eyes of our ancestors, if his mind and temper, the real objects of his mission, his blessed doctrines and promises, have not yet taken on a visible shape and won the reverence and love of the world he came to save ? St. Paul complains in effect that our Saviour still hangs upon the cross. And there he will hang, bleeding and in agony, until the world ceases from the murderous dispositions which originally put him there ! We, too, complain that Christ is not yet born ; that the nations still sit in heathen darkness, not even expecting the Messiah, or else only in half-intellectual Jewish longing, grieved and sad that he does not come. Oh !

were he yet to come in the flesh, might we not have a less heavy heart, than becomes us, when now it is only his spiritual birth into the world that we can hope for? For what triumphs of peace and purity, of brotherly love and truth and happiness, should we not associate with his personal appearing? We might naturally enough expect that glorious day to be the beginning of an all-triumphant era. But Christ has come in the flesh. Eighteen centuries have celebrated that wonderful event, and the world still gropes on in half-heathen ignorance and indifference—believing in immortality, and living only for the present—calling men their brethren, and treating them like thieves and robbers—praising the Prince of peace, and making war in Christ's name—emblazoning his precepts in gold, and proclaiming his promises in temples more precious than Solomon's, yet breaking the commandments with their daily bread, and grieving his Spirit with every breath they draw. What have we to comfort us under such a disappointment? Christ born! and the world neither glad nor pious? Christ is not born, then! The salvation of the world awaits his spiritual coming. He must come in the proper understanding of his character; he must come in the actual love of his spirit; he must come as the accepted guide and orderer of society; must come in spirit and in truth, before his birth will indeed have been accomplished! Now he is hid, not indeed in his mother's heart, but in the womb of superstition and worldly misconception; in the indifference and apathy of society. Is it Christ whom the Catholic world expects to-day, upon its tapestried altars, and in its perfumed temples? Is the bedizened doll, the sacred bambino, who in Rome walks in stately procession, with all the homage that silken robes and mitred bishops and the triple-crowned pope can bestow, the symbol of that Jesus, who is, or ought to be, the desire of all nations? Is it Christ whom the Protestant world expects to-day in its theological assemblies; the second person in the Trinity, God, the fulfilment of Mosaic prophecies, the antitype of Adam? Is it Christ whom the liberal school of thinkers expects to-day in its rational and intelligent congregations—the model man, the excellent example, the exalted Saviour? Alas! neither ecclesiastical mummeries, nor theological formulas, nor sensible opinions, can bring Jesus Christ to the birth. He seeks some other Bethlehem than these to be born in. The pious Romanist, the conscientious Puritan, the pure but cold worshipper of reason, have each and all seen him in their private vigils, though he comes not to any class, and knows no sect or order. But he is born wherever love unfeigned is found; born into every heart that sincerely and tenderly suffers and labors for humanity; born in every peacemaker's spirit; born in every soul that rises above the power of selfishness and worldly greed, and uses its means and powers to promote the good of mankind; born where humility, gentleness, purity of body and soul, trust and submission, faith, hope and charity are seen to dwell.

But who can hope to see Christ, or to know him, to-morrow, who can look upon the gentle lineaments of that holy babe as he sleeps in Mary's bosom, who does not expect him to-day? Bethlehem did not expect him, and she did not hear the angels' song that sent the shepherds alone to his manger. We shall none of us ever see Christ, till we strongly desire him. Would we make a Bethlehem in our hearts, we must see to it that they are not, instead of that humble place, the noisy cities of worldly care and covetousness. While we allow them to be filled with strangers, Mary will find no room there. Christ was born in a manger; rude walls and ill-furnished accommodations met his infant eyes. The soul must know itself to be a manger —a needy, ill-supplied, homely and unfurnished spot— before Christ will be welcomed to a birth-place within it. Yes! to drop all figure, Christ comes only to the want of the soul. We shall know him, love him, feel his saving power, the glory and the blessedness of his birth in our souls, only when we heartily desire him; when all we have, seems poor; and all we are, weak; and all we hope, uncertain and uninviting. Then when, with eager expectation, with sincere longing, with soul-wrung desire, like unto that with which the ancient handmaids and seers of Judea waited for the consolation of Israel, we prepare our hearts for our Saviour, he will come in the sweetness and beauty of his innocency —aye, in the power and plenitude of his truth—and make every woman another Mary, every man another Joseph, every house another Bethlehem; and new Annas shall prophesy and speak of him to all that look for redemption in Israel, and new Simeons bless God and say, "Lord, now lettest thou thy servant depart in peace, according to thy word, for mine eyes have seen thy salvation."

DECEMBER 24, 1854.

SERMON XVIII.

THE PREDESTINATION OF THE SOUL TO CONFORMITY TO CHRIST'S IMAGE.

A NEW YEAR'S SERMON.

"And we know that all things work together for good to them that love God, to them who are the called according to his purpose."

"For whom he did foreknow, he also did predestinate to be conformed to the image of his Son, that he might be the first-born among many brethren."—ROMANS viii. 28, 29.

How glorious are the doctrines of the New Testament—even those most associated with the narrowness and sourness of temporary creeds—when we liberate them from the fetters which deform their limbs and distort their features! The foreknowledge and predestination of God, the election and justification of the Gospel, have become so sadly connected with the partial and selfish conceptions of sectarists, that we hear the very words with a kind of shrinking and distress, as if they foreboded us no good, and heralded some forbidding and exclusive theory of salvation. Yet we do the Almighty goodness gross injustice, and the Gospel wrong, by all such apprehensions. It was in opposition to the narrow and exclusive hopes of the Jews, in correction of the partial and selfish notions of a limited compassion and arbitrary preference on the part of God, that the doctrines of election, predestination, and foreknowledge were originally taught. It was in behalf of the Gentiles—that is, of all who were not Jews—in other words, of mankind in general—that the apostle labored to prove that God had foreknown, predestined, and elected them to salvation by Christ. The whole import of the apostolic teaching is, that the Jews were a peculiar people, and the possessors of exclusive privileges, only temporarily, and with reference to the service they were ultimately to render the whole race; that God has no favorites, no plans or purposes which do not comprehend his whole family in heaven and earth; that he designed from the very outset to raise up his Son as a universal Saviour; made man to be saved, and predestined him to be conformed to the image of his Son, that Jesus might be the first-born among many brethren—that is, that all men might finally resemble him!

Do I not rightly say that it is a glorious doctrine, that God will have all men to be saved, and has predestined them to be conformed to the image of his Son? Is it not a thought full of encouragement and inspiration, that God has fashioned us with powers like our Master's, to know, and love, and serve him, and that he expects of us a life like our Saviour's? I know very well the coarse and sensual interpretation which such a generous statement admits of, and how eagerly those unconformed in purpose or mind to Christ's image, snatch at a doctrine which seems to throw the responsibility of our eternal well-being upon God, and relieves man of the obligation of personal fidelity and actual obedience. But this is no part of the New Testament teaching. What God wills is, that our hearts and minds shall be conformed to Christ's; that is the salvation he offers and promises. So long as we bear not our Lord's image, we have not, and cannot have, the salvation of God; for that is his salvation. If we be thinking about some external deliverance, some sensual happiness, some carnal advantage, resulting from the passage of time or the event of death, we are wasting our thoughts upon matters wholly foreign to the ideas of the apostle. His doctrine is, that God loves sinners as well as saints; Gentiles as well as Jews; and that he has predestined them all to be conformed to the image of his Son. But what then? Is a sinner a saint, because God loves him? and does God's love pay a man for being a sinner? Does God's choice, will, purpose, that we shall be conformed to the image of his Son, diminish in the least the necessity of our laboring with all our minds and hearts to achieve this likeness? If we leave it wholly with God, does he hasten to do any thing for us? Is *he* impatient? Can he not bear to wait better than we can? What are ages of expectation to him? What is not a year of sin and folly to us? If it be any comfort to a man to think that God will always desire, and propose, and favor his salvation, that he will never find any obstacle in that direction to his penitence and restoration, he can rightfully enjoy it. But it is quite another thing to believe that God has pledged himself to make us holy and happy, like Christ and himself, whether we will or no, and by instrumentalities aside from our own exertions. There is not a word in the New Testament to favor any such notion, while the whole spirit of the Gospel and the whole constitution of humanity are flatly contradictory of it.

But surely, it is a great and glorious fact to know that God has no partial, no sectional, no time-limited mercy and love; that his arms are open to all who seek him, everywhere and forever! God's love is fixed, and it is independent of what we do or forbear—universal, all-embracing, never-failing, and never-weary! His providence is everywhere directed to the promotion of truth, charity, goodness. Man is made and preserved, to the end that he may possess and enjoy these. And there is no law in the universe hostile to him, or to his pursuit and possession of these blessed graces. But while God is God, man is man; and man's nature and the conditions of its peace and welfare are as fixed as God's, by the will of God. When we say man, we mean a free, moral, and responsible creature; and when we say that a man is saved, we mean saved only as a man can be saved—that is, saved by the salvation of his manhood; saved in the exercise of his freedom, in the use of his conscience, in the rectifying of his heart, in the uplifting of his soul. There is no salvation in heaven or earth in which man has any concern, or with which the Gospel troubles itself, but this salvation of the soul from sin, from alienation from God and unlikeness to Christ, who is presented as the true and permanent model, and inspiration, and spiritual head, of humanity.

It is glorious to know that God has an eternal interest in our souls, and an eternal desire and purpose to have them conformed to the image of his Son. But is it not also appalling as well as glorious, to consider that infinite wisdom and goodness hold this design steadily in view, while we oppose, and hinder, and delay it; making it, perhaps, more and more difficult of accomplishment, requiring a far longer and more painful period of years and ages to effect it, and the use of more and more tremendous means of discipline? There are, I suppose, no limits to the time allowed an immortal soul to come into harmony with itself and God, and no end to the infinite resources of Almighty power and skill for rectifying, cleansing, and refashioning the perverted, stained, and crude character of man. But let it be well understood, that pain and restraint, remorse and self-reprobation, are medicines which the Divine Physician freely administers, and that the burning cautery and the bitter cup are not strange to the hand of the Almighty Healer. We sometimes talk of God's goodness and mercy, as if he shrunk from severity and an heroic treatment of our sins and folly. But he must have blind eyes and deaf ears who does not know that God is a wise Father, and not a doting mother; a Father who has the permanent interests of his children in view, and not their immediate comfort; a Father who can subordinate feeling to judgment, tenderness to duty. Pain, disappointment, sickness and sorrow, have had a great part to perform in the education of mankind. God has not treated the human race as though it were a toy, or a fondling. Fire and tempest, pestilence and famine, have swept its domain; the sea has raged at its gates and flooded its plains; lightnings have blasted and volcanoes deluged it with fire; war has emptied its bloody cup upon its head; tyrants have lashed it with their whips; superstition has prostrated its form in the dust, and sensuality buried it in filth. And out of this tremendous experience the civilization of the world has grown. God has counted nothing dear—no pain, misery, or ruin too costly—if only ultimate good was to come of it to the race. And every best blessing that the world now enjoys is the fruit of sorrow, and discipline, and severity. As the selfish passions of men are the motive powers of human excellence, when broken to their work, and have a glory and serviceableness under their true Master, precisely proportioned to their fury and injuriousness under their false one, so the destructive and primitive forces of the world, the scourges of pestilence, and war, and famine, the demons of misrule, oppression, and misery, are ever changing, under God's benignant but relentless hand, into the instruments of peace and plenty—the angels of love and mercy. We are weakly prophesying an end to God's severity, and wondering that he is not content with what satisfies us. We would gladly compromise with him for the present state of things. "Give us only peace," we cry; "let commerce only have an uninterrupted opportunity; let education and religion be the mild agents of civilization." But God does not take our timid counsel. When we are predicting the end of all war, and the inauguration of universal peace, he lets loose the swords of the great nations of Europe, and the cannon's roar deafens the ear of the world. Were we so little acquainted with the love and genius of God's providence, as to imagine him content with a policy that half-enslaved the whole Eastern hemisphere, and that his providence would shrink from war, rather than from an armed and oppressive peace? We do not know God, if we think him changed in his use of the costliest remedies for the highest ends. We ought not to be surprised if another thirty years' war should convulse Europe, and settle society there upon an entirely new basis. And so at home. Why can we not have domestic peace and abstinence from sectional dispute and the agitation of disturbing questions? You might as well ask, why the skilful physician will have his patient waked to take his medicine. What does infinite justice and goodness think of our temporary prosperity, our irritability of feeling, our mutual annoyance for a generation, compared with the triumph of a pure morality, a sound political justice, the respect in which we hold his image? There can be, there will be, no possible means of pacifying this country, but by beginning to do right. You may talk of contracts and constitutions, made of paper and ink; but what are they before the eternal contract written in human nature, and in Christ's blood?

Before the sense of justice, the obligations of humanity, once fairly roused, even in a minority, all interests of time and sense, all mere laws of policy, are as withs of straw. They are meant to be so, and God would see all our temporal prosperity ground to dust, before he would put out a spark of the conscience which inflames and threatens the tranquillity of our national affairs. Let there be one national step fairly taken in view of justice, humanity, respect towards the black race in this country, and the whole horizon would brighten with glory, and brotherly love and mutual respect return to bless the divided sections of our beloved land.

And if thus costly are the dealings of God with nations, when he would bring them to the line of justice; what are we to expect from him in his dealings with our souls, which he did predestinate to be conformed to the image of his Son? Doubtless, as you look about you and see in men the unpromising materials from which God seeks to make these likenesses of Christ—you tremble with doubts of his success! Perhaps you feel in yourselves the hardness and reluctance of the substance that he would fashion after the holy and lovely model of Jesus Christ. But surely we have seen the most rude and ungracious, the most awkward and unpromising children, trained into accomplished, gentle and noble men and women. What fruits of discipline, study, self-denial, patience, perseverance, have not fallen under our notice, in our general observations of society? There is nothing so remarkable about man as his improvableness. Shall not he, who improves every thing else, improve himself? Shall not he, who out of rude logs can frame a graceful ship, or from rough stones erect a shapely temple; or from the coarse ore of the mine melt out the iron, the silver and the gold, which he forges, shapes and polishes into the art and beauty of the world;—shall he have no power to fashion himself as he will, to purge out his own dross, to hew away his own knots and splinters, to build up his own being? Shall man be the miner of the earth, and not explore his own soul; the subduer of the forest and the sea, and not subjugate himself; the sculptor of adamant, and the liquefier of iron, and not the shaper of his own will; the architect of pyramid and cathedral, and not the designer and builder of his own character? We ought, my brethren, to gather faith from our observations of nature, commerce and art. Your own daily pursuits should teach you to believe in the possibilities of conforming yourself to any model you really love and reverence, and desire to resemble. Does distance or difficulty obstruct any genuine passion of your hearts? You will go round the world for the guano that warms your soil, the quicksilver that separates your gold, the spices that flavor your food, the seeds and gums that are your medicines. You bring your teas from China, your dye-woods from New Holland, your oil from the poles, your sugar from the equator. Distance and difficulty, deserts and depths, cannot deter nor defeat your designs. Nor can any unseemliness and roughness of Nature's products withstand the transforming powers of your mills and crucibles, your furnaces and cisterns, your saws and hammers. You put the cumbrous yellow cane of Louisiana into the caldron, and take out the glistening crystals of snow that sweeten your daily drink; you shear the shaggy sheep of the Green Mountains, and weave the delicate and various cloths you wear. You tap the trees of Para, and from their gums you fashion the defences of your feet—the impenetrable garments that defy the storms of sea and winter; and presently you mimic the woods and the metals, and give the softest pliancy or toughest rigidity, as you will, to the curious substance you have gathered. What transformations do you not effect in the substances you choose to work in? Is there any quality you wish to communicate to any substance, that you despair of finally effecting it? Will you have wood that will not burn, or water that will; iron that will float, or electricity that will talk, do you not attain these wishes? And is it only humanity that does not reward zeal, and labor, and thought? Is it only the soul's qualities that cannot be enriched, improved and refined? Can you transform the metals and the gases, melt the ores and solidify the airs, handle the lightning and fix the sunbeams—and can you not transform yourselves into the image of Christ; transplant his graces into your souls; import from Palestine the fragrance of his virtues, exhume his ashes and enrich your sterile clay; reliquify his spilled and precious blood to re-animate your hearts, weave his precepts into the fabric of your souls; catch his spirit, and fix it in the substance of your lives? Cannot you, who re-form and transform every thing else, be transformed in the spirit of your minds, and conformed to the image of God's Son?

Do not doubt your ability, my brethren. Nothing is so ductile, transformable, improvable, as the soul. The powers of Nature are dull scholars beside the powers of humanity. You can, if you will, do any thing, every thing, good and right, noble and glorious, with your nature and character. And, believe me, God will not let you do any thing else without solemn and painful remonstrance! You are quarrelling with his predestination, his sacred will and purpose, in every hour's neglect, disobedience or delay. All your sorrows, trials, misfortunes, sufferings, are his protests against your folly, obduracy, or shortness of sight! You are willing to be, or trying to be, what he would not have you; willing to be selfish, self-indulgent, base.

cruel, mean, slothful, low-minded. You are willing to be in the image of the world, or of the devil, to copy fashion, or shape yourselves into idols of pride, envy and admiration. You would run your sacred and precious faculties into moulds which the fleeting age has made, and take on the shape of your convenience, or your inclinations. You allow any strong hand that dares, to lay its forming finger on you, until you are marked all over with the tools and handling of the various circumstances and powers that would give you their own likeness. And thus you are hardening, deforming, mis-shaping yourselves, and making it necessary for God, would he save your souls, to deal from time to time with a severity which is only the beginning of a conflict which will never end but with your submission. Oh, how worse than wasted are a thousand human lives, all whose powers, cunning, labor, have been exhausted upon a resistance to the divine model of a true life?

Have you seen the costly preparations for some great casting of iron—the bed-plate of a vast marine-engine, for instance? The sooty workmen, at mine and furnace, have been long at work digging the ore and blasting the iron. There it lies corded in yonder piles of ugly crudeness and grim strength! Here, beneath this lofty roof, full of rough and shapeless materials, of vast cranes and monstrous tackles and chains from which the world might hang, with the dying light of day struggling in from windows in the roof, and the flaming light of furnaces flashing up from its floor, the preparations have been and are still going on! For months, the skilful workmen, in the moulding-sand that forms the floor, have been busy with firm and cunning fingers forming the mould, with every mortice, bolt-hole, groove, stay, inclination, anxiously adjusted and arranged ; and there it lies buried in the ground. Near by, the furnaces, heated seven times hot, hold the obdurate metal seething and boiling in their hellish jaws. From minute to minute the doors are opened, and out flows—amid flames and sparks that threaten the destruction of the building, and amid which the workmen stand as unharmed and unterrified as the three men that walked in the prophet's furnace—buckets of molten iron, that are borne with staggering steps and emptied into the vast caldron, from which the mould is finally to be filled. The long-expected and anxiously-prepared-for moment at length approaches. Nay, it is precipitated. For the door of the reservoir leaks with the immense weight of its raging contents. At a word, the channels for the molten iron are cleared ! the foreman stands at the bursting gate ! the workmen, with bars and tools suited each to its end, take their posts, while the master, standing over the mould, and looking calmly but earnestly round—finally gives the signal ! Up flies the gate, forth leaps the furious current, the channels blaze with fire, the mould trembles and smokes with the inrushing contents, the loosened gases explode from their tubes ! but silence and suspense hold the assembly still. The master stands intently watching the shrews for signs of any superfluity of metal. Perhaps there has been miscalculation, and not enough ? Perhaps the mighty weight has crushed the mould, and the metal is sinking into the ground ? Perhaps the casting is a failure, and the labor of months is to be repeated ? A moment must settle the results of a whole quarter's toil; the profits of years of industry are at stake; the pride of the engineer, the suspense of the workmen, all feelings of sympathy, are concentrated in this anxious minute. But lo! just here bubbles feebly up the tardy metal, rises a few inches above the surface, and stops—not a gallon of metal to spare, not a hundred pounds over, in a casting of forty tons! Success, proud, happy, glorious success, has crowned the arduous work! But had it failed! to break up the obdurate mass and prepare for another attempt, is a work of immense labor and expense—not to name the toil and time already wasted!

And is not this just what God must do, and will do, with our hardened and ill-fashioned souls, run into misshapen moulds and disappointing forms—when he is looking for the image of his Son! What hammers shall break up our souls; what furnace shall re-melt our substance? God only knows. But think of a life's labor thrown away!

My brethren, you are beginning a new year! For twelve months God has been at work with his providence upon your souls. He has done *his* part, and always with reference to one end—your conformity to the image of his Son. How have you done yours? Have you used the mould he furnishes you in his Son? have you been putting all you are into the furnace which is designed to prepare your souls to take on the likeness of Christ? Have you had God's will, Christ's character, your spiritual and holy destiny, steadily in view these twelve months gone? Have you been ceaselessly, patiently, regularly at work in the great object and aim of your lives through this period? I looked upon a steam engine last week, connected with a blast-furnace, which for thirteen months, day and night, had not one instant ceased its smooth, calm, powerful, efficient, and changeless motion. What an image of patient persistency! of laborious industry! of singleness of aim! —nay, what a triumph of human skill! There was a year's work well done. How much had that unconscious servant meanwhile earned for its master? And cannot the inventor and owner of that machine do a year's steady, telling, single-eyed and unwearied work? Is the brain a less perfect workmanship than the steam engine? Is the heart a less constant fire than the forge? Is the soul incapable of as firm a bed, as steady a motion, as resolute a task, as the mill or the machine? Let us see what another year can do to prove our spiritual competency to do a man's work for our characters. We want only that faith and courage and devotion which we show in our affairs, directed on ourselves, to bring miracles to pass in self-improvement, growth in grace and likeness to Christ. Let the labors of this year, which promises to be one of general prosperity in our outward affairs, be now deliberately consecrated to the salvation of our souls. Would to God that phrase had no technical, no canting, no false and misleading sound in it! I mean by it, nothing professional. It has no mere pulpit import. I ask of you to see and acknowledge, and consecrate yourselves to, the glorious and solemn destiny for which you were created. In the name of your rational fears and your rational hopes—in the name of your immortal souls—I beseech you to pledge this year to the realization of religion; to the study of your eternal destiny; to the acquaintance and emulation of Jesus Christ.

I am no believer in omens, and no conjurer of superstitions ; but God knows the need the teacher of religion has to turn into encouragements in his work whatever looks that way, and therefore you will pardon me for concluding my discourse with a personal reference, especially on the opening of the new year, which is the anniversary of the Sabbath that began my ministry to this congregation. Seventeen years—one fourth of a human life of seventy years—have I completed in your service ; and now, under fresh auspices, we begin together the new year and another term of religious co-operation. At such a time, might I not innocently convert the fact into a presage of cheer, that on the morning of the new year, the image of Christ, a copy from Thorwalsden's celebrated statue, found its way among other gifts, into my home, and stretched its benignant arms over my fireside, and cast its mild and consoling looks into my eyes ! "Begin the year," it said to my heart, "in the blessing of the Saviour. Be conformed more perfectly to the image of the Son of God, in life and conversation. Look on your model, and know that years come and go, only that you may have time and opportunity to grow into his likeness ! Go to the people of your care, and your early and later affections, with this New Year's greeting. Bid them be conformed to the image of Christ, and tell them God has predestinated them to this difficult yet glorious end. Comfort and warn, persuade and encourage them —and lo ! I am with you alway, even unto the end of the world."

JAN. 5, 1856.

SERMON XIX.

THE SUFFERING CHRIST AND THE LAW OF VICARIOUSNESS.

"Who now rejoice in my sufferings for you, and fill up that which is behind of the afflictions of Christ in my flesh, for his body's sake, which is the church."—Col. i. 24.

Paul thus rejoices in his sufferings for the Colossians. He was glad to do them good, and save them moral loss and wretchedness, by any amount of personal hardship, indignity, and sorrow. He felt that he thus made himself a partaker of Christ's sufferings, and filled out in part whatever had been wanting in his afflictions to consummate the great end of saving the world. A strong light is thrown by these natural expressions of Paul upon the true nature and object of our Lord's sufferings. If Paul could do any thing "to fill up that which is behind of the afflictions of Christ," it is very clear that, however great and transcendent his sufferings were, it was nothing peculiar in the nature of the sufferer which gave special efficacy to his pangs, for Paul's afflictions were to be added to them, and to reckon with them, and we cannot add things that do not come under a common denominator; and, if there *remained* any thing to be added, it shows further that the sacrifice, however grand and sublime, was not infinite and complete, and did not act after the manner of a charm, a bargain, or a mystery. Christ's sufferings, in short, were like Paul's sufferings—like the sufferings of every lover of his race and servant of humanity—the price which devotedness and consecration to the good of others willingly pays for the accomplishment of its benevolent and exalted objects. Christ's sufferings followed the law of all sufferings borne in the cause of humanity. They were peculiar only as all afflictions are peculiarized by the position, character, spirit, and circumstances, of the sufferer. Sustaining supernatural and extraordinary relations to the race, the promised Messiah and express Messenger of God, a sinless and holy being, a thoroughly and immeasurably devoted friend of man, a hero and martyr of unrivalled and surpassing greatness and goodness, every thing connected with our Saviour has vastly added importance and dignity ; and his sufferings partake the multiplicity and far-reaching value and efficacy which belong to his precepts and promises, his virtues and moral perfections. The significance of his words, his spirit, his example, his character and office, all give the measure of the significance which belongs to his sufferings. But, however much greater and more efficacious than any, or were it possible than all other sufferings of apostles, martyrs, and saints, Christ's afflictions may have been, the sufferings were yet the same in kind, and the same in design and effect, with theirs ; namely, by the law of sympathy, the example of disinterestedness, and the influence of costly service, to remove obstacles either in the circumstances, the wills, or the affections of others, to the practice of obedience and the pursuit of holiness. Paul's afflictions could properly be added to Christ's, without a change of terms. They may have been only as one to a hundred, or as one to a thousand; but their efficacy, however proportioned, was of the same sort. And what was true of Paul was true of all the other apostles, and has been true of all servants of God and humanity before Christ and since, and is now true of every laborer and sufferer in the cause of human virtue and happiness.

Furthermore, Christ's immediate sufferings upon the cross, the agonies of his death, are not properly separable from his other afflictions. His life was one long martyrdom for humanity. He died daily. Every hour had its cross for him. A perpetual and systematic self-denial of appetites, natural tastes, selfish inclinations, and personal hopes and fears; a crucifixion of ease, bodily shrinkings, and natural affections; an abandonment of sleep, food, and safety; a painful submission to the suspicions, taunts, and cruelties of his countrymen—all these forms of sufferings belonged to his ordinary experience. Doubtless the sum of his afflictions, any month of his active ministerial life, exceeded the anguish of his cross; and when we fasten exclusively on that, and expend all our gratitude on his mangled form, we do the less striking, but perhaps more patient and costly afflictions of our Saviour, a thankless wrong. Not, my brethren, that our instincts of affection are mistaken in lavishing upon the most vivid and expressive moment of his history, that last possible sacrifice of self, his suffering death, the tenderest and most abundant tears of gratitude and love! This is natural, and in accordance with the need we have of concentrating our feelings and recollections upon pregnant and characteristic moments. But it is because the cross was Christ's life-long posture; because his death was one with his life—always suffering, self-sacrificing, and devoted—always afflicted with wrong, violence, and persecution—that we are led to sum up all our memory of his sorrows in the last fatal agony of his death. But let us not superstitiously allow this natural and becoming sensibility to harden into dogma, until we end in attaching to the death of Christ a mysterious efficacy which did not belong to his life, and separate the anguish of his cross from the afflictions of his ministry. "For if, when we were enemies, we were reconciled to God by the *death* of his Son, much more being reconciled, we shall be saved by his *life*."[1]

Again: There can be no greater or more blinding heresy than that which would teach that Christ's sufferings, or any sufferings in behalf of virtue and human sins and sorrows, are strictly substitutional, or literally vicarious. The old theologies, perplexed and darkened with metaphysics and scholastic logic—the fruit of academic pride and the love of ecclesiastical dominion—labored to prove and to teach, that Christ, in his short agony upon the cross, really suffered the pains of sin, and bore the actual sum of all the anguish from remorse and guilt due to myriads of sinners, through the ages of eternity. To enable him to concentrate into a few hours of suffering what eternity alone could have suf-

[1] Rom. v. 10.

ficed to expiate in men, and to bear, in his sole person, what myriads, dead and not yet born, were to have divided among them all, he was pronounced a God—capable of infinite sorrows—of feeling in a moment what a finite being could feel only in an experience of utter misery, extending forever; and of suffering solitarily what the united race of sinners could suffer only in the added sum of their several endless miseries! What gain would the cause of virtue and happiness make by any such arrangement, were it possible, or rationally conceivable? There would be no diminution of suffering in the universe, even by an iota; and the quality and nature of the suffering would not be changed. On the contrary, our sense of justice and goodness, so far as God himself is concerned, is vastly more shocked by the proper penalties of sin being placed upon the innocent, than had they been left upon the guilty, where they belong. Had Christ, an infinitely holy and righteous being, been condemned to suffer in his own person the agonies of boundless guilt, and had the human race, wicked and sinful, come forward and offered to divide among themselves the woe that was to fall upon him, we should say that God's consent and acceptance of such a proposition would be worthy of his character and justice. But the truth is, literal substitution of moral penalties is a thing absolutely impossible! vicarious punishment, in its technical and theological sense, is forbidden by the very laws of our nature and moral constitution! The innocent may suffer *for* the guilty, but they cannot suffer *as* the guilty, nor *what* the guilty suffer. The truth-teller cannot bear the liar's penalties, which are shame, perplexity, and guilt; the pure cannot suffer the consequences of impurity, which are self-disgust, loathing, and degradation; nor the spiritually-minded, the afflictions which pursue the selfish and worldly, which are blindness of heart, decay of moral sensibility, dread of death, and fear of God. You can make a *good* man suffer as a *bad* man only by making him a bad man, and then he will suffer on his own account. Now the good, the benevolent, the holy, may and do suffer for the sinful, the bad, and the wicked; but they suffer in a way which actually increases the joy of the universe, and diminishes its threatening pains and penalties. Do you suppose that heavenly justice, goodness and mercy would permit any suffering to fall on its best beloved Son, or on any virtuous and holy persons, in a way that really and truly diminished either their worth or their essential happiness? No! the sufferings which virtue, disinterestedness, sympathy, humanity, bring upon the souls of their champions and glorious victims, are such as Paul, in our text, could honestly say he *rejoiced in.* And it is such pure and blessed sufferings that God, by his Gospel, is constantly inviting us to *substitute* for those sufferings which are evil, and evil only; the sufferings of innocency, which elevate and adorn, and sanctify and bless, which are joys in tears, blessings in disguise—for those sufferings of guilt which punish, degrade, waste, and defile—moral blindness, selfishness, malice, alienation from God, self-disgust, enmity with the conscience, and conflict with the race. Sin is suffering, and it is the only suffering which is dark and dreadful. There is no light in it. It harms, and only harms. It introduces confusion and chaos; it poisons personal and domestic peace ; it shuts out heaven ; it curses earth ; it converts men into devils, and brothers into enemies. It is the source of all the degrading misery and hopeless wretchedness in the world ! But pain, sickness, labor, loss, bereavement, self-denial, persecution, anguish of body, anxiety of heart, sympathy with others' woes, death, crucifixion by violence—why, consider for a moment what a changed, what a blessed world it would be, if these, the sufferings of innocence, these, the pangs of sensibility, these, the labors and toils of virtue, these, the tears and groans of pity, were the *only* sufferings in the world ? How much of these might not wisely be borne, to do away ever so little of the penalties of sin ? how much ought *we* not to bear, to save ourselves ever so little of the reproach and degradation of guilt ? how ready should we be to endure the contradiction of sinners, and to bear the cross, that we may extinguish, in any degree, the blight and curse of sin in our fellow-beings now in the world, or yet to come into the world ?

And this is the real substitution and vicariousness of that glorious and blessed system of relief, which is honored and illustrated so splendidly by Christ's cross—the transmutation of the sufferings of sin into the sufferings of innocency ;—not the making of the innocent guilty, or the treating them as guilty ; but the removal of guilt by the labors and sacrifices of goodness ; sufferings of the flesh, of the disinterested sympathies, of the humane affections, substituted for sufferings of the soul, the conscience, the very Nature. On these sufferings—guilt and degradation, blindness and selfishness, hatred and malice, lust and rebellion, cruelty and cunning, enmity, falsehood and fraud—the occupants of the sinner's heart—God looks with infinite concern and anxiety! If he can substitute for such hopeless, ruinous and corrupting sufferings—the pangs of virtuous labor, the groans of striving and pitiful goodness, the sorrows and tears of self-sacrificing mercy, the anguish of self-devoted love—what an enormous relief to the aspect of the world, and the honor, and beauty, and happiness of the universe? And this is the real change which Christianity is gradually effecting. It has certainly not *diminished* the suffering in the world—but it has altered its expression, and is transmuting its character. The suffering which sprung from brutal passions, from violence, intense depravity, and hatred, and malice—from positive sin and wickedness—is giving way, in some considerable degree, to the suffering which comes from aspiration, sympathy, sensibility to the imperfections and wants of the soul and of society. When men suffered most wofully and hopelessly, it was not always acutely or even consciously, that they suffered! Impaired in manhood, ungrown in thought, darkened in conscience—they were poor, mutilated or undeveloped souls, suffering the most serious and pitiable wrong, and ignorant of their misery! The most desperate sinners are not always remorseful;—but oh! what frightful penalties are they not daily paying for their wickedness? Like the worst physical injuries from frost or fire, which first destroy the sensibility, and then utterly devastate the human frame, sin, whether it be against light or in the absence of light, is often, in its most hideous forms, apathetic and horribly unconscious of its inhuman work. Have you not seen those low, painless fevers, which gnaw at the throat or drink up the blood? What acute disease is not less dreadful and less fatal? The world, in Christ's days, was filled with the dull misery, the painless horror, the stupid wretchedness of moral degradation;—of human guilt and sin that did not know its own name, or feel its own death-penalty! Enough of wilful sin, of acute remorse, of self-reproach, always exists to be deplored and relieved; but it is never the sum of human suffering. That lies dark and solid in the mountain of moral blindness, torpid conscience, wasted powers, perverted faculties; of ignorant alienation from goodness and God; and dreadful, dumb, and sometimes smiling, insensibility to honor, justice and duty! Oh! fatal selfishness! oh! stupid chill of moral death! blind unbelief! deaf inhumanity! "Oh! Jerusalem! Jerusalem! thou that killest the prophets and stonest them that are sent unto thee, how often would I have gathered thy children together even as a hen gathereth her chickens under her wings, and ye would not! Behold your house is left unto you desolate!"

In this great substitutional and sacrificial work, of putting innocent suffering and self-sacrifice in the place of guilty suffering and *soul*-sacrifice—all the genuine followers of Christ are engaged, and are thus made partakers of his sufferings and death, and "fill out what is behind of the afflictions of Christ." Whenever we crucify any appetite, or resist any impulse, or rescue any time or faculty, or strain any reluctant nerve, or whip any torpid muscle, or forego any innocent enjoyment, or encounter any physical peril, or defy fashion and custom, or confront censure and shame, for the sake of the moral enlightenment of the ignorant, the guidance and help of the erring, the softening of the impenitent, the encouragement of the struggling, the salvation of the lost—we are partaking Christ's sufferings and bearing his cross. And this glorious opportunity is not denied to any of us. We are surrounded by the degraded, the sinful and the blind. Their sufferings blacken the sky. The stripes with which they are beaten by sin half deface the image of God in which they are made. Is there any thing in reeking battle-fields, in festering lazar-houses, in heathen temples, more cruel and soul-moving than the moral degradation of thousands who live at our own doors? beings hardly more human than the dogs tackled with them to the carts they draw—their senses so brutified that filth is no longer offensive to them; their tastes so low that they riot in their bestiality. Talk to them of God and they stare with stupid wonder! of Christ, and they think you speak of some neighbor! of their souls, and they feel about as for their knife or purse! And perhaps *their* loathsome state is not so helpless as that of a class greatly above them in outward condition—the rude, ferocious, defying youth of our cities—their symbol, a bludgeon or a pistol—the vigorous, rebellious, insolent product of our own crude institutions—just taught enough to be doubly dangerous—to whom God and Christ are merely the convenient counters of profanity; virtue, the standing mark for jests; daylight, the name for the labor they hate; night, the synonyme of drunkenness, riot, violence and crime. Nor are these young banditti, that infest our streets and make our walks dangerous at early evening, the most alarming portion of the community! The very places of legislation and government have lately been, and even now to some extent are, in the hands of the shameless and the violent; nor do any combinations or remonstrances of the wise and good suffice to prevent or control the bribery and corruption, the peculation and crime of those whom the community have placed in power. If good men are joined to the city councils, their hands are tied by majorities, and their interference rendered null. We know not from which quarter we have most to fear, from the thieves or the government; the illegal or the legalized crime of the city! And what is all the peril to life and property which such a state of things involves, horrible as it is, compared with the degradation and accursedness which it implies in large classes of the community! For remember, that for every man that is knocked down and robbed in our streets, there must have been beforehand a thousand souls knocked down and trampled under foot and robbed of human dignity and worth;—that for every victim of the gallows, there are ten thousand men tugging at the rope that chokes him; and they know not that it is round their own throat! The worst, infinitely the worst, of a corrupt government, is the dreadful consideration, who made and who supports it; the worst of all the crime, violence and insecurity is—that it implies so much ignorance, desperation and recklessness behind it! If men murder when bread is scarce, or in violent and unsettled times, or in communities ridden with priestcraft, or in nations oppressed with vindictive and unjust institutions; if degraded Italy and Spain turn out their bandits, or India nourishes her thugs; if France raises up the inventors and engineers of infernal machines, or arms the hands that shoot one archbishop at the barricades and stab another at the altar, or waylays the assassin of liberty with weapons caught from his own blood-stained hands and treacherous arts—we do not wonder. Such classes and such crimes belong to a humanity pent up in superstition, political thraldom, and desperate circumstances. But the violence and crime, the robbery and murder of a community and a country like ours—comparatively free, well-fed, at ease, with open ways for labor and thought, with quick rewards for industry and virtue, with lavish opportunities for instruction and preferment, with every prize open to every man—seem the spontaneous products of innate depravity, the very riot of reckless folly—the most inexcusable, hopeless and alarming sort of wickedness! And what a matrix of moral ignorance, and blindness and sin, has this now molten stream of crime ripened in? Can we be easy in our consciences or hopeful in our faith, and not feel that we have got to meet this dreadful state of things with sacrifices and sufferings—that we must fill out what remains behind of the afflictions of Christ, would we stay the flood of public corruption and redeem the souls of our brethren? Rich men must sacrifice their fortunes in this work; strong men must crucify their intellects; loving hearts must pour out their sympathies; the easy must forsake their ease; the unoccupied their leisure; woman her fastidiousness and her fashion; the young their carelessness and gayety—all must join in the work of expiating the sins of our people, ransoming the guilty, redeeming the lost here at our doors. We must ply with tears and toil, every engine of redemption, and afflict ourselves in every necessary manner to abolish this death of sin, which rests like the curse of God upon our brothers and sisters—on the brutal boyhood, the abandoned women, the hordes of idlers, thieves and beggars ; the unschooled, unchurched and unvisited ; the heathen and inhuman classes of our fellow-citizens, of our should-be fellow-Christians. The public and the industrial schools, the societies of employment, the hospitals and charities, the means of political reform, the opportunities of private influence, the teaching of all servants to read and write by the hands of our daughters ; the resisting of excesses in dress, in manners, in food and drink ; the support and encouragement of all measures which soften, enlighten and win the rude and envious ; the actual superintendence of special families, and the rescue of particular persons ; these are the means and opportunities still left to us, never more open, never grander since Adam fell or Christ rose, for filling out the afflictions of our Lord, for his body's sake —which is the Church—of which we must see that all men are made members. *Our* Calvary is the mountain on which our moral intelligence and gracious privileges have lifted us, in the midst of this spiritual wickedness and destitution ! Our cross is the stretching of our hands for the nails which this violence will drive—that they may tear us innocent, and not the souls of the guilty ! We must suffer, suffer in the sweat of thoughtful brains, in the anguish of perplexed and palpitating hearts, in the labor and sacrifices of contriving, sympathizing, never-weary and never-despairing exertions for the salvation of our community and race.

And, brethren, we must learn, like Paul, to rejoice

in this suffering! It is the only secret of victory over the world and ourselves. The key to joy we have lost! Sin and folly had broken its wards, and filled up its entrance-way. But suffering is still within our power, and in our hands. Serenity, satisfaction, steadfast friends, permanent relations, health, kindred, satisfying success, gratified ambition! Ah! ye bright illusions! phantoms of youth and inexperience! whither have ye gone? All faded and wrecked! But suffering, laboring for the race, bearing with the wrong-headed and the bad-hearted, spending and being spent in the service of humanity and Christ and God—suffering! Ah! thou once overlooked and spurned form! cloaked with the pall or folded in the shroud, skeleton at the feast, mocker at the wine, but still disguised angel, marred and rejected messenger of God—suffering! *thou* remainest, and provest our only constant and evermore precious and satisfying friend! Yes! it is our privilege to suffer! And woe to the heart, woe! woe! to the heart, that spurns that cup; that knows not how to suffer; that refuses to suffer. How blessed the sensibility that feels the woes of the world, and carries them, painfully and tenderly, as a mother bears her sick child in her weary but clinging and grateful arms! And, believe me, no great good is done without suffering. Out of its agonies have come the works of genius, and the deeds of heroes and martyrs, poems and reformations, discoveries and revelations! Beauty and truth, love and worth, have all hung on the cross, and ripened there, as on their natural trellis, into the fruits that refresh and inspire humanity. Christ has not trodden the wine-press alone. Other garments have been dyed in blood, and the world will not follow any colors that have not the purple stain of suffering in their folds. Yes! and it must be *vicarious* suffering, a suffering not in one's own cause, or for one's own sake—a suffering not in the service of greed, ambition, self-preservation, not in expiation of the inexperience, folly, or ignorance of one's own heart or life, but a suffering *for* and in the place of others—a suffering in behalf of principles, which are the property of humanity; of institutions, that shelter the race; of hopes, that are the heritage of the future; or of sorrows, wrongs, injuries, misfortunes and crimes, that crush and afflict our whole generation.

Such sufferings are the filling up of that which is behind of the afflictions of Christ, and they are for his body's sake, which is the Church. It is the law of God's universe; the innocent must suffer *for*, though not *as*, the guilty; the lamb must die for the wolf; the good must expiate the wretchedness and wickedness of the bad! Suffering, the suffering of virtue, piety, love, must creep into the place which the sufferings of wrath, of selfishness, of sin now fill, as the secretions of some mineral pool creep into the rotting tissues of the woody knot fallen into its bosom, and convert it, fibre by fibre, line by line, twist by twist, into precious stone—the same, yet saved from decay, glorified, and made immortal. So, suffering is suffering still! but now beautiful, holy, blessed, and full of eternal life.

Thus is the world changing into the Church, which is the body of Christ; the brutal suffering of its sinful life—coarse, cruel, horrible—a mass of writhing deformity, and shameful corruption, and self-wrought violence—like the body of a malefactor, full of black and cruel blood, with marks of guilty wounds and disgraceful sins, the gyves of the jail, and the rope of the hangman—gradually changing under the transmuting and redeeming powers of our Lord's suffering followers and faithful co-workers, into the likeness of the dying Christ, bleeding and wounded still, suffering and sorrowing yet; but oh! with what beauty in that melting eye, what glory on that thorn-crowned brow, what triumph and salvation in those pierced hands and feet!

Welcome the sufferings of innocency, the sacrifice of love! Welcome a state of society, a world, all whose griefs shall be those of sympathy, all its wounds those of charity, all its afflictions those of submission! For the end of such a world must be the end of Christ's sufferings, a perfect redemption from moral evil, and a quick ascension into the perfect joy and undimmed glory of the city of God in heaven.

February 1, 1857.

SERMON XX.

CHRIST—"THE HEAD OF ALL PRINCIPALITY AND POWER."

"——the head of all principality and power."—COLOSSIANS ii. 10.

IN the present discourse, I design to exhibit the nature and influence of those principalities and powers so often spoken of in the epistles, in a language vague and vast, and fitted to excite the religious imagination to the utmost. And this I shall do, not by a fatiguing comparison and criticism of the texts in which these words occur, but by an appeal to your inmost consciousness—endeavoring to make you *feel*, and thus recognize and understand, the principalities and powers that rule and largely constitute our life.

The world we most truly live in, my brethren, is not the world of earth, water, and sky; nor the world of men and women and children; nor the world of immediate experience, sensation, and thinking. It is the world of spiritual realities and spiritual relations, the world of principalities and powers, with a history as old as God's own being, a past as remote as the unbeginning eternity, a future as distant as unending time; a world of thoughts, feelings, tendencies, influences, which the immediate generations that occupy the planet—important as their action or influence is—have only a very small part in originating or controlling. The visible inhabitants of the globe—how small a part are they of the minds and hearts that still live in the hereditary influences they exert, in the impulses they communicate, in the thoughts and passions they animate! How little of the actual philosophy, science, art, government, religion, manners—nay, how little of the total civilization of the nineteenth century is *our* work, due to our unassisted and underived minds, or hearts, or wills! The dead govern the living. The past controls the present. The visible generations of men, the thrones and nationalities and populations, that seem to regulate affairs, are but the agents and representatives of venerable powers, and mighty wills, and great experiences withdrawn from view, that still truly reign, leaving us little choice in action, because communicating to us the most decisive impetus and direction of their own. The principalities and powers that carry on this very age, and maintain this very life of our own, are not alone or chiefly our ideas, our passions, our wills. *We* are not the great activities of the world! We are merely the instruments, channels, and vehicles of the mighty will of a great historical past, doing what the accumulated passions, desires, purposes of our race will have us to do—moulded, shaped, inspired by invisible wills and voiceless influences, from the whole countless myriads of humanity, so vastly mightier than the petty fraction of the race that now possesses the earth.

Does it often enough occur to us to think, in our

skepticism of spiritual realities, how profoundly spiritual is the life of the most material community, or of the most stupid and irreligious individual ? We are all—for good or evil—living under the perpetual dominion of an invisible world. For the evil powers and prejudices, the inherited enmities and antipathies, the superstitions and predilections that govern the lowest tribes and the worst men, are just as spiritual, in their lack of all local habitation or palpable form, and in their viewless methods of influence, as the Holy Spirit of God, or the powers of the world to come. The crimes and vices and wickednesses, the political tyrannies and false religions, the shocking customs and terrible maxims that deform the world, are not chiefly the products of the depravity of our own day. They are the result of accumulated powers and principalities of darkness, that from their invisible thrones in the past, still sway the unhappy spirits of living communities with an irresistible malice. If you go to India, and find there a vast population under the religious conviction that women must be kept in a perpetual state of mental childhood, do you fancy that it is the men of this generation that keep those women in that degraded state ? Is it not a power stronger than all the men in India, or all the missionaries in India ? And yet it is a purely invisible power ; the power of an idea ; a false idea, a prejudice, a spiritual thing ; but a terrible reality, nevertheless !

Do you imagine that it is Louis Napoleon, and the king of Sardinia, and the emperor of Austria, who are creating and making the doomfulness of this general war that now threatens Europe and Asia ? Alas !

that terrible logic of events—of which politicians now speak—what is it but the irresistible power and reality of national antipathies, ancient grudges that taint the very blood of remote generations, passions communicated by mighty men, that from their crumbling urns still sway their sceptres of ambition, and brandish their swords of vengeance or conquest ? It is the one frightful thought connected with this already opened conflict, that the principalities and powers that conduct it are invisible ; that it comes against the will of existing rulers and generations, a fearful necessity of foregone conclusions in a wicked past ; and that no man can tell by what complicity of invisible powers the heirs of old transgressors may be forced into the *mêleé* of inimical races and conflicting ideas !

Do not suppose, my brethren, because ideas, superstitions, national hatreds, are unsubstantial in form, that they are unreal in essence. If unrealities can sway and cut and carve the world, can change the map of Europe, stop national industries, and occasion the widest misery, in what attributes of reality are they deficient ? The world is full of these invisible principalities and powers. Could the spiritual nerves and fibres —subtler than electric wires—that move and animate the world, be made visible, in what a complicated, busy, and far-reaching network of powers and wills should we not find ourselves immeshed ! How far back would many of these lines be seen to lead, and in what forgotten hands would the reins that still control the world be still seen firmly grasped ! Is the living or the dead Napoleon now on the throne of France ? Is it the Italy of to-day, or of Dante and Cæsar, that is springing to its feet ? You may call these powers prejudices, shadows, imaginations ! I call the spirits and the ideas that do the actual work of the world—whether they lie in the still dust of their graves or move in their ruddy flesh—the veritable realities of to-day. Powerful prejudices, influential errors, great superstitions, mighty names, are as real as climates and soils, mountains and rivers ; for they characterize the moral geography of the globe, they bound nations, they make wars, they establish customs, they set up dynasties, they rule posterity. The visible forces—the present people, the existing amount of mind, and will, and passion, and conscience in the world—form not a tithe of the real world ; would not account for, do not decide, cannot make nor unmake, that mighty world of principalities and powers, of faiths and feelings, of social tendencies and currents of opinion, in the midst of which we live ! Instance our own government. Let the names, the wills, the inspirations of our founders, be for a moment withdrawn from it, and it could not stand a day in *our* wisdom, patriotism, and care. Instance society itself—its foundations in the family tie, and all the invisible inheritance of usage, blessed prejudice, and viewless sanctity that give it power ! Suppose society depended on the wisdom, the worth, the will of this generation, for its existence ? That is, supposing it to be dissolved, call on the worth, will, and wisdom of this generation to reframe it and set it a-going upon another model, and see what an impossible task you allot to the incompetency of one age ! Or, suppose that the education of the world were dependent alone on the intentional and conscious training each generation gave its successor ! Suppose, in short, that *society* were no more and no other than the associated people now in the world; that humanity were no more and no other than the men and women now living; that *law* were no more and no other than *the laws;* that religion were no more and no other than the existing worship of the world; and the Church and Gospel of Christ no more and no other than existing religious institutions! Why, it would be just as mad and empty a notion as to affirm that the Mississippi river is that amount of water now in its bed, and not that mighty configuration of the globe which affords a perpetual channel to floods, that constantly renew themselves from the ever-busy mists that rise from the ocean, descend in snows on the mountains, and melt into the bosom of that Father of waters!

Men can manufacture fountains, but not rivers; they can make monuments, but not mountains; and so they may build cities, but not society; they may create laws, but not law; they may erect churches, but not the Church. It takes *divine* powers to do any creative work, and the family, the State, the nation, the Gospel, the Church, are creations, not conventions, agreements, and compacts. They are the principalities and powers that rule the world for its good, subject as it is to many other principalities and powers of darkness and sin, that are mightier in malignity than the palpable evils and wickednesses of the world. The good and evil in this world, my brethren, are neither of them most potent as immediate and palpable things. If we had only to contend with bad men and women, it were a comparatively easy struggle; "but we wrestle not against flesh and blood, but against principalities, against powers, against the rulers of the darkness of this world, against *spiritual* wickedness in high places."[1] It is the mighty selfishness of a gross and degraded past history; it is the malignant superstition of a long-established heathenism; it is the tremendous authority of diabolic genius that intoxicated the past with its evil charms; it is the thraldom of great conjurors in malice and pride—men like Napoleon, who bewitched the world with the admiration of glory, or like Mohammed, who built an altar out of the burning senses of his race; it is the organized and instituted selfishness, sensuality, and malice of the whole past, that corrupts the very veins, dwells in the brain, and lives at the heart of the present generation, and makes the invisible powers of evil vastly more fearful and hopeless to contend with than the actual and conscious dispositions of living sinners, or the real and overt acts of present wrong.

Ought we not to realize that our souls are the platform on which these invisible powers and principalities, for evil and for good, are now continually confronting their forces? Would not our spiritual position and our lives, in that aspect, have some greater dignity and awfulness in our eyes than when we consider ourselves, as it were, a generation without any relations to the past or the future—beings whose natures have nothing in them but seeds and elements; not also the old and mighty life for good and evil of the past! I stand awestruck before this astonishing relation I bear to the common humanity, of which I form a part. I find my

[1] Eph. vi. 12.

nature is not mere private will, intellect, heart, but that I am also the subject of mighty wills, intellects, and hearts, both good and evil, that possess me, and either intoxicate, pervert and degrade, or inspire, enlarge, and elevate my soul. I find that as the earth has a necessary motion of its own all the while that we move freely upon it, so our nature has a compulsory motion of its own, while our characters have their own independent motion, too. I find that I am the subject of ideas, affections, powers, that are not me nor mine, infinitely greater than I am, and the source of all that is best and noblest in me, or worst and most perilous. I discover that my boasted independence is a very small domain—the freedom of a bird, that occupies a fixed stratum of air, a mile or two thick, in an infinite and forbidden space, and seems to itself only, to have the liberty of the universe. But I finally rejoice in the glorious discovery, that what I thought at first my insignificance is my grandeur; what I thought my loss is my gain; that in place of my poor private life, God has destined me for the great life of humanity; that in place of my own freedom, he has given me his; that instead of a soul innocent because inexperienced, he has communicated to me a soul fraught with the life of the whole race, and connected with the whole universe—with memories, influences, powers and principalities of good and evil, angels and devils, at work upon it; that I am endowed with the knowledge of good and evil, both tempted and inspired, and have spirits of evil for enemies, and greater spirits of good for allies—with the HEAD of all principalities and powers for my Saviour and immortal friend.

Such a position would be terrible and awful, if the powers of evil were equal to the powers of good. But while God is on the throne of the universe this can never be; and while Christ is his great spiritual representative and the Gospel continues to be "the power of God," we have nothing to fear, if we accept our deliverer, and trust "our high fortress and tower of defence." "For I am persuaded, that neither death, nor life, nor angels, nor principalities, nor powers, nor things present, nor things to come, nor height, nor depth, nor any other creature, shall be able to separate us from the love of God which is in Christ Jesus, our Lord."[1]

Christ is "the *head* of all principality and power." Christianity, which is the name for his influence, the Church, which is the channel of his power, has more determining sway upon the thoughts, customs, and character of men, and has had for eighteen hundred years, than any single element or impulse in history or civilization.

In Jesus Christ there broke into the world a mighty and shaping influence, a holy will, a spiritual sovereignty, an illuminating, warning, inspiring principle of mingled thought, affection, and volition, which was, among the other moral and spiritual influences at work upon the world of feeling and opinion, what the mighty gulf-stream is among the other currents of the ocean—changing the temperature of the most distant seas, ameliorating the climates of far-off boreal shores, and modifying the navigation and the commerce of the globe. We often dwell upon what the world is doing

[1] Rom. viii. 38, 39.

for the Gospel, to propagate and diffuse its influence. We talk of upholding and supporting it. We make serious question of its evidences, are alarmed at the doubts that assail its origin and reality. Would it not be better for us to consider what the Gospel is now doing, and has always been doing, for the world—what a self-asserting, self-proving reality it is—how truly and deeply it confirms itself, and how mightily it shapes the thoughts and destinies of men?

Will you reply that false philosophies, and religions not of divine origin, have manifested a similar, if not an equal, power? Will you point me to the tremendous sway of the Oriental fatalisms, to the religions of China and India, to the still potent sceptre of Mohammed? I should be mad to deny the pertinency of your rejoinder. Nor, as the advocate of Christ's headship, have I any need to do it. Who thinks it necessary to question the tremendous influence of powerful error, of organized evil, of passionate malignity, of grand and awful superstition? It is a childish and undignified philosophy of history and humanity that allots power and influence in this world and in humanity, only to what is good; that denies any continuity of evil, any hereditary sway to dangerous and misguiding powers. There is no appetite, no faculty of soul or sense, no imagination nor impulse of which humanity is capable, that may not by a mastering spirit be evoked with such power, and organized with such effect, as to influence and mould whole generations and races of men. Dynasties, social systems, religions, have been built up by mighty spirits, giants in will and in impulse, upon any and every quality in our nature—

now on fear, then on hope, now on the senses, then on the imagination, here on the ignorance, and there on the intellect of men. And he would be a very unskilled and superficial decipherer of the moral and spiritual hieroglyphics of history, who so read the past as to declare that any broad stream of religious, social, or political influence, determining the character of ages and nations, had come from a feeble fountain, or did not have a mighty well-head of thought and will for its source. The prejudices which once denied Mohammed, Confucius, or other founders of false, or merely human religions, to be men of prodigious and earnest enthusiasm, true principalities and powers in the development of humanity, are fast disappearing. We do not, we must not, deny that effects so mighty were due to causes of tremendous efficacy. A conjunction of an extraordinary personality with some equally extraordinary want or sensibility of our nature at the time, is necessary to account for every great spiritual or religious movement. As one illustration, take Mormonism—the only faith which, on any considerable scale, we have had a chance to see the origin and growth of, in our own day—and certainly the most characteristic and philosophically curious phenomenon in the history of the nineteenth century—the relapse of modern civilization into its original barbarism; the untimely return of patriarchal ideas; the reappearance of Oriental weaknesses in the Western wilderness; exploded, effete polygamy, springing into fresh vigor in the new world and the nineteenth century, under the sanction of a new revelation! We shall wonder less at this, if we consider what has always deeply impressed me, that the most extraordinary triumph of mingled reason and religion ever achieved over the human race, was the establishment of monogamy as the law of civilized society. Polygamy, either under the protection of law and legal forms, or in spite of them, is the impulse and ever threatening tendency of the human race. Against this surge of passion Christianity erected her invisible but mighty breakwater, and civilization has fortified this sacred sea-wall. Mormonism is the frightful leakage of this dyke—a moral crevasse—the giving way at a point of ignorance and stupidity in the sacred levee that dammed out this ever-threatening stream. Divine Providence, perhaps, saw in the periodical reaction which overtakes the sentiment of sacredness in the marriage bond—and which is now, under more decent forms than Mormonism, but from the same impulse, agitating society at large—the necessity of exhibiting the effect of polygamy under modern conditions and in the western hemisphere, in order to warn and save our general civilization from so dreadful a peril. The vigorous and unscrupulous minds that seized upon this ever-latent tendency and converted it into a religion, are truly great in their sagacity, will, and administrative faculties, and I doubt not that the limited channel in which their influence runs, may serve to sewer and empty into the wilderness the feculence and pruriency of our modern disloyalty to the family state. Mormonism is spiritism and Free-loveism in their natural connection, logically carried out—the fine theory done into coarse practice—the sophistry and subtlety of restless Socialism reduced to practical absurdity, and made palpably disgusting, because thoroughly obvious. Thus it is that the evil powers and influences of the world get to be organized principalities and powers—tremendous engines of evil.

But, because we do not deny the reality of the mighty founders of false religions and false civilizations, nor call them divine, because they were great in their effects; because we do not worship power and success, and deify all the principalities that have swayed the world, let us not be drawn from the ground that Christianity is of God, and that Christ is the *head* of principalities and powers, and proved so by the place his person and influence has taken in the world. It is not merely the greatness and extent of his influence, but the nature of it, it is not his success, but the character of his success, that establishes this point; and that influence and that success have always been on the side of truth, goodness, peace, order, brotherly love, superiority to the senses, purity of life and devotion to duty. That influence and success have always assimilated with, accompanied, strengthened, and inspired, when they did not wholly occasion and cause, the movements of liberty, knowledge, truth, and progress. The track of the Gospel has been the path of civilization; its triumphs have been the emancipation of serfs and slaves, the elevation of woman, the growth of equality among men, the reign of law, the progress of knowledge, and the increase of peace. Its institutions have been the refuge of innocency, learning and worth, in times of violence and wickedness. And although the Church is spotted and stained with the mire and the blood of the ages through which it has passed, it has been, like Christ himself on his way to that cross that saved the world, clothed not in its own chosen robes of purity and love, but arrayed in such garments as its crucifiers have given it—marred and mocked, yet always laboring, and most effectually, for the salvation of its enemies and the improvement of its half-enlightened friends. Christ's influence, called the Church, has poured a pure and purifying stream into a polluted and polluting channel, and it has not been easy to distinguish between the feculence of the channel and the filth of the stream, except by observing that wherever Christianity has poured, it has, sooner or later, made civilization, however turbid at the start, run clear in the end.

My brethren, amid the evil principalities and powers that are still influencing the world and above them all—amid the good principalities and powers that are helping us on, and above them all—is the head of all principality and power, Christ and Christianity, a principality and power, the immeasurable significance and value of which cannot be exaggerated, and which it becomes us most gratefully and humbly to adore and glorify. I wish you to feel that this saving power is mightier than your wills; that it is a glorious, an active reality, the occasion and cause of all that is best in your convictions, your faith, your hope, your trust. I wish to feel with you that when we speak of the Gospel, we do not speak merely of a book, but of a power; not of a dead piece of history, but of a living fountain of spiritual influence. I wish to feel with you that the Church is not a building, nor an organization of individuals, not your Church, nor our Church, but the grand embodiment of Christ's will and Christ's truth, inspired by his authority and his heart, fed with continued life from his Spirit, and invigorated with the prayers, the faith, the blessings, the experiences of all who have joined it in past ages, and who now lend it their influence and power in heaven. The Church is alive! If the state live not in one generation, if the family live not in one household, but in that continuous and vital unity which a common humanity allows and secures, how much more the Church? The question, how far one generation can bind the faith, the conscience, the pecuniary responsibility of another, is a question mainly asked by shallow political and spiritual philosophers. The life of humanity is one. Every age inherits the responsibilities of its predecessors, as every noble son inherits his father's honest debts, along with his fortune. To be jealous of the past, to think we derive all our strength from ourselves, and all our weakness from our connection with it, is nearly the precise opposite of the truth. Those are greatest who know most of, and receive most from, the past; who are best acquainted with the principalities and powers of the world, and welcome in the largest measure of their good influence, while most strenuously resisting their evil. It is the great weakness of the unread in history, the unenlightened in the fellowship and communion of recorded thought and departed spirits, to indulge in original, and crude, and thin speculations. The mere instincts of the utterly unthinking, who carry in their organizations, and in the shaping influence of their very blood, or derive from the social atmosphere, much of the wisdom of the past, are more sound and saving than the speculations of minds that, on discovering themselves to be individuals, immediately set up on their own account, dissolve partnership with their fellow-men, sign off from institutions—the family, the state, the Church—and attempt to live in their own wisdom, will, and might. But if there be one folly greater than another, it is in our day, the attempt to pronounce the Gospel outworn; Christ a mere name among other great names; Christianity a superstition, and the Church a prison for the intellect, and a strait-jacket for the will. It is the Church that is now freeing the Churches! It is Christ that continually purifies Christianity! It is the largeness and nobility he teaches and inspires, that is forever widening the bonds of charity and intelligence. Summon pure Naturalism, and exhibit, if you can, in her doctrines, a spirit of charity, toleration and breadth, in worshippers of science and law, such as the Gospel cherishes! The deifiers of law are among the narrowest of philosophers. What they usually mean by law, is the few favorite laws they choose to recognize, as if the laws of God and nature were not infinite in number, and did not include spiritual influences, and miracles, and social institutions! Do you suppose there are no laws governing what we call exceptions, because we do not know the law for them? The eddies are as much under law as the main stream; and the unnatural is often only a name for our ignorance. Those who bring us the first volume of God's revelation, and deny the value of any other, need not boast their breadth. We accept that, and rejoice besides in every successive volume he pleases to issue, whether it be called God in History, or God in Christianity. Those who deny the Church its place, because they see so fine a place of worship in outward nature, have yet to learn that the love and the worship of nature is itself the fruit of that sensibility which Christianity has communicated. The whole heathen literature has not a single recognition of what we call "the landscape" in it, and the enjoyment of God in his works is a Jewish and a Christian satisfaction, due, above all things, to the influence of instituted and organized faith.

Open your hearts and minds, then, to the Head of all principality and power! Expect inspiration and salvation from your faith in Christ, your welcome of his spirit, your fellowship with his disciples, your communion with his life, your union with his Church! Already, in spite of your indifference and distrust, Christ is saving you, and blessing you! Already the Church encloses and comforts and feeds you. How much better and more thorough, and blessed its influence, if you would, with all your hearts and minds and wills, yield yourselves to Christ's inspiration! "For ye are complete in him, which is the head of all principality and power." "Beware, lest any man spoil you through philosophy and vain deceit, after the tradition of men, after the rudiments of the world, and not after Christ. For in him dwelleth all the fulness of the Godhead, bodily."

May 21, 1859.

V.

THE HOLY SPIRIT AND THE CHURCH.

V.

THE HOLY SPIRIT AND THE CHURCH.

SERMON XXI.

THE SOUL'S RENEWAL—A NEW-YEAR'S SERMON.

"Create in me a clean heart, O God, and renew a right spirit with me."
Ps. li. 10.

THE first Sabbath of the New Year has returned to us, and we are here to welcome it, and to receive the blessing it offers. Yesterday we celebrated the arrival of the New Year in our homes; to-morrow we shall mark it in our places of business; to-day we observe it in our sanctuaries. Yesterday we asked ourselves, who were missing and who were spared in our domestic circles; what friends had gone from the greeting of our eyes and the pressure of our hands; from whom we heard no more the New-Year's wish, and who were still left to pour that affectionate salutation into our ears! To-morrow we may ask ourselves how we stand with the world; what losses we have made, and what gains; how much of our custom has gone, and how much remains; what we have to fear, and what to hope, as we ponder the annual balance of our accounts. To-day the more important and pregnant consideration is, what the year that is past has done for our souls ; how it leaves us in our relations with our God ; what the opening year says to us as moral and spiritual beings, passing through time to eternity, through life to immortality. Not, my brethren, that our domestic, our religious, and our business affairs, are separate or separable interests ; not that our experiences, our successes and reverses, our joys and trials, at the hearth-stone and at the counting-room, are not part and parcel of our spiritual life, educational in their aim and in their effect ; not that the times and seasons as sickly or sanative, as peaceful or warlike, as prosperous or adverse, do not reflect themselves in the sky of the soul ; but that our religious interests are our supreme interests, to which our domestic and our commercial are alike subordinate and auxiliary ; and that, however we may have suffered or prospered in the health of our households, or the condition of our affairs, we have truly suffered and truly prospered, only as the beginning of the New Year finds us better or worse men and women—nearer to, or farther from, our God and our Saviour.

Before taking up the main question, a few words are due, on the score of patriotism and citizenship, to our civic, social and commercial condition, at this season of review. In respect of the public health, the mortality of our own community, the safety of our own households, we have much to be thankful for in reviewing the past year. While pestilence has severely visited our Southern cities and coasts, we have, amid many fears, escaped all contagious disorders. And two events of much consequence to the future safety of our city, mark the departure of the old year: the proposed removal of the Quarantine to a safe and distant anchorage, and the establishment of a Sanatory Association, to be devoted to the carrying of all needful measures of reform in the cleansing, ventilating, and sewering of our streets, and the regulation of the tenant houses occupied by more than half our total population. If to this we add the rapid forwarding of the Central Park, which this very next spring will begin to be in use, and afford a most needed resort for the leisure of our pent-up population, we may mark the present as a season very flattering to the future health of our community. It is one of the few encouraging things in our municipal affairs, that an enterprise of such magnitude and pregnancy as the Central Park—so essential to the highest interests of the city—should thus far have escaped the opposition and perversion of demagogues, and been able to establish itself in the confidence and affections of the whole people. Nothing can be more intimately connected with the moral and spiritual interests of communities than the state of the public health. Pestilence is frightfully demoralizing, and a filthy and over-crowded population makes morals and piety impossible. Drunkenness and lust are the inevitable attendants on a poisoned air. Clean streets, abundance of pure water, good drainage, open squares, well-lighted and well-ventilated tenant houses, economical conveyances to the neighboring country, innocent amusements within the reach of all, cheap bread—these are the primary external conditions of a virtuous, because a healthy and happy, community.

These things do not make people moral and religious, but they give education and religion their most favorable conditions of influence; they are the first things to be looked after, not as ends, but as means; not as results, but as conditions. But I do not propose to dwell upon them now.

In respect to the commercial record of the year, no doubt it must be called a year of great disaster; of enormous losses and unexpected disappointments; of general depression and universal anxiety. I suppose the general balance-sheet looks as discouragingly as it has done any New Year's Day this twenty years past. The universal panic of eighteen months ago left such paralysis, timidity and distrust behind it, that the real causes of business depression have been doubly aggravated, and their effects greatly protracted. The poor harvest of the West, due to the floods and hurricanes of last spring, has crippled our best customer; manufactures lie crushed beneath a policy which our legislators seem not free enough from party theories to abandon; and commerce finds her ships empty and rotting at the wharves. I suppose an untold degree of mental distress and anxiety has afflicted our merchants the past year, the more, perhaps, from the general and brave efforts made to keep up appearances, and go boldly over the sandy bar of panic, scraping the bottom, but not lowering the top-sails, much less casting the anchor. I have no doubt that the dreadful pressure of the last year has consolidated the foundations of our commercial credit, and that those who, by every sacrifice, have maintained honor and faith, are, though stripped of nearly every thing else, in a condition to reap a glorious harvest on the inevitable renewal of business, upon the succession of two or three fair crops. I believe in, and predict, a season of prosperity, setting in before the second return of this anniversary, which shall atone for the losses and anxieties of the two years of paralysis which have preceded this date. And I hope that the lesson of the past year will not be lost—namely, the peril of living so thoroughly up to the last notch of our ability, as to render a year of commercial disaster one of the utmost strain in the whole economy of life; for a general domestic and social machinery, adapted only to the full tide of success, can be kept a-going at the ebb of our fortunes, only at the sacrifice of temper, happiness, and almost of honesty. Undoubtedly we have set our standard of living too high. Insensibly the whole community is strained by the high pitch the leaders of it have taken. Nobody is to blame in particular, and few individuals can venture to resist a general custom. But that an over-expensive, showy, self-indulgent, ostentatious and uncomfortable style prevails among us, to an extent not found in other cities, cannot, I think, be denied. Is it necessary that our business should be done in palaces of marble, or that our homes should be so very grand and stately? I am afraid we are sacrificing too much of the substance to the show—too much reality to an empty seeming.

Permit me to remind you, that if you find your own capital seriously impaired, the industrious poor find their little reserves entirely gone by the waste of the last year, and that a more serious, if a less open distress, is, without the unexpected relief of a mild winter, likely to afflict the honest poor this season. than that from which they suffered during the last. The admirable Association for Improving the condition of the Poor never had greater evidences of threatened want, nor greater proofs of its own usefulness. I earnestly commend it, to-day, to your careful consideration, and beg you not to abridge your ordinary contributions to its resources.

But now, leaving all merely social and public interests, let us give our thoughts to the supreme concern, and ask ourselves, not how the New Year finds our business, or our health, or our domestic state, or our recollections or our prospects as citizens and merchants, but how it finds our souls. "Create in me a clean heart, O God, and renew a right spirit within me," is a much more appropriate petition for the New Year than any other sort of renewing we can ask for. An unclean heart and a wrong spirit are the worst burdens, the most serious evils, we can desire to have pass away with the old year.

What matters it how clean our streets, how free our air, if our hearts are unclean, and bound in sin? What matters it that business is renewed, if a right spirit within us is not renewed? What congratulation belongs to that New Year that does not bring the new man of the heart with it? And how can we triumph in any changes for the better, which the fresh date may promise, if it does not promise or record the inauguration of a right spirit within us? I believe that this opening year is attended with more of the joy which belongs to the consciousness of hearts that have been newly cleansed, and spirits recently made right, than any previous one within my own recollection. There can be no dispute that the great event in the old year was the very general revival of religious life in the churches and the world at large. In the midst of commercial disaster, and perhaps through the way which calamity and the sense of the uncertainty of all earthly possessions opened for it, the spirit of truth entered into the souls of men! God became a solemn and tender reality to thousands who had been living without him in the world. Christ found entrance to hearts that for long years had kept him knocking in vain at their doors. Religion, from a dull formality, confined to the Sunday, became a lively concern, pressing into the week, and imperatively demanding some portion of every day for its social cultivation. Many whose anxieties till this time had been about their threatened fortunes, found themselves a hundred times more anxious for their threatened souls, and for the first time realized the whole import of our Lord's great question: "What shall it profit a man to gain the whole world and lose his own soul?" Thousands whose lives had flowed along without any marked change for tens of years—satisfied, decent, orderly, moral—found themselves suddenly conscious of sins they had not before charged to themselves, occupying an attitude of indifference or hostility towards their Sovereign which they had not before suspected, and impelled by an inward awakening to seek a forgiveness from God and a new relation of friendship through his Son, which till now they had deemed fanciful and unreal.

I envy not the religious sagacity nor the spiritual experience of the man of any creed who can look with suspicion, ridicule, or contempt upon the refreshing from on high which fell upon the Churches last spring!

Doubtless the *occasion* was natural, but the *cause* was supernatural. The conditions were human, but the influence and effect were superhuman. If any causes are to be judged by their effects, then why not superhuman causes by superhuman effects? And if any effects are superhuman, it is when human obstinacy, indifference, faithlessness—producing cold, selfish, and worldly hearts and lives, and resisting for years and lustres all that instruction, entreaty, warning can do to arouse or to change them, suddenly, under no special influence from these intermediate instruments—are made tender, filled with self-reproach, dissolved in penitence, become exquisitely sensitive to the divine presence, devotedly grateful to Christ, and conscious of a continued support and renewing from the Holy Spirit. That such has been the blessed experience of thousands during the past year is no more doubtful or deniable than that the year has been a year of commercial disaster. If a year of changing fortunes, it has been as evidently a year of changed hearts. The religious crisis was just as obvious as the business crisis; and the successes of the Church and the Holy Spirit quite as plain as the failures of the banks and the spirit of trade. Nor were the effects of the revival of religion any less marked than the effects of the decline of business. The material harvest did not fail more remarkably than the spiritual harvest flourished; and the consequences of the short crop in one have not more unmistakably survived, than the consequences of the abundant yield in the other.

If our canal and railroad tolls have declined; if our western trade has fallen off; if our freights are low—because of the failure of the wheat and corn in the great valley of the West—so our churches have been thronged, our ministry quickened, our communion tables enlarged, our young men brought into religious activity, our friends, in not a few cases, made over again into the likeness of the master, and thousands of reliable, conscientious, and devout persons, contributed to the ranks of business, of good citizenship, and family life, because of the heavenly rain in the great valley of God's kingdom. If the great river of the West swelled disastrously and swept the seed away at the sowing, and ruined in advance an enormous breadth of the harvest—the river of God swelled beneficently, and swept away the seeds of death, and left in their stead the fertility of the blessed spirit of grace and truth. I deny that the effects of one freshet are more obvious than those of the other. And I cannot understand why liberal and rational minds and hearts should feel themselves pledged or interested to deny that God has visited his people. It is little better than Atheism to believe in a God that *cannot* touch his creatures except in accordance with some law of nature, laid down by our imperfect science. If we are to believe only in ourselves, and in the God which is in us; in the Holy Spirit only which we carry in our consciences; in the answers to our prayers involved in the mere benefit of repeating holy words; in the conversion which comes from a mere change of purpose, and the regeneration of a self-evolution of the heart, then we may consistently deride and discredit the existence of peculiar seasons of visitation from on high; scoff at years of special religious revival, and turn our backs upon any pretences to fresh spiritual experiences. But I confess that a God in us, who is not the shadow and echo of a God out of us; a Holy Spirit in our hearts, which has not an existence independent of our hearts; a God so subordinate to nature and laws that he can do nothing except science and order give him leave, is not my God and Father, nor the God and Father of Jesus Christ, nor a God whom you can safely lean upon, trust, love, and look to, to help and save you.

If it be superstition to believe in a living God, a personal God, a prayer-hearing and prayer-answering God, let us be superstitious! If it be liberal to doubt or deny, or reason away, or keep out of sight, or in any way resist the influence of a living God, a personal God, who rewardeth them that diligently seek him, who answers prayers, who gives deliverance to the captives of sin, and lends strength to the morally weak, and breaks the chains of habit for those who, discovering their own inability, ask sincerely his aid in achieving their liberty, then let us have done with so liberal, or rather so illiberal, a faith. For liberal Christianity it is not, which binds God to loose man, and imprisons the Creator in his own works for the sake of emancipating science from any thing above itself. Long enough has such a spurious imitation of religion been permitted to pass for the reality. A child's watch—all face, with no spring of motion from behind—is not a more foolish substitute for a time-keeper, than is a self-inspired, self-evolved, self-moved religion a substitute for a God-given, God-maintained, God-filled religion. The bowman might as well say the arrow he shoots into the air came from another archer in the sky, when it falls to his feet, as the offerer of prayers think himself answered from above by the pleasant frame of mind his devoutness of words produces, when he does not really believe any God listens to his cry! My brethren, we may better doubt our own freedom than God's! If we think our own minds superior to the brute matter about us; if we find our wills capable of an independence, even in the presence of the most determining motives; if we sometimes triumph over bodily decay, resist and conquer enormous obstacles, and prove ourselves freemen of the soul, shall we for an instant believe that our minds and wills are the products of a spiritual force, that is itself not as free as ourselves, that is not as victorious over nature as we often are, not as independent of brute laws and material conditions, as the creatures it has formed? It is the greatest folly of reason, the greatest presumption of self-conceit, to entertain such an opinion!

My brethren, thousands of believing and devout minds are to-day rejoicing with joy unspeakable that this New-Year finds them, for the first time, conscious children of God, heirs of a divine grace, subjects of a heavenly kingdom—in new and peaceful, in sustaining and blessed relations, with God—in tender, genuine, and comforting communion with Christ—forgiven, accepted, adopted, beloved, sanctified, saved! I rejoice to believe that not a few of you have this year tasted the grace of God, which has made you wise unto salvation. Without participating directly in the special excitement which has spread through the country, we have lived under the same heaven from which the grateful showers were falling, and have felt at least the fringes of the clouds dropping their fatness upon us. I think I have never known, among ourselves, so much apparent seriousness of inquiry, eagerness for guidance, and willingness to be moved in a right way, as during the last few months; and it ought to be a source of common congratulation with us that God has not left us out of his kingdom, when so visibly enlarging its boundaries.

But, brethren, a general participation in a mild awakening of spiritual life is not enough. The prayer of our text, the prayer of the sinful and conscience-stricken David, is, "Create in *me* a clean heart, and renew a right spirit within *me!*" He does not say, Help the community to which I belong to improve itself, and let me share a general interest in our mutual advances in truth and goodness. Religion, though a domestic, a social, and a public interest, is, primarily, a personal interest. All sin is individual. There is no abstract, no public, no common sin. All virtue is individual. There is no abstract, public, common virtue, except the aggregate of individual virtue. All sense of sin—penitence, confession, regeneration, sanctification, salvation—is personal. Sympathy, community of effort, fellowship, help and perfect individual struggles. It is far easier, in the midst of striving consciences, aspiring hearts, prayerful souls, to maintain our private struggle for the spiritual crown. But, after all, every man, every woman, every soul, must seek unto God for itself—must have its own direct, personal experience, its own act of submission, its own welcome to the spirit of truth, its own adoption as a child of God. Every one must say, "Create in *me* a clean heart, and renew a right spirit within me." And blessed are those among you who have made that prayer from the depths of troubled and sin-torn hearts, and have prevailed with God to answer it! I need not tell you that I have no foolish disparagements to offer to the great principles of morality; no unworthy slights to cast on common honesty, social amenity, rectitude in business, neighborly kindness, regular habits, freedom from vices. As well might one disparage ploughing and sowing and cultivating, because they are not sun and rain, and nature's great chemistry; or neglect barns and fences and tools and methods, because they are not the great gifts of the soil. But certainly all the good habits, and all the good principles in the world, do not by themselves succeed in sweetening the temper, subduing the will, elevating the soul, and making men and women conquerors of their selfishness, their tempers, their self-dissatisfactions. I know nothing, alas, more discouraging than the dead stop in the growth of character, the unchangeable fixity at a certain point, in the souls of the self-culturing class so-called, the people who are trying to find their way to heaven on a road they make as they go along. Instead of taking the wings of a dove, and mounting on the breath of God's Spirit, ever buoying them up, and supplying them with incitement and support, they creep on their hands and feet along the dusty road; instead of opening their sails to the wind of heaven, they feel their way along the shore, safe and sound, in their own estimation, only when they can touch bottom and push themselves with their own oar!

"But oars alone can ne'er prevail
To reach the heavenly coast;
The breath of heaven must fill the sail,
Or all the toil is lost."

There is nothing unnatural in this fact, much less any thing incredible. How should men hope to rise above themselves, except by the aid of a power external to, and above, themselves? Can we save ourselves, pray to ourselves, conquer ourselves, free ourselves? We might just as well attempt to jump off our own shadow! And this is the fatal mistake of all attempts to substitute a system of social ethics for a system of true religion. Religion represents a bond, a partnership, between man and God. It contains offers and promises of aid and deliverance. It gives assurances of the existence and presence of infinite powers, willing and anxious to do for man what he cannot do for himself. Can he be said to be a religious man, in any proper sense, who does not believe that God has any access to his soul, or care that he has any access to it, or who makes no dependence on God's help in his struggles with sin and his aspirations towards excellence? Yet men and women with excellent intentions, who want to do their duty, and to have right affections and clean hearts, go on for years, discouraged at finding themselves still the slaves of their own faults and weaknesses, and all because they have never sought with any sufficient faith and earnestness God's aid and Christ's spirit, to support and make adequate their own efforts. They are children of the law, trying to fulfil in their own moral strength what it requires the grace of God, his free spirit flowing into the soul, to accomplish. Why, even a dog can, in the inspiration of his master's presence, do what he is utterly unable to do alone. A child, supported by the voice and eye of his mother, is another being. And is a man, unconscious of God's eye and God's Spirit, truly himself, or to be expected to be able to accomplish those moral and spiritual transformations, which convert the selfish into the disinterested, the passionate into the self-restrained, the vicious into the virtuous, the careless into the believing ?

If, my brethren, there be any good news in the Gospel, it is this, that God is willing and able to save to the uttermost ; willing and able ! All that is necessary on our part is to be willing to let him do it, and believing that he can and will do it. Discard, I beseech you, from your thoughts, all those caricatures of this radical truth of the soul's dependence on God for its moral and spiritual life and ability, which prejudice the rational mind against the doctrine of divine grace. I do not ask you to believe that it is the native or total depravity of your hearts that makes this help of God necessary, or that it is to escape the fires of eternal punishment that you need God's deliverance ! I ask you only to see and acknowledge this, that man is, by his original constitution, a child of God, dependent for his support on his Father ; dependent on him for his education and his setting up in the true life of the soul ; and that, forgetting or denying this, he loses his courage, his confidence, his ability to make a true man of himself, and goes about like the prodigal, feeding with swine, an outcast and an alien. Away from God, he is in a most unnatural state—shorn of his strength, his wisdom, his only adequate guidance. And yet, every now and then, whole generations swing away from their faith in God, either in some tremendous reaction upon superstition, or through the attractions of science and art, and the allurements of self-worship. We are, I hope, near the close of a violent recoil upon Puritanism, aided by a powerful spirit of self-assertion, which a new world, and the victories of our enterprise and knowledge, and our democratic institutions, have produced. Our present alienation from God—the practical distance at which we keep him—our little genuine dependence on his inspiration and support, are not natural; they are most unnatural. They occasion a world of wretchedness, weariness of life, inward unrest, secret infidelity, and suicide. They allow the soul to be crushed with self-imposed burdens; they make our temptations irresistible, our sins unconquerable; they leave us without refuge or repose! We are the victims of our constitutions, our temperaments, our circumstances! They drive us to think and to say, "I can't help being what I am! I can't get into a right frame. I can't be what I approve, or what I desire. It is a matter of constitution." And so we give up the controversy. Very well. It is true. *We* can't do any of these things. If we could, we should not need any God, nor any Saviour, nor any religion. The whole theory of Christianity is that we can't do any of these things in, and of, ourselves. But God and Christ can do them all, and we can do any and all of them, God helping. I can do all things, Christ strengthening me! Our great wisdom lies in knowing where to turn; what to look to; how to get the moral and spiritual help we need. Suppose the miller, instead of opening the gate and letting in the stream, should attempt to turn his wheel by main strength! This is what we do when we cease from prayer, fail to put our souls in communication with God, and to open our hearts to the glorious visitations of his power! And this is what is wearing us out in so many ineffectual efforts at self-conversion. This is what is taking away our joy in our faith; that blessed religious enthusiasm which is, as the eagle's wings, renewing its strength day by day, and enabling the soul, in place of delving and digging its way, to mount and fly to heaven.

Do you ask how you shall find God in your long alienation from him; how you shall close up your broken relations, and renew your filial communion? Has he not sent his Son for the very purpose of answering these questions? Is He not set forth, to be the way, the truth, and the life? Because God is an unseen spirit, he has chosen to make himself visible in his Son! Because we cannot visit the distant fountain of all our strength, hid in the everlasting hills, he has established a well of living water in Christ, kept ever full from the eternal head, and made accessible in his church, a truly supernatural institution, a city of God dropped upon the earth! Practically we lean on God, when we lean on Christ; practically we have God's help, when we have his Son's help. "He that hath the Son, hath the Father also." And, practically, we cannot hope to get the Spirit of God into our hearts, except through the mediation of our Lord and Saviour. The man that really knows and feels the meaning of that word *Saviour*, that accepts Jesus as his Saviour, that clings to him, and loves him and trusts in him, has found God's salvation ; for Christ is the mediator between God and man. Not that direct communication is intercepted or impossible, but, practically, indirect communication is often easier, even when direct is possible. And, as a mere fact, the experience of the world has taught it that no Saviour is equivalent to no God. My brethren, ought you not to joy in God through Christ ? And instead of feeling reluctant and indifferent and suspicious—as if you were going to compromise your moral and intellectual dignity in the act—ought you not, with your actual knowledge of yourselves, to feel the glorious privilege, the vast relief, the unspeakable consolation, contained in the faith that you have a Saviour able to save to the uttermost ; a God and Father, willing always to do exceeding abundantly above what you are able to ask and even to think, if you will only abandon vain self-reliances, and "cast yourselves on him that careth for you ?"

Would to God this New-Year's Sabbath might date the return of some wanderers to the Father's house ; that on the threshold of the New-Year, some heavy-laden hearts might cast their burdens on the Lord, exchange their galling chains for his light and easy yoke, and go on their way rejoicing in a heavenly deliverance. Then, indeed, would we together set up a new stone at this stage of our pilgrimage ! and celebrate with joy the triumphs of our faith over our sins and our sorrows. Then might I have less reason for self-reproach and sadness on this day, which precisely marks the twentieth anniversary of my ordination and ministry, for you would be my hope and joy and crown of rejoicing!

JAN. 2, 1859.

SERMON XXII.

NATURE, ORIGIN AND WORTH, OF RELIGIOUS EXCITEMENT.

"Father, glorify thy name. Then came there a voice from heaven, saying, I have both glorified it and will glorify it again.

"The people therefore that stood by and heard it, said that it thundered. Others said, An angel spake to him."—JOHN xii. 28, 29.

IT is more probable that the thunder was mistaken for a voice, than that an articulate voice was mistaken for thunder, in this case; for thunder is a voice from heaven. The deeply religious and exalted mind of Christ turned all striking natural phenomena into divine language, and the devouter portion of his followers, lifted into a sense of God's presence by his society, no doubt often supposed the natural events connected with his career to be supernatural, and this was the more likely, because of the actual miracles which he did.

I wish, at this time, to examine, with reference to the prevailing state of religious excitement, first, the relation of the miraculous to the natural in Christianity; then, of the extraordinary to the ordinary, in religious moods and methods, that we may understand how much and how little importance to attach to the alleged supernaturalism in the movement of the popular religious mind at this time. I begin with the relation of the miraculous to the natural. Our text is an illustration of the difficulty which exists in times of religious excitement in distinguishing between natural and supernatural appearances. And this is a universal difficulty. It is not easy to define natural laws and miraculous exceptions satisfactorily, even in the abstract; but vastly easier than to distinguish them positively as actual occurrences. Not being thoroughly acquainted with nature, we are prone to attribute new, or hitherto unobserved phenomena, to exceptional causes. Thus, until the theory of comets was understood, their eccentric movements so entirely refused to come under any law common to the other heavenly bodies, that it was almost unavoidable to regard them as portents of coming disaster, moving by a miraculous interposition across the heavens, in defiance of gravitation and the laws of nature.

Again: What less than a miracle must a vessel, moving against wind and tide, seem to a savage on a Pacific island, as, for the first time, he views a steamer moving swiftly by his coast? Again: Suppose one of our Pilgrim Fathers, waked from his sleep of two centuries, and placed in a telegraphic office in Wall street, to converse with one of his descendants at New Orleans without having the wonderful process explained, but only the actual facts proved beyond question, that he did communicate and receive intelligence through that thousand miles instantaneously. Can we conceive an actual miracle which could surprise or confound him more? What distinction could he draw between such a fact and the prophecy of future events—the raising of the dead, the healing of the sick, by a touch?

And yet there *is* a distinction. Although we are ignorant of *many* things, we know others well. There are doubtless new, or rather undiscovered laws of nature, and probably great regions of natural law, with which we are as yet unacquainted. Discoveries as wonderful as steam, electric language, photography, are probably in store for new generations of inquirers and humble questioners of nature's secrets. Still, there is a realm of positive knowledge. We know that heavy bodies gravitate to the ground. We know that blindness cannot be cured by a touch; that withered limbs do not recover at a word; nay, in spite of the phenomena of trance, and sleep, and catalepsy, we know, with sufficient care, how to distinguish death from all its mockeries. It is possible, therefore, to conceive of a genuine miracle that is a positive, unmistakable repeal and contravention of a well-known law of nature. A man actually dead restored to life; a man actually blind restored to sight by a word; water actually changed to wine; bread actually multiplied at the word of command—these are miracles, and it is idle to say that these events could not occur under circumstances in which the suspicion of fraud would be unreasonable; foolish to affirm, that no amount of evidence could render them credible. What a rational faith in them properly demands is, a sufficient object to make such an interruption of natural laws reasonable; their connection with such persons and purposes as to furnish us with supporting grounds of faith in them, and then such careful, copious, and exact evidence of the fact, as events of so improbable a character require. Christian believers maintain that all these circumstances conspired in the planting of our religion; that the object was worthy a direct interposition; that the character and conduct of Jesus Christ make his possession of miraculous powers not unreasonable, and that the positive evidence that he had and used such power, is precise, copious, and overwhelming.

Miracles being thus possible and actual, though most rare, and receivable only under stringent criticism, we can see how equally possible, nay, how unavoidable, imitations, and echoes, and pretensions of miracles must be. I have no doubt of the genuineness of the positive miracles ascribed in the New Testament to Christ and his apostles, but I find in the record evidences of a disposition—an honest and natural disposition—to exaggerate the miraculous element; to attribute to miracle what fell out in the way of nature, and to throw a wavering, supernatural light, over things ordinary and normal. It would be very strange if this were not so.

If we go back and place ourselves in the society of Jesus—a being from time to time working *actual* miracles, we can at once see how disposed we should have been to ascribe *all* his conduct and speech to miraculous influences; how excited and exalted our whole frame of feeling would have been, and in what honesty we should have become credulous, and reported many things in a strained way. Nor must we forget that the natural powers which Christ had—his power of realizing the divine presence, and seeing God in nature, in man, and in all the operations of his own and the human spirit—gave a preternatural, or exalted tone and temper to his most ordinary moods; for he was, doubtless, as exceptionally grand and gifted in his nature as he was peculiarly and miraculously supported in his office.

And here let us distinctly understand the real value of the miraculous element in our religion, judging it from the estimate which Jesus put upon it himself Our Lord did not value his miraculous powers for themselves, nor use them for himself. They had no spiritual significance to him. They were useful to him in proving his official relation to God and men, and nothing more. I suppose he knew as little of the way in which his own miracles were wrought as we do. For God is the only worker of miracles, and those through whom they are wrought by him, merely derive thence a seal of their authority as messengers. Then, again, although there may be miraculously communicated knowledge, as well as miraculous power, yet the inspiration of the intellect with the knowledge of facts or future events, or of the truth of laws and precepts not otherwise known to be binding, is not that moral and spiritual inspiration on which Christ really valued himself, though he possessed it. His real everlasting superiority as a spiritual head, lay in his nearness to God as a spiritual creature—a nearness which, though extraordinary, is not miraculous—for moral inspiration or spiritual influx is a question only of more or less, since it is open to all moral beings. Christ's miraculous powers, then, whether wonder-working or prophetic, are not the attributes which make him sublime, holy, and saving. It is the vast moral power, the spiritual insight, the divine disinterestedness in him, which we venerate and love, and wonder at; and this is not miraculous, but a merely increased measure of that inspiration which accompanies every human soul, and grows with fidelity and obedience in the heart of every faithful child of God.

I press this point for a special reason. We must not, with the impatient and knowing, deny miracles; but we must not, with the credulous and marvel-loving, exaggerate them. We must not deny Christ official inspiration, which is miraculous, but we must not exalt official inspiration, because of its superior historic importance, above moral inspiration, which is not and cannot be miraculous.

The great and ever-glorious method by which God communicates with his children is by natural and spiritual laws. The ordinary, regular, normal events and operations of life, are infinitely more important and instructive than any interruption of them can be. If Niagara should, on a certain day, stop its flood in full tide, and hang suspended in mid air for five minutes, it would be a miracle; and if it did this at the command of a wise and holy man, who claimed to have a message from God, we should listen to him with docile and reverent ears. But what would the stoppage of Niagara for five minutes reveal of God, compared with what its flow for five, for forty centuries, has done, and is daily doing, to show forth his glory and might? The multiplication of five loaves and two fishes into the food of five thousand men, is a proof indeed of the official power and place of Christ; but what is it, considered as a showing forth of God's power, when compared with the yearly resurrection of nature in the spring—the growth of the wheat over millions of acres, the spawning of the finny tribe in all waters, and the perpetual multiplication of loaves and fishes, by the ceaseless will and power of the God of nature? In like manner, the descent of the Holy Ghost, however real, falling on the disciples at Pentecost, and enabling them to speak in various tongues, is a marvellous thing, pointing out the apostles as authorized teachers of the new religion. But what is it, after all, to that communication which God has with the human soul, when he originally inspires it with thought, affection, conscience, reason; or which he continually has with it in supporting and increasing these powers, and revealing himself, by means of them, to every docile and patient child of the Great Parent? Remember that Christ, in the chief relations he had with God, was upon the same human footing—of a God-created, God-inspired soul, in a God-created, God-supported world—that every other human spirit is; and that all that the supernatural or miraculous can add to the natural and normal is, however important for official purposes, small indeed, considered spiritually and absolutely.

We shall never be able to do justice to the New Testament, or to the religious phenomena either of past history or of recent occurrence, until we recognize more distinctly the wonderful spiritual basis of ordinary human life. The soul, by its very constitution, is near to God, and lives in and from him. God is not afar off, but here with us—permeating our very being, and communicating strength, wisdom, and peace, according to our willingness to receive him. Instead, therefore, of wondering at the communication of good suggestions, noble impulses, a strength not our own, an insight new and piercing, we ought to know that these are steadily and uniformly waiting to enter our souls, as the beams of the sun are to penetrate the soil of that earth which turns away from them, or sends up clouds and mists from its own surface to hide and quench the solar ray. God is always waiting to be gracious ; always whispering truth, peace, joy to our hearts. It is not he that goes away from us, or intermits his care and shuts off his inspiration, but we that go away from him, and refuse his messages, and stop our ears to his constant voice. He speaks to us in a thousand ways—sometimes through outward nature, where he stands clothed in beauty or sublimity, and uses the form of mountain or flower, of ocean or dew-drop, to arrest the eye and win the heart ; sometimes in the form of humanity, as [illegible] urges reason, love, or pity, through the lips of rever[illegible]t age, or lovely innocence, or weeping sorrow ; sometimes by our consciences, in their derived light, flashing reproof and approval on our pathway ; sometimes by mysterious breathings, that, like zephyrs from a spiced shore, woo our souls with heavenly sweetness to some unexpected port of bliss. But in whatever form it be, God is near—a besetting God, on the right hand and the left, ever educating, disciplining, helping his child, and striving to save and bless him. The world is full of God ; the soul is full of God ; for he is the omnipresent and all-pervading spirit of the universe. It is, then, only a coarse and exclusive, and half-religious notion, which makes only the extraordinary, the miraculous, the irregular, the inconstant, the peculiar—the presence and influence of God—the cause of religious life and the means of spiritual growth.

At this moment a strongly-marked religious interest

pervades the public mind. The extent of it is indicated by the fact that the secular papers contain regular and long accounts of revivals in the churches, and we may be sure that they know too well what is interesting to their readers to make the mistake of dwelling upon topics that are not popular at the moment. It is an unquestionable fact, then, that the relations of men with God are more on their hearts and minds, and their willingness to hear and solicitude to profit by the Gospel of Christ, are much greater than usual, at this time. And doubtless, instead of seeking to account for this, or to discuss the causes, whether natural or supernatural, the first disposition of serious men should be, to take advantage of it, and improve the season of moral sensitiveness to the awakening of the sleepers and the sowing of the harvest. When, for any reasons, the minds of men are open and their hearts soft, we should fling in the seed of truth, and endeavor to lead those who for the first time are willing, to the source of truth and the feet of Christ. It should be, then, the universal aim of religious teachers, at this time, to bring the duties and privileges of religion home with special earnestness and tenderness to the souls of men. I cannot sympathize with those who think it unwise to multiply, to some extent, occasions and means of religious instruction and quickening at such a time, or who suppose that great harm is likely to accrue in the end from the special attention given to religion and the special excitement felt about it now. Reaction upon vigorous action we expect ; apathy will follow excitement ; but it is equally true that action ensues upon inaction, and excitement grows out of apathy. It will not do to object to religious excitement, that it is followed by religious apathy, unless we object to religious apathy, because it is followed by religious excitement. None can or will deny, that a state of settled and healthy interest in religion is the state above all to be desired ; that excitement and apathy are both highly objectionable ; but certainly, while we have one extreme, we must look for, and even welcome, the other. And I do not doubt that the present excitement is a wholesome reaction upon the general and obstinate religious indifference that has for years prevailed in this country.

But some doubtless will ask, if this present excitement is not a mere nervous panic —a moral St. Vitus's dance—spreading, by pure physical sympathy, through the community, and gathering new force with every success. There can be no manner of doubt that the nerves have their part in the matter, and that a contagious emotional element, capable of an evil and perilous direction, is at work at this time. But who gave us our nerves, and planted this sympathetic power in our constitution ? When I see a boarding-school suddenly afflicted with a general agitation of the nervous system, instead of saying only, with the physician, this is a common morbid symptom, which needs tonics, and an immediate dispersion of the parties to it beyond the reach of mutual excitement, I reflect, with the philosopher, upon the origin and meaning of this wonderful sympathetic organization, and am confident, that though in this case a painful and diseased activity, it possesses some great and benignant power, and has an honest and wholesome place in the human constitution. And so with all the enthusiastic and emotional elements in our nature—all intimately connected with the more delicate parts of our physical organization, they have their proper and necessary place in our experience, and are not always and everywhere to be suspected and outlawed. If the nervous and sympathetic thrill happens to be struck in the service of truth and duty; if the contagion of feeling is of a right feeling; if the excitement, partly physical, partly moral, is an excitement in favor of repentance and newness of life, I shall not, for one, content myself with exclaiming, mere excitement! as if that ended the matter. Nor can I wholly object to what is called the machinery of the occasion, so long as it is not concealed and dishonest, and overworked. I take it that it is only a question of more and less. All religious institutions involve machinery. The ministry, the Sabbath, the exercises of public worship, earnest speech and exhortation, are kinds of machinery. I can see no reason why this machinery may not be properly increased at special times. That it may be, and is greatly abused, admits of no question. But a judicious use of machinery in behalf of religious interest, is as legitimate and as necessary as in behalf of political interest. We have political revivals; why not religious? political exhorters and successful orators; why not religious? times and seasons when excitements are diligently sought to deepen the popular interest in special principles of policy and patriotism; why not of duty and worship? But thoughtful and instructed natures will feel it and need it very little, whether in politics or religion.

But is any or much good to be expected from the sudden and temporary stir of religious feeling? Is there not a great deal of animal heat and false excitement in it? and must not a work of alleged grace, done in haste and under the contagion of enthusiastic feelings, soon show its emptiness and instability? I have already said that physical excitability and nervous sympathy have no small part in this matter. Of course, when they subside, those who were animated by nothing else, will be seen to have experienced no moral and spiritual change. But many who feel the nervous excitement keenly, feel a general moral excitement likewise; and under the influence of a sensibility which required body and soul for its creation, really awake to convictions that shape and bless their future lives. It is probable that in the conversions of camp-meetings, not one in ten effects any useful or permanent change of character. A Methodist class-leader told a friend of mine, that in his village there had been an annual revival for eight years past, and that of sixty or eighty persons each year claiming conversion, three-quarters had experienced the same change every year, and regularly backslidden. The Church, however, steadily gained genuine converts, and was content to go on upon this system, which, considering the ignorance and stupidity of the parties, was, perhaps, the only system possible. Under the moderate style of chastened excitement which prevails in the churches of this community, I should expect the measure of reality and worth in the alleged conversions would be strictly proportioned to the degree of cultivation and intelligence marking the subjects of it. If men of sense, possessing a tolerable acquaintance with their own nature, fall under religious excitement, it is likely to do a more thorough work;

and although a subsidence of excitement leaves them less changed than they hoped or thought, it does not leave them without some substantial and important experience of spiritual things fitted to renew, and perhaps radically change, their lives and characters.

Because a great deal of backsliding, a great deal of self-delusion, of false profession and mere superficial piety, is sure to ensue upon this movement, yet it is not hence to be concluded that its general drift is not wise, and wholesome, and genuine. It is with religious excitement as with other social and political movements. You recollect the great Free Soil excitement, and how many of its first earnest converts have since eaten their words of earnest profession of anti-slavery faith; still, that movement bore fruit, and will survive the backsliding of some of its prominent early disciples. When an excitement is based upon the real importance of the subject of it—when the attention it arouses fastens upon a truth, and not a falsehood, it does good; and that was the case with the Free Soil excitement. Contrast it with the excitement of the Harrison campaign, when a universal bankrupt law—wrong in principle and accidental in policy—was the real cause of the stir—a stir which left no effects whatever but a dangerous precedent in legislation—and you will see the difference between the excitement in a good and in a poor cause. The present excitement is in a good cause—the cause of repentance of sin, acceptance of God's offers of mercy to penitents, newness of life, and pureness of heart—and I can see no reason why, if a large proportion of the converts are spurious, the small proportion of the genuine should not repay the labor. For it is not only spurious converts that religion has to contend with, but spurious pupils, spurious hearers of the Word, a spurious attention, a spurious interest, spurious good resolutions, spurious decorum, and all sorts of spuriousness. Because not one in ten of the hearers of a rational preaching show any decided fruits of the teaching they profess to receive, approve, and enjoy, are we to abandon it? Why then make spurious *converts* the exclusive objects of our suspicion? Moderation and calmness, reason and good sense, have their failures and fruitlessness as well as emotion and excitement.

It is interesting, my brethren, to observe that this revival, like all others of a general sort, has come quite gradually upon the community, and with less external preparation and expectation than usual. No doubt the general commercial distress, the social trouble, mortification and sorrow which the previous six months had brought with it, had produced a very wide-spread sense of the importance of a more substantial dependence than fortune and external success can offer. It is common to say, that when men can get nothing better, they turn to religion. It is true; and God, I question not, is glad to win their hearts on any terms. No doubt, too, that lack of other engrossing occupations leaves the mind more open to moral influences. All the secondary, external causes of this interest, ought to be freely and honestly acknowledged. There is nothing to be ashamed of in them. They act in accordance with the recognized and established laws of human nature. I can believe, too, that the disused and almost-forgotten emotionality which a long suspension of religious excitement in this community had produced, adds to the attractiveness and force of this passionate sensibility, now that it is once in motion. But this revival is, mainly, the honest reassertion of the place which piety and faith ought to have in the souls of men; and from all I can learn, it is marked with unusual freedom from excesses, fanaticism, and the extravagances of speech and behaviour, not uncommonly connected with such movements. It is particularly interesting to notice, what is not strictly peculiar to this occasion, but is more than usually marked in it—how universal, unsectarian and simple are the doctrines upon which the revival proceeds. The Trinity, the vicarious atonement, everlasting damnation, election—with the spirit of denunciation, and fear—are for the time put utterly aside. Men are urged to repent of their sins; to accept Christ as a sufficient Saviour, to give God their hearts—and thus the ordinary truths of religion, in which Unitarians and Trinitarians, Universalists and close-communion Baptists might unite, are the powers alone depended on to accomplish the conversion of souls. In proof of this fact, it is a truth, that the *Christ*-ians,—an anti-Trinitarian body, but with Methodist habits of preaching and discipline—are largely and constantly engaged in this work, and are as successful in raising the intensest religious enthusiasm as though they believed and urged the whole Westminster Catechism. It ought to teach Christendom that if Unitarianism seeks, cultivates and enjoys a soberer and more regular religious life and habits than the prevailing bodies of modern Christians, it is not because of any lack of power in its doctrines to move the emotional nature, but because of the general culture of the whole man which it promotes, the balanced and complete development it seeks, and the class of discreet and cultivated persons who compose its sect.

But now, having done ample justice to the reality and the importance of the present popular religious excitement, I return to the general principle from which we started. It is this: what is exceptional, occasional and extraordinary in religious exercises and experiences, or in the means of knowing and serving God, or of receiving and living the Gospel of Christ, is always of little dependence, little importance and little claim, compared with the regular, usual and permanent institutions, habits and sentiments of Christendom and Christians. Religious instruction, good, regular and steady, is more important than religious impulse—as food is more important than artificial stimulants or medicine. A moderate daylight is more favorable to the discovery and pursuit of our spiritual journey than flashes of lightning. Intelligent principles of religious conduct are more useful and decisive than the most enthusiastic emotions. The habitual application of unexcited conscientiousness to the daily duties of life, is a far more acceptable and more saving experience than any exalted frame of sensibility into which the soul can be raised for a few hours, or days, or weeks.

The world is indebted for its real progress in truth, virtue and godliness, to religious knowledge. I do not mean the illumination of one faculty called the intellect, but of the whole soul; and religious knowledge is like all other kinds of knowledge in this respect, that it is the fruit of patient, long-continued, unexciting instruction. You cannot educate a youth in chemistry by dazzling him with a brilliant experiment; nor in mechanics, by taking him into the engine-room of a transatlantic steamer and moving his astonishment at the play of valves and pistons and levers; nor in literature, by reading him a tale that dissolves him in tears. All these exceptional aids of education may have their place in arousing attention, firing zeal, and melting out by a white-heat some obstinate apathy; for it is not to be denied, that the most sudden surprises of feeling, brief glimpses and accidental words, sometimes permanently affect the whole course of life and character. But no wise man proposes to depend on these for education. We feel the vast necessity of a regular schooling, a patient, plodding training, in all the practical professions and callings. And why should that greatest of all callings, our Christian vocation, our spiritual education, be trusted to any thing less than a systematic culture? This is duly felt by all religious teachers, of wise and sober thought, in all bodies—and is not forgotten, probably even at this moment, by the most earnest and active movers in the religious excitement. But there is no doubt that the common people in this country have acquired an unfortunate sense of the relative importance of the extraordinary to the ordinary grace of God—and of their own relative dependence upon what is called sudden conversion, to what ought to be their main dependence, the regular converting influence of religious truth, taken as the steady nourishment of life. If we had an ideal Church and Christianity, conversion, in the early sense of that word, would be impossible. The apostles could not have been converted if they had been brought up Christians. They were Jews, and Christianity was new, and they could only receive it by a change of opinions and affections. But what room is there in the heart of a child carefully and successfully brought up in the faith of Christ, conscientious, devout, affectionate, pure and good, for any change, natural or supernatural, entitled to the appellation of conversion? It is true, every man, no matter how carefully educated, has crises in his spiritual experience, on account of the growing nature of his mind and heart. He experiences many successive changes of views and feelings, which are more or less critical and important—and he may, in his desire to harmonize and parallelize his experience with apostolic penitents or Bible characters, name them by the scriptural phrases. But they do not accurately and plainly correspond to them. It is, however, unfortunately true, that through parental neglect or filial indocility, a large majority of men and women grow up to their full maturity in a sad ignorance of Christianity —with undisciplined wills, undevout affections and dull consciences;—and the awakening of such minds to a sense of their own immoral and unspiritual condition is often as great a revolution as the conversion of a Jew to Christianity. But, as a rule, it is commonly not revival seasons, but the providence of God in some great calamity, bereavement or sickness, acting upon a nature which the long and seemingly ineffectual influences of Christian instruction had been steadily preparing for this result, that accomplishes the awakening work. I suppose there is rarely a Sabbath in a large Christian Church, where religion is faithfully and devoutly administered, in which some single soul does not see and feel, as if for the first time, the truth and power of the Gos pel, and bring itself to a sort of spiritual new-birth. If nothing be said about it, if not made the subject of special confession to any one, perhaps so much the better. But this will depend upon temperament and circumstances. I cannot doubt, that, as in a field of whitening wheat, some head attains every minute its critical perfection and ripeness, of which it gives no marked indication to the distant eye—so, in a congregation of Christians, the real conversions, though special and individual, are, as a rule, noiseless ; they occur in the ordinary course of religious instruction ; are not best and most permanent in times of excitement ; and are less marked and formal in precise proportion to the thoroughness of the general training of the moral powers and religious faculties.

No candid observer will deny that the expectation or theory of conversion, which is given out and maintained by theologians and preachers, will be likely to color and shape the alleged experiences which occur under the guidance and inspiration of that theory. Suppose it be given out, boldly and persistently, that a religious experience has two great phases ; that it consists, first, in very heavy and despairing feelings, in which the sense of sin presses like an insupportable burden on the soul ; and second, in a sudden sense of relief, a feeling of pardon, of inexpressible lightness of heart and joy in God, accompanied by a sensible and half-material illumination called *glory ;* is it not in accordance with all the laws of human nature that the actual, honest experiences of the souls under a religious excitement directed by the propagators of this theory, will be in precise accordance with it ? If, moreover, those who have been mentally manipulated into this double experience send out their groans of despair, and then shout out their *glorys* of deliverance, as their souls experience these easily excited feelings, what enormous propagation to this theory and its corresponding experience will not be given! Does any one believe that, not having heard of the theory, *the experiences* would take this precise form? No student of mental phenomena can for an instant ignore the operation of the general principle by which this delusion is maintained. The reality of the despair, or of the joy, is not denied, even in the cases where no permanent religious effects follow. All that is denied is the divine or supernatural, or even the peculiarly Christian character, of these well-known dualisms, or oscillations of feeling, known to all religions, practised in all delusions, whether political, spiritualistic, or dramatic, and based upon well-understood operations of human nature.

If, on the other hand, religion be administered upon the theory of no violent changes; if the attention of the people be steadily guided to the importance of fixing their principles by regular reference to the will of God, illuminating their consciences by habitual self-examination and prayer, and establishing their lives in sound, moral, and religious habits, their interest, sensibility and affections, will all expend themselves in this diffusive way. They will not be waiting on times and seasons; expecting freshets of feeling, or postponing their religious emotions and duties to some hoped for, but uncertain period of revival. And if any such period come in the communities where they dwell, they are not likely to be greatly moved by it, because they are *at home* with the Spirit of truth, not in the excitement of entertaining a rare and mysterious guest.

To sum up, then, the whole matter. A judicious, thorough, and truly evangelical ministry would be one in which religious education, instruction, and training would be the grand and patient dependence, and in its ideal perfection special seasons of religious excitement, or great crises in personal character, would be impossible. The souls of the flock would have their daily bread and their ever-running well of water, and never experience either the intoxication or the gorging which follows abstinence from both. It is a sign of unsuccessful and imperfect religious training, when sudden conversions occur in adult age. It is a blessed thing to have the thoughtless awakened, but it is a melancholy fact, and a terrible criticism on our Christian systems, that so many thoughtless souls remain to be thus awakened under Christian institutions and influences. The great harvest that is now gathering in, is a sad commentary on the multitude of sinners which have escaped the sickle these many years past. And it is a dangerous error if those who are converted under sudden pressure of popular feeling, imagine that any thoroughness of revolution, any sincerity of conversion, can do the work of these long years of self-neglect, these thoughtless, soul-spoiling, spirit-blinding years of misspent time and feeling. Emotion can do something, can do much for the soul, but it cannot do time's great and solemn work. It cannot form habits, nor break their power. It does not break their power, even when it breaks them up. The drunkard who quits his cup, after years of self-indulgence, is a hero, but he has a drunkard's body and a drunkard's soul. And the old and hardened sinner, converted and truly turned round by an awakening providence of God, has a sinner's body and soul. He carries the stiffness, the narrowness, the inexperience of his old life into his new. He may well be called a *child* of God, if it be not truer still to call him a *babe.* His religious character will be not childlike, but childish ; sincere indeed, and blessedly changed, but not entitled to take its place on the level of long and patiently disciplined religious characters.

We must welcome, then, religious revivals, as we welcome a violent thunder shower after a long drought. True, it tears up the roads and injures the bridges, but it saves the crops. But this is the best it can do. It does not produce the effects of the early and latter rain. The farmer does not want occasional violent thunder storms, but frequent and gentle and steady rain. He cannot have large and fine crops upon any other condition. But if rain will only come in thunder-gusts, better these than drought and famine.

Let our own attention, my brethren, be directed to the importance of a better improvement of the ordinary and usual means of divine grace—a better use of the calm and sober views and instruments commended to us by the rational system of faith it is our privilege to find in the New Testament. There is none too much excitement in this community about religion. It is a sadly irreligious community ; and I believe that the one-sided, half-enlightened, half-honest notions of religion, maintained by the creeds of our churches—views which keep up the mysterious, irrational, unscientific, and incoherent ideas of a past age—are to no inconsiderable view responsible for the gross immorality, the gross infidelity, the still grosser materialism, and the astounding apathy of the people at large, to the real significance, the practical breadth and thoroughness, the noble symplicity and rationality of the religion of the New Testament. I believe, with all my heart, that an erroneous theology is, to no small extent, the cause of the weakness which organized religion exhibits in its contest with worldliness ; and that the present arousing of the people from their apathy is not due to the zeal and skill, or even to the leading of religious teachers, but to an irrepressible outburst of the pent-up religious sentiment, which has at length reacted upon an indifference which material prosperity and false doctrine together have brought upon the community. The people are ahead of their teachers in this matter, and their teachers are compelled to follow their lead. It is laymen who carry the whip and the spur in this race, and laymen, some of them fresh from nefarious transactions and atrocious sins. How wise their guidance is likely to be, how permanent their zeal, you may judge ! But of their sincerity I doubt not. It is the sincerity of a God-given religious nature, that now and then bursts forth in the worst men from the bondage of years of apathy, and like an overloaded blood-vessel, spurts forth with startling energy its gory current into the very faces of men, amid general panic and universal wonder.

Amid these events, it is the vast and glorious part which true religion has, or ought to have, in our hearts and lives, and in those of our children, which should arrest or sharpen our attention. Let us carefully consider whether we are true to our own glorious faith, faithful to the blessed conceptions of God, our holy and righteous and all-loving Father—of Christ, our head, exemplar, teacher, inspirer, elder brother, shepherd, bishop, and Saviour! of our human nature, image of God's own, with its transcendent wealth of faculties and affections; of the world, great school-house and play-ground, symbolic gallery and heaven-tuned orchestra that it is; of life, divine gift, significant and portentous endowment, open mystery and perpetual miracle, that we find it; of society, outgrowth and incarnation of human nature, full of lessons, warnings, gifts, and consolations;—are we faithful to our large, broad, thorough, and ennobling conceptions of these splendid and holy truths—the conceptions of the honest, brave, and pious men who achieved our spiritual independence and founded our liberal Christianity, and the heritage of the coming generations, if we transmit them with the eloquence of a courageous adhesion, and a conscientious embodiment, in our lives and characters?

Let us hold fast to what is good, and from the serene heights of our own clear and beloved faith look with piercing eyes into the face of error and fanaticism—acknowledging whatever good is found in their company, and welcoming every indication of progress, of sincerity, of vitality, but steadily plying our own well-tried means and instruments for our own moral and spiritual good—relying on our own views of duty, truth, and godliness, while we give a fresh and invigorated attention to our religious duties and self-discipline, and a more careful heed to our daily walk and conversation, in the light of that pure Christianity we profess.

MARCH 14, 1858.

SERMON XXIII.

SPIRITUALISM AND FORMALISM: THEIR RELATIONS TO THE FORMATION OF THE RELIGIOUS CHARACTER.

"Woe unto you Scribes and Pharisees, hypocrites, for ye pay tithe of mint and anise and cummin, and have omitted the weightier matters of the law, judgment, mercy and faith; these ought ye to have done and not to leave the other undone."—Matt. xxiii. 28.

A considerable portion of the Christian world is now passing through its annual season of special attention to religious offices. For the space of forty days, known in the Catholic and Episcopal Churches as Lent, a more or less rigid abstinence from carnal indulgences, public pleasures and worldly pursuits, is enjoined, and a round of devotional duties prescribed, some of a public and others of a private nature. It is not my purpose to disparage this custom, although the text may seem to threaten it. A truly thoughtful mind, acquainted with the slippery hold which moral and religious duties and sensibilities have upon our inconstant nature, could not object to this usage of the Mother Church and her English daughter; but could only regret that it did not better accomplish its object ; that the minds and hearts of men and women were not, by its method, fixed more decidedly upon serious themes, and correspondingly withdrawn from frivolous, or selfish and temporary pursuits. For certainly there can be no real dispute among intelligent people as to the end aimed at in religious institutions and usages, whether among Catholics or Protestants, by formalists or spiritualists, by advocates of times and seasons, or by despisers of both. That end is the moral and spiritual elevation of man ; his subjection to the will of God ; the formation within him of a pure, noble, conscientious and reverent character, which shall outwardly show itself in the beauty of his daily life and conduct. This is what the enlightened Catholic and Episcopalian seeks, what the intelligent Protestant and Puritan seeks. Their disagreement is mainly one respecting means, and not respecting ends. In one sense, there is among them, it may be confessed, a dispute about ends also ; but it is rather a question about words than things. It is this : whether life be for religion, or religion for life ; whether man lives to glorify God, or to be glorified by God ? The old Church, with most of its derivatives, has maintained that the end of life is religion ; that to know God, and love and worship him, is the final cause of our being ; that God created man for his *own* glory, is literally jealous of his service, and has made salvation wholly dependent upon obedience to his arbitrary sovereignty. The new Church, to which we belong—with a large portion of Protestantism that does not yet accurately know its own real position—maintains that the Almighty made man, not for his own glory, as that phrase is popularly understood, but, in the exercise of his perfect benevolence, that the creature might share a rational and moral existence with his Creator ; that God might *communicate* his glory, and thus increase and multiply the blessedness of the universe. According to this latter theory, God's glory is in no peril—gains and loses nothing by us, our obedience or homage being in no degree essential to the Perfect One. "God is not worshipped at our hands, as though he needed any thing, seeing he giveth life and breath and all things." The benefit of creation is essentially our own. God presents himself for worship, not for his own sake, but for our sake ! He makes himself known, not that he may enjoy the glory of our obedience, but that we may have the privilege, through the knowledge and obedience he allows us, of discovering the secret and enjoying the blessedness of a divine life. Religion, therefore, is not the end, but the method, of a true life. A true life is a life of mental and moral activity, of sympathetic friendship with men, of aspiration towards the highest, of love for exalted intelligences and characters, and a supreme love of God, as the alone perfect and absolutely good. According as men have thought God jealous of his own glory, or thought him jealous of our happiness, desirous of being worshipped for his own sake, or desirous of being worshipped that he might thus draw his children towards the only fountain of undying joy, have their ideas of religious methods and usages partaken of a theoretical or a practical character ; of a sentimental or a beneficent form. The old sacrificial system of the Jews, and that new sacrificial system of Christians, called the atonement, is based upon the notion that God has his own glory to tremble for, and is largely though not exclusively concerned to save his own honor and conscience; while the new light that is springing to its meridian, discards these puerile conceptions of a God whose throne can be shaken by pigmies; and makes religion a concern of our own, from the neglect of which we are the only sufferers—a system and method that seeks our spiritual development and glory, not the suspended happiness or the unperilled honor of Him "with whom is no variableness, neither shadow of turning," who dwelleth in light inaccessible and full of glory.

This, certainly, is not an unimportant difference of opinion; and yet, among those who seriously adopt either view—that man is made for religion, or that religion is made for man—a not dissimilar result of character may be looked for. For, we cannot live to God's glory without finding it to be for our own happiness; nor can we live for our own highest happiness without living to God's glory. He who consecrates life to religion with an intelligent sense of what religion is, "Love to God and love to man," and he who uses religion to guide and glorify life, although they have different ways of stating their aim, will really both arrive essentially at the same goal—a pure, humble, loving and worshipful character. To one, worship may be the most imperative and the most formal of duties; to the other it may be only the greatest of privileges and the most varied of offerings; to one God may be the most jealous of sovereigns, to the other only the most attractive and exclusively lovable of intelligences; yet the effect of the contemplation and adoration of perfect goodness and holiness must always be essentially the same. And whether man were seeking God's glory or his own bliss, experience would sooner or later teach all persevering pursuers of either, that their paths were identical; that whether God were seeking his own glory or our happiness, he could do only one thing in relation to ourselves, i. e., lay upon us the ennobling obligation of the first commandment, "Thou shalt love the Lord thy God with all thy heart, and with all thy mind, and with all thy strength."

It matters, therefore, less than at first appeared, whether we make worship an end in itself, or a means. Practised as an end, it is found to be a means; adopted as a means, it is proved to be an end. We cannot be happy without resembling God; we cannot resemble God without contemplating his character; we cannot contemplate his character without adoring him; we cannot adore him without experiencing the bliss of worship; we cannot taste this bliss without discovering that God is the fountain, and joy and glory, of our life; and that to praise and love and adore him, is the real business and the true pleasure of moral existence—the beginning, and middle, and unending direction in the pursuit of blessedness and immortality.

Nor can there be any essential difference between those who begin with worship to end in practical benevolence and brotherly love, and those who begin with fidelity in duty, to end in adoration. I do not believe that anybody was ever faithful to what are called strictly religious duties—that is, to meditation and prayer, and the contemplation of Christ and God—who did not soon perceive the necessity of strict truth, exact justice, active usefulness, and practical goodness towards men; nor was there probably ever a truly scrupulous lover and server of his kind, a man deeply and heartily in earnest in regard to right and just and virtuous living, who did not come to feel the presence of God in his soul—the need he had of knowing, and loving, and adoring his Maker. There is no such gulf between the duties we owe God and man—no such partition between morality and piety, beneficence and adoration—as it pleases some theorists to lay down. Because some devoted lovers of their race have not been churchmen, or even open worshippers of God, it has been rashly concluded that they lacked the experience of inward devoutness. It is a misfortune, indeed, when any man separates himself from the religious customs and external worship of his day and generation. It is never wise to indulge such eccentricities of conduct. But these deviations from usage are not to be considered necessary proofs of irreverence, or even of actual neglect of worship. And as a matter of fact, every truly good man is devout at the core, and if he pray not with his lips, has a hidden shrine where he meets God, and where God meets him.

We return, then, to the point we started from. There is no real dispute as to the end aimed at by sober Christians in the use or disuse of times and seasons. As the Apostle Paul says, with noble liberality, "He that regardeth the day, regardeth it to the Lord; and he that regardeth it *not*, to the Lord he doth not regard it." He that keeps Lent, keeps it for the deepening of his religious nature, the better knowledge of his duty, the more patient contemplation of his Saviour, and the more connected worship of his God. He that keeps it not, keeps it not because he fears that the setting aside of a special forty days for this duty may seem to imply that it is less incumbent on him for the other three hundred and twenty-five days ; he doubts the wisdom or necessity of emphasizing times and seasons, and is afraid of public forms and ecclesiastical appointments.

Those who sincerely observe, and those who sincerely neglect, this Church season, then, are equally Christian in their reasons ; and perfect respect should be paid to the convictions of both. I suppose the disrespect which those who neglect it express or feel towards those who observe it, is really based upon the conviction, that they mostly do not observe it "in spirit and in truth ;" that it is, after all, with the majority, rather a form than a substance, a show than a duty—superstition rather than piety ; while, on the other hand, the disrespect which the observers feel for the non-observers, is based upon their notice, that the disuse of formal religion does not mend practical piety ; that they do *not* make the three hundred and sixty-five days—all of which they profess to consecrate—any the better for neglecting the forty days of special piety. And this is the real question between the upholders of ecclesiastical religion and the defenders of spontaneous religion ; between the formalists and the anti-formalists. It is wholly a question of fact, and not a question of principle.

It is conceded by both, that the true aim of man is the supreme love of God and the brotherly love of man—that a devout, just, affectionate character, is what we are all to seek—a real character, internally and externally upright, pure, aspiring, reverential. How to form this character is the question. And on this point there are two answers. Commit man to the Church, says the formalist; pass him through the discipline of times and seasons; stamp him deep with early religious habits; frame his lips, before he knows why, into prayers; work upon his imagination with symbols, pictures, architecture, costumes, until it is inextricably intertwined with sacred associations. Make him the subject of a ritual which shall remind him, every time he rises, or eats, or lies down, every time the hour of the day is struck from the bell-tower, of his relations to his Maker and his Saviour, and thus fashion him, by a lifelong discipline, into a religious being! But, replies the anti-formalist, how has this system worked? Worked? answers the ecclesiastic. Look at its fruits! Whence came the piety that has built up the magnificent hierarchy of the Roman Church? What a mighty sense of religion must have produced the splendid cathedrals, the glorious pictures, the hospitals and retreats, of the Catholic world, and given the transcendent power to Peter's successor to abase emperors and monarchs at the feet of the Papal throne! Look at the fidelity to that faith, which, in a free country like ours, could rally such a procession as we beheld on Thursday last,[1] in honor of one of its patron saints! Or, look at the glories of the Church of England! Yes, replies the anti-formalist, but is not this splendid ritual, and this self-sacrificing fidelity to the Church, rather a substitute for true religion, and a bar to the understanding of the

[1] St. Patrick's Day.

real essence of piety, than a true expression of the actual faith of the Gospel? May not men be excellent and devoted churchmen, and still none the better for it in their real and spiritual character? And do we find, as a rule, among undoubting churchmen, purity of life and the fruits of the religious character? Have we not "the form of godliness without the power," in ecclesiastical usages and in the characters they nourish? Of course, the formalist cannot concede this. If he is frank, he will say, I own that ecclesiasticism, in its best present successes, leaves the character of the majority who come under its sway too little affected. But I deny that any other system could do as much as the Church system has done to sanctify and redeem the world. I allow that a vast proportion of all Romanists or Established Church-men—English, Greek, Russian—are poor specimens of the Christian life and character. But do you consider the ignorance, crudity, and social degradation of those whom this great system tries to help? and could any other system do half as much with them? On the other hand, in proof that this system does not hinder practical or spiritual development in those prepared by other culture to receive it, the ecclesiastic may point to the vast works of charity, the immense personal sacrifices, the exalted purity and worth of thousands of saints, martyrs, and missionaries, exhibited within the fold of the Church.

But now, let us hear what the anti-formalist has to say for his principles. He starts from the same ground with the formalist. The object of religion is to form a Christian character, in which love to God and man shall first enshrine and then manifest themselves.

How shall this character be created and established? Let a man commit himself, says the anti-formalist, not to the Church, but to his conscience; let him find a temple of worship in this glorious universe which God has built—an altar of sacrifice, wherever a duty is to be done, or a service to humanity to be rendered. Let his religious symbols, his times and seasons, be the great signs of the zodiac, the coming and retreating seasons, the starry hosts, the mighty ocean, and the tender flower. Why should he hold one day specially sacred, when all are holy in God's sight? Why any one act of his, specially religious, when all acts are so, if done in a spirit of obedience and faith? Why retreat from the world into a cell of prayer, or a cathedral of worship, to find God? Is he not as present in the din of the workshop as in the silence of the cloister; in the stirring crowd, as in the solitude of the mountain height? Why seek Jesus at the table of communion, when his favorite walks were among the fishers at their nets, the reapers in their harvest-field; by the wayside, or among the multitudes at city festivals, or with great gatherings on the hillsides of Judea? Where is his example to be followed, if not in the ordinary life of the world; where his work to be done, within us, or around us, if not in the practice of virtue and piety, rather than in the profession of it? Are we to believe that God peculiarly dwells in temples made with hands—he who is a spirit, and occupies all space; that he needs articulated prayers—he who knows our thoughts before they are framed into words; that sprinklings and washings, that bread and wine, that mediation of trained priests—in short, that religion as a ritual, something in itself and for itself, with its own times, seasons, customs, and feelings, is acceptable to him or necessary to us? Away with such husks of form, such superstitions of the world's childhood! Let religion henceforth be a life; and life a religion. Let the heart, the conscience, the intellect, worship God and serve man, and the bondage of rites and times and symbols and external sanctities wholly disappear. Thus far the anti-formalist.

But here interrupts the churchman: I agree with you entirely in the desirableness of thus universalizing religion, and making all days, all acts, and all emotions worthy of God and sacred to man. You have only described the common aim which all intelligent Christians seek. Allow me to remind you, however, that the point at issue is entirely as to the means of attaining it.

Have you tried your purely spiritual and unsystematic style of religion? Is there any kind of anti-ecclesiasticism, anti-ritualism, anti-external religion, which has fully and thoroughly carried out your principles, and if so, what have been its fruits? The world has millions of people who despise and neglect all religious usages and forms—all church-going, all formal prayers, all rites and seasons! Are these the people whom you adduce as the proofs of the beneficent influence of an uncreeded, unchurched, informal piety? Are these the thorough spiritual Christians with whom not one day, but all days, not one place, but all places, not one act, but all acts, are sacred? Surely not. And so far as these people are concerned—whom you will confess to be both immoral, careless, reckless and irreligious—would it not, on the whole, be better, even if for them

17*

we could make *one* day holy—though all the rest were desecrated—or any *one* set of their feelings or acts serious, or even less frivolous and profane than the residue?

But leaving this melancholy class, for whom religious institutions—and the more formal the better—seem wholly indispensable, let us in candor consider how your anti-formal principles work, even in the best hands. There are thoughtful, cultivated, excellent people, who once had all the advantages of special religious training, and who now believe themselves entitled to emancipation from rules and symbols, and days and weeks; who think they can trust their own consciences and their own hearts, and who mean and strive to make the whole of life useful to man and worshipful toward God! Now, as a matter of fact, is it this class of persons whose moral heroism, disinterestedness, and Christian elevation, have so far exceeded the rest of the world that we turn to them as the regenerators of society, the hope of humanity, the leaders of the race, the great successors of Christ and his apostles! Where are these holy men who are too good to need Church or ritual? Where are these saints, whose constant prayers no seventh day suffices to contain; where are these reverent spirits, to whom all of life is so sacred, that one thing cannot exceed another in the tender piety it awakens in their bosoms? I am afraid, my brethren, that we should be obliged, after all, to go into our churches in search of the most honest men, the most active philanthropists, the most lowly and spiritual Christians. I am afraid that the souls found most free from the dominion of forms would turn out to be those who most faithfully used them; that the most pious Mondays and Tuesdays and Wednesdays would be found to be in the society of the most pious Sundays; that those who most punctiliously said their prayers in Church would be found to be those who most truly observed our Saviour's injunction, "Pray always;" and that those who reverenced rites and seasons most would be found to be those who were consecrating life in general, most entirely and successfully!

The real, radical difference between the formalist and the anti-formalist in religion turns out practically to be this: belief or unbelief in the use of *means*. The religious character acknowledged by both to be the same thing, the churchman insists, will not grow, without a specific culture, a regular systematic attention paid to it at fixed times and by fixed methods. The anti-formalist insists that it requires no specific attention, but will grow better under the influence of broad general purposes of right living and right feeling; that it is narrowed, hindered, and weakened by forms and ceremonies, and that thus religion, from a life, is converted into a ritual.

Now, my brethren, I am not going to say that forms have not tended to great excess—have not often run into superstitions—hardened into chains for the mind and heart. The Church has at times become a prison. Protestantism was a violent and necessary reaction upon the externality of religion, and liberal Christianity a still plainer protest against the bondage of the intellect, exercised by creeds, and priests, and ceremonies. But I hold that the abuse of forms, and symbols, and externals in religion, forms as silly and weak an argument for their abandonment as the abuse of food would for its disuse, or of pleasure for its extinction, or of liberty for its suppression. Every great attribute of our nature, besides its general play, must have its particular and exclusive sphere. We trust neither morality, nor law, nor amusement, nor social intercourse, nor business, nor domestic economy, to informal and spontaneous operations. They all require to be fastened down to rules. We take our meals, not when we are hungry, but at fixed hours ; we visit, not whom we please, but where we are invited ; we seek our pleasures, not at all hours and everywhere, but at appropriate times and places ; we do our business within bank hours ; we wash, we iron, we bake, we brew, we settle our accounts, we change our clothes and our houses, we pay our bills, our rents, our taxes, at fixed times and places. We get our secular education within certain fixed limits of age, and by means of certain established customs. We acquire our commercial and professional training by careful apprenticeship. Is it only religion that is of such general, profound, and universal importance, that we need not have any particular and careful methods of cultivating it ? Is it only our consciences, affections, mental habits and wills, that need no special instruction, training, support, and encouragement ? There never was a greater folly in the world. You might as well say that wine and vinegar and medicine, being seldom used, required care in their preparation, importation, and protection ; but that water was worthy of no attention, no expense, no care in procuring, protecting, and keeping it, because we want it every day ! Let us, therefore, neglect the costly aqueduct that brings it, the pipes that feed our dwellings, the tax that secures our right to its use! If we wanted it only once a month, we might then devote some thought to it; or if it were not of universal use—if we wanted it only for drink, and not for cooking, for washing, for cleansing—then we might establish some methods for its supply. But being of universal importance, why pay any special attention to it? Is not this about the nature of the argument against the formal, systematic culture of religion?

Religion is a matter of daily life; of universal importance; of practical living and feeling. It ought to regulate every minute of existence, and every act and thought of the soul. *Therefore* we will pay no specific attention to it; we will have no appointed means of studying its truths, of considering our relations to it; of quickening our consciences, stimulating our imaginations, and regulating our hearts; no sacred places, no holy symbols, no form of prayer, no days of rest, no seasons of special consecration! As if a man should say, I am going to farm on so very extensive a scale, that I can afford to devote no time to studying agriculture, or to collecting the best tools, or to arranging the order and method of my business!

There never was a more dangerous sophistry than that which defends the modern outbreak of contempt for religious forms, times and seasons, methods and disciplines! It is equalled only by the argument against order of all kinds, in the French Revolution. Must we always be running from one extreme to another? Can we not abolish gold lace, and feathered hats, and cumbrous trains, and the folly and extravagance of ancient costume, without bringing the worth of clothes into question? Must George Fox go naked, because the king's courtiers dressed like dolls? Can we not do away with superstition, without doing away with worship? get rid of poor forms, without giving up the principle of form itself? I hesitate not to say, that the spirit of religion, in our day, is perilously involved in the neglect and suspicion of religious forms. There is too much indifference to externals for the good of internals; too much religious license for true religious liberty. Parents allow their children to act, in their ignorance and levity, upon their own responsibility in religious things; to think what they please, to go where they please. They fail to indoctrinate them; to form their religious habits; to teach them that reverence for external piety which is so essential. Nay, they do not watch their own spiritual state, and guard and cultivate it within the fences of correct opinion and judicious customs. They despise the great experience of the world in regard to the aids to be derived from rites and usages. They cannot shut their eyes, nor bend their knees, nor bow their heads in public worship. To raise their voices in a responsive service would be the height of acquiescence in anti-puritan customs; to observe the days consecrated by the use of the Christian Church for a thousand years and more, would be popish; to keep any season of the year with more fidelity than another in respect to religious self-discipline, would be rank superstition; to attach any serious importance to baptism or the communion, a kind of puerility; or to hesitate to do any thing agreeable to oneself on Sunday, out of respect to the day, a piece of formalism unworthy these enlightened times!

Let us be above these weak prejudices, that drive vulgar minds only from one extreme to another. Human nature demands liberty *and* law—spirit *and* form. It needs emancipation from old ways and usages, that it may establish new ones. It does not pull down its religious house to live out-doors, but to build a new and better one. We want not the old Jewish or Puritan Sabbath back, but we want Sunday to be a day of rest from secular cares, and of religious culture and worship ; we want not the old creeds back, but we need a new creed that shall express the mind of Christ as we now know it—leaving other generations to discard our reading, if they can make a better. We want neither the Romish nor the Episcopal forms of prayer, but we need a new Protestant ritual of worship, that shall not leave the worship of the Lord's house at the mercy of every accidental, incompetent, and eccentric individual who may chance to occupy the pulpit. Surely it ought to be enough for the minister to have his individual opinions fully expressed in the sermon, without tyrannizing over the whole congregation with the moods of his little, and mayhap peculiar mind, in the whole remaining services. It is a source of unfeigned astonishment, that congregations are willing to trust the great exercises of their public worship to accident, and not know, or have any choice in settling, what they shall pray for, or what praise and confess !

We want a church year—a regular and well-understood improvement of the events in our Saviour's history, sunk into the mind and heart of the rising race, by days consecrated to their notice and keeping. We want, too, some book containing the doctrines, the prayers, the means of religious improvement, of which experience has proved the worth, to be the representative of religious ideas and methods in the home ; a book to carry from the house to the church, from the church to the house, binding both together, from which children could easily learn the methods of piety, and which would be an external support and guide in the life of faith.

I doubt if candor, liberality, and enlightenment exist in adequate degree to bring about these immensely needed reforms in our denomination. But no amount of prejudice on the part of those who have superficially considered the subject, ought to prevent the freest expression of opinion on the part of those whose lives are consecrated to the study of the religious wants of the community. Happily, all changes in public worship, all improvements in church usages in our plain congregational bodies, are entirely at the disposal, and according to the choice, of the people themselves. Nothing can or ought to be done, against the wishes even of a respectable minority, in matters involving so many nice feelings and respectable prejudices. But it is the duty of those appointed to teach, to suggest improvements ; of those with whom the legislative authority lies, to order and act according to their sovereign pleasure. You must appoint your own worship as you will. It is my duty to conduct it according to your directions. But I hope you will seriously consider the general direction of thought, and the sober suggestions of this discourse, and be prepared, when any definite question on the subject shall arise, to act with the discretion, the unanimity, and the intelligence becoming so grave a body and so serious a subject.

MARCH 20, 1859.

SERMON XXIV.

THE APPLICATION OF WORLDLY WISDOM TO UNWORLDLY THINGS.

"For the children of this world are in their generation wiser than the children of light."—LUKE xvi. 8.

MUCH of the language of the Scriptures, as well of the world, is antithetical, and intelligible only in the mood of mind in which it is uttered. It is perfectly true as meant, and as understood, by the parties to it; but it is misleading, when considered as the prosaic ground of doctrine or practice. "If any man come to me and hate not his father and mother and wife and children and brethren and sisters, yea and his own life also, he cannot be my disciple," is an instance of this. The text, as commonly used, is another: "For the children of this world are in their generation wiser than the children of light."

This language is often quoted to sustain and eulogize that ignorance of the world and absence of practical judgment not seldom evinced and gloried in by those deeply engaged in the religious life. "The children of light" are commonly supposed to be here indirectly praised by the unfavorable comparison they are made to bear to the "children of the world," in respect to soundness of views and discretion of conduct in the ordinary concerns of life. The opinions which make this contrast popular are deeply laid and widely spread. The child, much more the man, "of this world," studies the world he lives in, learns the character and ways of men, explores the human heart, is an adept in weighing and gauging motives of action, in applying means to ends; is prudent, forecasting, judicious; does not expect to reap without sowing, nor to fly without wings, nor to buy without money; does not disdain expediency and compromise; would sooner any time have half a loaf than no bread, and shows himself a cautious, calculating, and time-serving person in all his maxims and methods.

"The child of light," on the contrary, taking one of the most saintly degree, has little interest in this world; his hopes and affections are in another; he does not wish to know men, or their ways, motives, or character, for fear of corrupting his own simplicity; he despises forethought as a distrust of Providence, calculation as a base selfishness; prudence as a mean timidity. He that feeds the ravens will supply his hunger; he that clothes the lilies will furnish his wardrobe. Expediency is the snare of worldlings, compromise the collusion of infidels. The children of light are guided by principle, not by experience. They deal with ends, not with means; and would sooner die straining after the unattainable than live in tranquil possession of any thing short of it.—Is not this a fair statement of the opposite qualities and tempers which the world, on the one hand, and the Gospel on the other, demand from their children?

Accordingly, the children of the world have usually had the practical conduct of human affairs in their own hands. Who should, or could govern society, but those who believe in it; who would or could carry on the world, but those who think it worth carrying on? Who but the wise and prudent should possess places of power and means of influence? Indeed, to attain means of influence, to aspire to and reach position and power, to have any real part in holding society together, is it not in itself proof of that prudential and worldly temper supposed to be condemned by the essential spirit of the Gospel?

"The children of light," on the contrary, if they pay any attention to this world, or to any existing institutions and terrestrial things, can do it only in the way of criticism and disapprobation; they can know just enough of politics to denounce it; just enough of commerce to testify against its corrupting and unchristian character; just enough of money-making to show its wholly poisonous and base tendencies. But their thoughts are mainly given to an invisible kingdom, and to interests beyond the bounds of time and space.

At any rate, such is the way in which "the world's people," meaning all who are not professedly pious, and the people of God, are commonly contrasted. That there is some seeming authority in the language of the Scriptures for this contrast, and the separation it implies between things terrestrial and things celestial, between the children of the world and the children of light, need not be denied. But whether there be any real foundation in the nature of things, the will of God, the Gospel of Christ, and the actual meaning of the Scriptures, or in the actual state of things now, for a permanent distinction of this character, is the real point of practical inquiry. If "godliness be profitable unto all things, having the promise of the life that now is, as well as that which is to come," are prudence and good sense profitable to our present interests only, and inimical to our eternal ones? Is the wisdom of this world essentially and necessarily fatal to that "wisdom which is from above?" And can the children of light continue to be such only by a steadfast quenching of all the rays which the experience of this world would mingle with the beams of their heavenly lamp?

It throws much light upon this question to observe, at the very outset, that it was not in the way of commendation, but of reproach, that our Saviour said, "the children of this world are in their generation wiser than the children of light." The very object of his parable of the unjust steward, is to exhibit the importance of that practical wisdom, solidity of judgment, and sagacious employment of means, so often used in the furtherance of purely selfish objects, for the attainment and advantage of the unselfish objects of a religious life and character. Christ desired to stimulate the zeal, enterprise, sagacity, and prudence of his spiritual helpers who were to be founders of new religious institutions, by pointing out to their emulation the judicious, prudent, and enterprising methods, to which an enlightened selfishness gave birth. In recommending the imitation of the judicious means employed by selfish and worldly persons, of course he did not approve and commend selfish ends or worldly aims. But injudicious and wicked ends may be sought by judicious and sagacious means. You may admire and approve the beautiful style which conveys dangerous ideas, without approving the ideas themselves, or praise the handwriting of a forger, without being properly suspected of approving forgery. You may surely commend industry, zeal, sagacity, persistence, even though the end to which they are perversely directed has your utter detestation. And it is clear that all the energies and tastes, appetites and faculties—with all the experience, observation, tact, and wisdom—ever possessed by the most consummate and accomplished man of the world, might be employed in and directed with the highest advantage to the pursuit and establishment of the Christian character, and to the living of the Christian life. The child of light, that is, the soul that loves the truth of God, welcomes its full beams, and lives to reflect them in his own character, and to put all other souls under their blessed illumination—cannot know too much of the world he lives in, nor understand men too well, nor have too balanced a judgment, too sagacious a policy, too comprehensive a plan, too nice a tact, too sweet and engaging manners, too many accomplishments! Let his aim be what it should be, let his heart belong to Christ, and then, if he were on the throne of an empire, and had the wealth of Crœsus, the accomplishments of Bayard, and the policy of Metternich, it could only be for his own good, and for the blessedness of the world and the glory of God. Nay, the more the high and holy sentiments and aspirations of such a sagacious and lofty spirit were turned to practical affairs, and made to flow into the actual channels of the world's immediate life, the more truly spiritual and Christian would such a soul be. To direct the thoughts and efforts of the soul away from time, as though this were to raise them to immortality; to close the eyes to the visible, as if this were any help in seeing the invisible; or to disparage the earth, as if that were exalting the sky, is a childish and superficial way of cultivating a religious and Christian character, which the true children of light must be very blind not to see through.

I do not suppose that you, my brethren, are in any particular danger of overlooking or neglecting prudence, calculation, and worldly wisdom, in the general conduct of life; or that you are so likely to sacrifice these in the pursuit of religion, on enthusiastic and mystical principles, as to make it incumbent on me to warn you seriously against the danger. It is not for that purpose that I am engaged in discussing the question before us. But for this, namely, that the idea still maintained by popular and prevailing superstition, that the true religious character is one opposed to the exercise of sound discretion and worldly wisdom, does a great deal to excuse men from the duties of religion, a great deal to bring religion into practical contempt, a great deal to make the opinions of religious men disregarded and despised. For just consider what an imputation on divine and spiritual influence it is, to say that it drives men out of their practical senses; unsettles their judgment; makes them less valuable as members of existing society; less reliable co-operators in the actual business of life; poor advisers in the great concerns of statesmanship, commerce, education, political economy, and the conduct of nations and cities! It would, according to this notion, be most unsafe for society to have all its members come under the influence of religion! There could, then, be no enterprising trade, no efficient government, no accumulation of wealth, no diligent and sagacious men of business, no thrift, forecast, nor calculation. Such an amount of faith in God would be dangerous to civilization. Men would not sow the harvest if, in general, they took so little thought for the morrow, nor weave clothing enough to cover the nakedness of the world, if they commonly accepted the doctrine which makes the care of Providence the best of raiment. Nine-tenths of the world must be irreligious to make it possible for the other tenth to be so pious as this! So long as the worldly and wicked will maintain and support society by their shameful industry, their sad anxiety to grow corn and wine, to spin and weave, that they may sell and hoard; to lay up, in an impious distrust of Providence, against failures of the crop, or sickness, misfortune, and old age, the means of their own and other people's subsistence, it is safe for a few to devote themselves entirely to lives of faith and prayer and aspiration, to unworldly theories, and to a lofty contempt of prudence and the vulgar excellencies of terrestrial prosperity! But the possibility of such a self-forgetting and unworldly class is entirely dependent upon the continued existence of a much larger class who continually *remember* themselves and their enthusiastic, self-oblivious, and sacredly rash brethren besides! Thus the unworldly may thank the worldly for their title to live in this planet at all. The pious, after this fashion, may thank the impious for the opportunity of displaying their graces !

I am very well aware, my brethren, that many noble, aspiring, and truly Christian souls, are actually deficient in sound judgment and worldly wisdom, and that their disinterested piety and sweet and holy graces are a greater benefaction to the world than even their prudence and discretion could be. I know that moderation, sobriety of judgment, worldly wisdom, are far more common than a childlike trust, a holy aspiration, a self-forgetting moral enthusiasm. Admit this, I beseech you, in the fullest and frankest way. But do not go on to think and say that it is the elevation, purity, and disinterestedness of religion, that disturbs the practical judgment of men, or that religious men and women are the better for these serious defects of character, or that the union of sound sense, sober judgment, balanced opinions, with moral aspiration, spiritual insight, and self-consecration, is an impossible, an unnatural, or an unholy alliance ! It is not the love of God that makes men fanatical and indiscreet, nor the love of truth, holiness, and heaven, that drives men into extremes of imprudence and folly ! It is not the love of Christ that unsettles the reason, confuses the feelings, and unbalances the faculties ! Men, indeed, have truly loved God and Christ, and yet had fanatical and unsettled minds ; but their fanaticism and unsettledness came not from their light, but their darkness ; not from what was true, but from what was false in their views ; not from the pure and heavenly, but the corrupt and earthly portion of their faith. It was not their religion, but their irreligion that left them in a marked imperfection of manhood. Do you suppose it is the *love* of humanity that makes the ultra-abolitionist of our day such a wild and visionary personage, such a general and reckless scold? Not at all! I do not, on account of his faults, deny his love of humanity, for I see it in the many noble sacrifices of worldly advancement, and of public reputation he is willing to make; but his bitterness and his scorn and his uncandor and unreason, I ascribe wholly to his weaknesses, his partisan temper, his necessity or passion for creating a sensation, his wilful intemperance of character. Is it, moreover, his self-sacrificing devotion to his race, his burning love of the black man, that sober society disrelishes and frowns upon? or is it rather his destructive treason to the constitution, his mischievous assaults on the religious and social institutions which, we all so well know, underlie the real and permanent interests of the country? And suppose, for a moment, we should all become like him —should all cry, "Down with the Union!" "Away with the Church!"—how long would he himself be safe from the bloody violence and the malignant passions his own intemperate views and reckless speech excite? It is under the shelter of the law that he is able to denounce whatever laws he dislikes; under the protection of the Union, that he can safely assail the Union as the compact of hell; and under the reign of the very order and peace which he pronounces infidel and inhuman, that he is able alone to find a platform from which to vomit his scorn of the whole Christian world and its united governments and people. And precisely so it is with the Church, when she thoughtlessly disparages prudence and thrift, and what she is pleased to call worldliness, in an indiscriminate manner! She owes her own temporal support, her edifices of worship, the education and the leisure of her teachers, their support and their means of charity, to the very pursuits, the very calculation and foresight, the accumulations and the occupations, she disparages. Of course, it is not the Christian piety, the true spirituality of the Gospel, that moves this cheap kind of denunciation; this unmeaning and insincere, or else empty and indiscriminating, censure. It is the sloth which will not take pains to clear up its own views; the professionality which will not risk, for truth's sake, its own reputation for sanctity; the rhetoric which cannot afford to sacrifice so easy a style of sonorous commonplace, that begets that pseudo and inexpensive sort of heavenly-mindedness which consists in calling the necessary, and useful, and beneficent pursuits of society, by hard names. To show enterprising and zealous men of business the guards and cautions they need to carry into their affairs—to persuade them to see and find a noble school of honor and integrity in their commercial pursuits, and to regard themselves in their success only as treasurers of the interests of society and almoners of the Lord—this is too thoughtful and difficult a work for those who trade in religion and make a business of creating strong sensations. But this is precisely what religion itself, or the Gospel of Christ, undertakes. She does not for a moment allow that any of the genuine interests, or natural occupations, or civilizing pursuits of men, are under the ban of piety. On the contrary, she takes them all into Christ's kingdom. She wants the industry, the sagacity, the enterprise, the wealth, the intelligence, the culture, the happiness of the world within the Church. But it is her duty and sacred office to separate the chaff from the wheat, not to burn the wheat to get rid of the chaff; to purge the motives, not to change the callings; to elevate the views, not to disorganize the relations of men; to regulate their appetites and passions, not to eradicate or destroy them; to bring moderation, symmetry, and a true order into the minds of all men, not to expurgate any of their qualities, or pronounce any part of their nature, or of the world they occupy, or the society they constitute, profane and diabolic.

There is such a thing as worldliness, certainly, and there are thousands and tens of thousands of worldly people; but their worldliness does not consist in their industry, their thrift, their sobriety of judgment, although these are all used to gratify their selfish egotism and greed. Worldliness is the love of self, as opposed to the love of God and man; and as this world had possessed this for its prevailing spirit for ages, when Christ came, it was a characteristic description of selfishness to call it worldliness. So far as men are now selfish, greedy, unsympathetic, hoarding, thoughtless of the claims of their fellows, and unmindful of God, duty, and immortality, they are worldlings. But their worldliness does not dwell in their interest in business, or politics, or pleasure, or society, but in the nature of this interest. This interest may be, and is in many, pure, peaceable, and full of good fruits, favorable to the finest and soundest character; but it is in still more, impure, contentious, unprincipled, selfish, and vile. Some men grow, on their business pursuits, their social relations, their political, literary, and professional avocations, more and more honorable, benevolent, disinterested, and aspiring ; acquire a truer brotherhood with men, a closer fellowship with Christ and with God. Other men dwindle, on the same pursuits, into self-seekers, rivals, and antagonists of their race, doubters of religion and defiers of God. It is not their pursuit, it is not the world, considered either as a place or a providential scene of mixed occupation, that makes or unmakes men ; it is men that use or abuse, that convert to food or to poison, the opportunities and means which a gracious Providence leaves to their choice. The world is good enough ; it is we who are wilful and mad, that make it corrupting to ourselves and others, and then call the evil we have infused into our circumstances, an evil inherent in the things themselves.

Let me guard you against one fatal misuse of the truth I have brought before you. I have endeavored to show the necessity and the feasibility of bringing all the prudential and practical wisdom and enterprise, afforded by the opportunities, the discipline, and the occupations of life, into the formation of the religious character and the perfecting of the Christian life. What an abuse of this important truth would be made, if those who are only prudent, industrious, and zealous in their worldly pursuits, should thence immediately declare, or think themselves to be religious ! If, because the wisdom of the world may be ministerial to the wisdom from above, it should be made a substitute for it, or be confounded with it ! And yet this is the error constantly endorsed or experienced by those who are forever crying up decency of life, as if it were the substance of piety. But, on the other hand, because industry, prudence, worldly wisdom are not the love of God and man, are they opposed to the love of God and man ? are they nothing, because they are not every thing ? are they not useful means because they are not good *ends ?* It is this false depreciation of them, on the side of the Church, which leads to as false an exaggeration of their worth on the side of the world. But let us not be tossed to and fro, from one extravagance of opinion to another. The human race ough not to be divided between fanatics of religion and fanatics of worldly success. Fanaticism of any kind is weakness and folly ; and there is no proper excuse for those who will not be at pains to keep a balance of judgment, and a proper medium between the relative claims of the present and the future.

We are living at a time when sober men have got tired of half-truths, and are not quite patient of the labor of getting at whole ones, and so maintain a sort of suspended animation of the higher life. Religious discussions and philanthropic debates are carried on to the very small satisfaction of men of sense, really anxious for the truth, because the mouths of the earnest men are too small to hold any thing but partisan and ultra opinions, fighting superstition with skepticism, and not with truth, and attacking one kind of injustice with another kind of injustice, instead of arraigning it at the bar of eternal equity. The errors of orthodoxy, forsooth, are to be met only with the errors of heterodoxy ; the follies of formality with the follies of informality ; the excesses of worldliness with the excesses of unworldliness. If there be a false spirituality in vogue, all spirituality is to be decried; if prayer in the corners of the streets is to be discouraged, prayer in the closet is given up; and if we are not to believe in the dogmas of local councils, we are not to believe in the doctrines of Christ and his apostles. Because our religion is a spirit and a temper, it is therefore to have no definite opinions, no regular methods, no helpful symbols connected with it; as if the question, "what is *Christianity*," were not very different from the question, "what is *truth?*" It is as much a different question, as what is heaven, and what is the road to heaven, or what is Boston, and what is the road to Boston. Religion may be a very indefinable thing; but *a* religion may be a very definite thing. The spirit of the Gospel may be hard to confine in articles of belief; but the truths, or facts, or methods by which that spirit is to be attained may be as capable of statement, as the chemical methods of creating a subtile essence, or distilling an evanescent gas. We know as little about the secret of a blade of grass, as we do about the secret of God's being, for mystery and infinity are at the bottom of every thing, whether it be a grain of sand, a world of light, or an intelligence like God's own. But how to raise grass requires some definiteness of belief in the season of planting, the methods of sowing and of culture, and the enriching of soils; and so, how to secure the Christian spirit, how to acquire the religious character, requires some definiteness of belief, some opinions, some methods of self-discipline, some training of intellect, conscience and heart; and it is the confounding of things that differ, the lack of patient and candid discrimination, that is doing so much mischief now-a-days, when truly religious men, in their zeal for a neglected side of the truth, talk in a way that sounds like infidelity, and which is welcomed by infidels with approbation.

Although church-going is not religion, it nevertheless remains church-going; and church-going ministers to religion. Although theology is not religion, it still remains theology, or the theory of religion and of the application of religion, and surely, as such, it is immensely important to religion. Because Christianity is not absolute religion, is not religion itself—nor belief in Christianity, practical piety—it does not change the fact, that Christianity is a system of revealed truth, by the study, the belief and the application of which, practical piety and sound morality, and all personal and social interests, are promoted as by nothing else! Why, then, this foolish confusion of thought, this indiscriminate mode of speech, by which means are disparaged because they are not ends, and methods and forms and symbols and statements of faith are sneered at and waived aside, because they are only educational and preparatory, or temporary and ministerial, and not absolute? Or what proper controversy is there between principles and methods; lofty aims and humble means, a spirit too great for statement, and directions for the promotion of that spirit, most explicit and simple; a faith in the absolute and ever-unattainable truth; and a faith also in *truths* touching Christ and Christian growth and culture, that are not absolute but relative, and therefore precisely statable.

If we applied to religion and the religious life and character, the pains-taking thought, the prudent enterprise and sober weighing of things, which sagacious men of the world apply to their trade, their ship-building, their railroad making; if we made the accurate distinctions they make in respect of what they give for their goods and what they take for them, who they trust and who they do not, what they believe and what they doubt; if we exercised their patience, address, devotion, wisdom, in our religious concerns; we should find a wonderful dissipation of the clouds that now hang over this great subject; we should get beyond the reach of the vague thoughts which leave us at the mercy of eloquent but incautious lips, that unsettle our convictions and destroy our hopes. We should be driven to neither extreme—whether of worldliness or unworldliness—but maintain the rights of humanity in the presence of the Church, and the rights of the Church in the presence of humanity; reconcile reason and faith; interest in life and self-consecration; freedom and law; emancipation from the letter, with reverence for the Scriptures; spirituality, and the use of rites and symbols; progress with fixed foundations; and the use and improvement and enjoyment of the whole of this world, with the love of Christ and man and God, and the best and noblest preparation for the world of spirits.

MAY 14, 1859.

SERMON XXV.

COMPARISON OF THE CLAIMS OF ENLIGHTENED SELFISHNESS AND UNCALCULATING LOVE.

"For what if some did not believe? Shall their unbelief make the faith of God without effect? God forbid."—ROMANS iii. 3.

THERE is a serious doubt in the minds of many intelligent and well-disposed people in our day, whether religion, considered as distinct from morality—that is to say, decency of conduct and worthiness of life—has any existence, except in the imaginations of well-meaning but deluded persons. By religion, as thus doubted, is meant, I suppose, what is ordinarily understood by that word ; namely, a relationship between man and God, kept up by conscious obedience, prayer, and aspiration ; and for Christians, an interior intercourse of the soul with its Sovereign and Father, by means appointed in the Gospel of our Saviour. And this familiar and popular definition of religion is, I suppose, the correct one. Religion is universally understood among plain people, and by ordinary, average minds, to be something different from morality. Morality is well described as that kind of just, honest, and correct behaviour, which it would become men to practice, if their lives began and ended with the world they now inhabit; if they had no obligations outside of it, and no knowledge beyond it, and no connection with any powers or authorities except the visible ones of this terrestrial globe. It is perfectly clear, that were there no God, no Saviour, no immortality, and, of course, no judgment to come, it would still be necessary to have rules of good conduct, and means of promoting considerate and righteous manners among men, in behalf of the general good and for the sake of individual happiness. Furthermore, there can be no doubt that a virtuous and noble life, seeking truth, rectitude, and the common welfare, would be the dictate, whether obeyed or not, of the most enlightened selfishness, were there no supernatural authority to enforce it, no Bible to recommend it, no Saviour to illustrate it, no immortality to reward it. Accordingly, a small body of highly intelligent people exists in England, distinguished, also, for correctness and elevation of life, whose adherents call themselves *Secularists*, to mark their distinctive opinions—that is to say, people of this world in opposition to people seeking another; not *worldly* people, in the sense in which that phrase is used by religious persons, but those who think that motives enough for virtue and philanthropy, and whatever else goes to make good people, are to be found in the contemplation of actual affairs in the present plane of every day life, and in the recognition of themselves as beings destined only to an earthly existence. They, therefore, systematically ignore and abandon all hopes and all thoughts of a future existence; all obligations to any unseen or supernal authorities—in short, all religion; and devote themselves to morality, to good citizenship, the elevation of the poor, the advancement of pure manners, equal laws, and practical happiness. It is their conviction that hopes of heaven and fears of hell are alike selfish and ignoble ; that interest in a future life diminishes fidelity to present obligations, and subtracts from the improvement of earthly affairs the energy and zeal which they so pressingly require. They think that even if there be a personal God, He cannot want their service as much as their fellow-men do ; and if there be a future world, it will be time enough to attend to its duties and enjoy its pleasures when we reach it. Meanwhile, both being uncertain, it is not prudent to waste thought and feeling upon them. These people—Secularists as they style themselves, in contradistinction to Sacredists, if the word may be pardoned—are, I repeat, among the most truthful, genuine, and excellent people in England ; distinguished for intelligence, beneficence, and thorough kindness of heart and life. I suppose they merely carry out, and boldly embody in a system, ideas and feelings that are widely prevalent in a less conscious and unsystematic form, here and there--opinions with which some of you, for instance, may more or less heartily sympathize.

And you may well ask, in view of this statement, if there can be thorough goodness and real unselfish conduct in this world—intelligent, useful, pure, and correct living—inward elevation of mind, heart, and conscience, devoted usefulness—without faith in a personal God, belief in a revealed religion, docility to a divine Saviour, hope of a future life—does it not prove religion to be somewhat of a superstition ? to be, at any rate, an exaggerated influence—or to say the least, not the essential and indispensable thing the pulpit so uniformly pronounces it? Is it not at best a means to an end which it is now proved can be attained without it? Moreover, as the end which religion professes to aim at, and to furnish means for reaching—that is, a good and righteous life on earth, as preparatory to a blessed and eternal life in heaven—is by no means the universal, or even ordinary result, in those who come under its teachings, and who profess to respect and reverence its doctrines and spirit—is it not worth while to consider whether the attention up to this time given to faith had not better, in future, be given to practice; the time spent in worship be devoted to philanthropy, and the thoughts and energies expended in gaining heaven be used in improving earth? If there be a just, and wise, and holy God, surely he cannot fail to approve faithful services to his needy children, more even than devotion to himself, who needeth nothing; and if there be a future life, who so well prepared to enjoy its privileges and fulfil its duties as those who have most faithfully used the opportunities and discharged the obligations of this present life?

There is something in this style of reasoning which seems to me not easily answered by minds of only ordinary reflection; something taking and conclusive to persons of quick and off-hand judgment. And yet it is truly fallacious, though widely and secretly convincing to thousands of frank and generous hearts, all over the world! I shall endeavor to point out the flaws, in the fair presentation I have sought to give, of the argument for dispensing with religion. "For what if some did not believe? Shall their unbelief make the faith of God without effect? God forbid."

I begin with restating what it is, under the name of religion, which, in opposition to the Secularists and their unconscious disciples everywhere, I am about to show cannot safely or wisely be dispensed with.

And I repeat, that by religion I do not mean a refined and subtle something carefully adapted to the present sensitive state of the public faith—in which divine persons, and divine hopes and fears, and divine commands and sanctions, are so exquisitely veiled and so adroitly manipulated, that it is difficult to say whether they are or are not believed in, or whether they belong to heaven or earth, or dwell in the region of the natural or the region of the supernatural. I hold a religion which is only a thinly veneered morality, a faith which is unbelief varnished with believing words, to be not half so safe for its disciple as an honest denial of religion. I suppose that a religion of this sort—as a seventh day interlude, a change in excitements, an æsthetic or intellectual luxury—might find supporters, if not disciples, among utter skeptics. Indeed, it is stated that a Free-thinking club, composed in part of avowed Atheists, has looked with favor on a religious society which has reduced a positive faith to the vanishing point, without abandoning its assembling together for purposes of spiritual improvement. No! it were easy to find patronage for this sort of religion among Secularists themselves. But the religion I contend for is the ordinary kind, which simple, unmetaphysical, sober folks—so superstitiously, in the estimation of the Secularists—still accept and believe in; the religion of

Catholics and Protestants, Methodists and Baptists, of orthodox and heterodox Christians ; that religion which commands the fear and worship of God, the discipleship and imitation of Jesus Christ, the necessity of repentance and forgiveness of sins ; which makes the soul a dependent on God's pardon, arouses and pains the conscience before it quiets it to rest, excites the spiritual affections and fixes them on God in Christ, creates a trembling hope of salvation, and makes the longing and desire for immortality and heaven, the perpetual and patient struggle of our mortal pilgrimage.

Nay, further than this, the religion I contend for is that familiar, prevailing religion, which many of the foremost thinkers of the day—the poets and political economists and moralists and philosophers—disuse or despise—which puts into catechisms and creeds and forms of faith, and embodies in positive rites and usages, and fixes down to holy days and times and seasons, its instructions and disciplinary methods ; and sustains a class of religious teachers, and builds churches, and has prejudices about their use, and distinguishes between things secular and things sacred, and values doctrines and rites, simply because they are connected with a hope of salvation. If this popular, ordinary kind of religion cannot be defended, it is not worth while to contend for any other. If the world can dispense with what commonly passes for religion, it can dispense with any superfine edition of it, which, at the best, must be confined to a very few hands.

What, then, is the grand reason for believing and maintaining and using religion as thus defined—what the necessity and the occasion for it? I answer, in the first place—directly and unequivocally—*its truth.*

If there were no personal God and no immortal life, and no moral issues of life and death, and no actual Saviour—if God had not made man as he is, for purposes which he has revealed, and had not chosen to bring him into such personal relations with himself as are implied in the very words Religion and Christianity—then, I might confess, that men were presumptuous in supposing God cared very much for them, or that He could concern himself directly with their present or their future. Then, the hope of immortality might be esteemed a rash and delirious longing; then, the connection between this world and another, a vague and improbable invention of human vanity; then, the possibility of actual intercourse with God by prayer and communion, a questionable or unreal pretension; then, religion itself an uncertain speculation, not to say a dangerous delusion. But, allowing for a moment, that it is *true* that God lives, and actually asks and demands our obedience and homage; that he offers the gift of eternal life upon certain moral and spiritual conditions; that he has sent his Son into the world on a mission of mercy and salvation;—allowing, for a moment, that it is a *fact* that God really hates our sins, and is concerned for our escape from their power, and that having perfect wisdom and love, he has devised and laid down his own methods for saving the world from folly and blindness, and the consequences of disobedience; allowing, in short, that Christianity is *true*—why, surely, any theories based upon the hypothesis that it is not true, or that nobody knows whether it is true or not, are liable to most serious objections! I confess that were we without any revelation of God, or any experience of man's spiritual constitution and wants, had the race and the world experienced a different history from its actual one, I should see a great deal of reason in the ideas of the Secularists and their unnamed sympathizers. As it is, their whole plan proceeds upon an hypothesis totally different from that presented in the real case. They say, in effect, How *can* God, an infinite Being, be interested in our mortal worship of him? How *can* he have placed us in this world for any purpose but to improve it? How *can* he have desired to interest us in another life before we have exhausted this? Well, I reply, how he *can* have done it, I am not wise enough to answer. That he *has* done it, is the point nearest and most important to me and to you. It is amazing, all but incredible, that God, who made the countless worlds, should have distinguished this by his peculiar favor! It is confounding that man, beginning a helpless, unconscious babe, should end a mighty, immortal seraph! It is awing and overwhelming to think that the only begotten Son of God should have been clothed in mortal flesh, should have toiled and sweated beneath the burdens of a persecuted, a reviled and forsaken life, and died upon a bloody cross, for creatures so ungrateful, so sinning and so worthless as we mostly are, or seem! It is passing strange that God should task the resources of an infinite nature, and blend in the fortunes of his own throne, to save a race of creatures that doubt his own existence, repudiate his Son, and are disposed to bury themselves beneath the oblivious dust after they shall have finished their short and erring career above it! But, if God really *does* live, and if he *does* thus love, and if he has, in his Son, thus revealed his boundless interest and concern for us; if religion is true and Christianity real; if communion with the Father, fellowship with the Son, inspiration from the Holy Spirit, be possible and actual things—are we, then, in a condition to make light of faith, to question piety, to abandon the study and practice of our purely religious duties, or to relinquish any of the defences and customs which bring them regularly, persuasively, patiently and persistently before the minds and hearts of our children, our fellow-creatures and ourselves?

I do not here undertake to prove that religion is true. I assume that it is true, on the strength of general consent, and on the authority of the vast majority of the wise and learned and good in all the Christian ages. If it is true, you will concede the adequacy of the basis for treating it as true. If it is not true, really it seems to matter little what is, or what is not, what we do, or do not do. But let not a temporary and exceptional skepticism disturb our confidence. "For what if some did not believe? Shall their unbelief make the faith of God without effect? God forbid."

But, in the next place, religion, considered as the name for man's relations to God and the future, and the doctrinal discipline and worship which is founded upon them, possesses a claim on our utmost respect, not only as *true* in itself and connected with our future salvation; but also because it is true to man's immediate nature and present wants, both as an individual and as a social being, and in the very world he now lives in. Do away religion, and you fling man back upon his meagre understanding and feeble reasoning powers for his whole guidance. An enlightened selfishness, the rarest thing in the world, becomes his best and highest rule of life. Considering that virtue and justice, honor and truth, are always for the interest of each and of all. perhaps you think that no happier reign could be inaugurated than that of a thoroughly intelligent self-love that the whole object of religion—which is a complete human development—would be fully secured, if men only saw clearly what their interest required. But this proceeds upon a fallacy now very popular, that it is ignorance alone that causes wrong-doing—that the chief source of vice and crime, folly and selfishness, is mental and moral blindness—that sin is the stumbling and wandering of people that know no better—that are only mistaken in what they want, deluded by their passions and led through pure but profound self-ignorance, to grasp their ruin in their bliss. Show them how much pleasanter right is than wrong, innocence than guilt, disinterestedness than cupidity, goodness than money, peace than pleasure—and, according to these worthy but credulous people, the drunkard will at once become sober, the miser a beneficent citizen, the angry and violent man gentle and amiable, the sluggard an ant in industry, and the self-seeking public-spirited and philanthropic ! An enlightened self-love, it is assumed, would do away with selfishness, which is the root of all bitterness and strife and wrong in the world. Admitting this for a moment, a proper rejoinder would be, that religion leaves all the motives of a utilitarian kind wholly unimpaired by those she adds to them, and, by showing that our salvation in the future depends upon our dutiful and pious behaviour on earth, certainly does not diminish the inducements to virtue and honor, which spring from the fact that they are felicitating and useful in themselves. "Godliness," says the apostle, "is profitable unto all things, having the promise of the life that now is, and of that which is to come."

But this is not the fundamental answer. The truth is, that ignorance of what our real interest requires, or where our genuine happiness lies, is not the chief, nor even a principal cause, of our disobedience to the laws of brotherly love, or of the neglect of our divine obligations; and the theory that makes it the chief obstacle to goodness is one of the shallow notions of our age that blindly and perversely worships intelligence, instead of studying the human heart, reverencing conscience, and fearing and loving God. Man, after all, is not so mean and calculating a creature as these proposed elevators of their species would make him out. He is far more than an incarnated balance-sheet, or organized interest-table; he is a creature of powerful passions, enormous desires, strong affections, and independent will, who is capable of acting against his interest with a noble contempt; who is very seldom at any time ruled exclusively or chiefly by his interest, but rather by his passions, his impulses, his affections, and his will. Mainly he does as he pleases, and he pleases to count a little immediate ecstasy worth years of promised peace; a little imperious self-will worth a great deal of blessed subordination; a little pride, or passion, or prejudice, or love, or spite, more than all the reason, and duty, and utility in the universe. Men know that they are fools to be angry, and suicides to yield to their sudden appetites and violent passions—know that it costs them long repentance, broken friendships, stinging regrets, .and permanent failure. There is not a young man of dissolute lusts and bad habits here present whom I could enlighten a ray on the folly and madness of his passionate course ; nor a greedy accumulator of money, who does not know that a few years hence, as he lies on his death-bed, his fortune will not be worth to him one of the straws he gasps away his empty life upon ; nor an idle, frivolous girl, nor a hardened worldly woman, who does not know, as well as Dr. Paley, and Mr. Bentham, and Mr. Combe, and all the Utilitarian philosophers that ever lived or ever will live, that no real happiness, no true wisdom, no enlightened self-interest, is promoted by gew-gaws and feathers, by laces and upholstery, by folly and show. It is not ignorance that binds these victims to their vices and their follies, as to a funeral pile. It is want of moral strength to break away from their ruin. It is a state of paralytic will, of rebellious or reckless affections. Until this passionate, pleasure-loving, eager nature of ours, is reached by objects that kindle nobler desires, fix profounder affections, electrify the heavenly will ; until something stirs the conscience as no calculation of interest can, something starts the will to do right as no mere enlightenment of the understanding can—there is no chance of an emancipation from the ruinous, heaven-defying follies and vices, and the mean, earth-clinging weaknesses, that commonly describe our race ! Do you hope to set the reason and the conscience and the selfishness of man against his passions, affections, and desires, and so win the day? You might as well fight fire with straw, or the wind with fans! The passions are withstood only by the help of the passions; the emotions by the emotions; the affections by the affections. The baser will yield only to the nobler in its own kind. To restrain the bodily appetites, the moral appetites must be aroused; to arrest the unlawful, the lawful passions must be set to work; to purge the baser, the purer affections must be animated. And this is the work of religion, and nothing but religion can do it. Her appeal is to the heart, and the conscience, and the will. She aims to arouse the admiration, the enthusiasm, the passionate fears and hopes, the grateful affections, the self-condemnation, the sympathy, the heroism of the soul. To this end she presents her all-holy, all-wise, and all-loving God, and gives the affecting history of his long-suffering dealings with his rebellious children; her gentle, heroic, martyred Saviour, dying of wounds from the very hands he was filling with life and happiness; her noble ideals of character, her attractive and glorious future! She appeals to the conscience, not as to a slave of interest, but a noble witness for God, and calls upon man to hate and despise himself for his treachery to his better nature and his divine original. She speaks to the will as Christ spoke to the palsied arm, when his voice of power put nerve into its stringless muscles. She speaks, not as to the base beam of the grocer's scale, that will only yield to the preponderate weight that inclines it to either side; but as Moses spoke to the dead rod, when it leaped out a living serpent, and devoured the meaner vermin that crept around it. Man's will is free! free as God's lightning, as it sleeps in the silent, motionless cloud, which at any moment may dart from its lair to shake the mountains with its voice, illuminate the concave with its glaring eye, and cleave the centuried cedar with its falchion of flame! And religion alone knows and feels this, and so alone can catch man halfway down the precipice of ruin, and summon forth the angel's wings, now folded to his faithless body, that will arrest his fall, and send him with a swoop of victory up the very face of destruction itself.

Do you doubt it? Alas! were it not true, what could have made the world tenantable at all, or saved the race from the utter ruin of its selfish indolence or mischievous activity? Oh! if enlightened self-interest, if intelligence and reason, had been the only or the main dependence of the world! Alas! If noble passions, grand emotions, spiritual awakenings, and sudden visions of heavenly truth and beauty, had not come to its rescue!

Thank God, there is not a simple, heart-Christian in the Methodist or the Baptist, or the Christian ranks, who tells the love of God and the compassion of Christ, the bliss of heaven and the base ingratitude of sin—in sentences of tangled grammar, and words, half of which cannot be found in the dictionary—who, in his passionate, loving soul, with eyes streaming with pity and tones that have been caught from the cross—pleads with and condemns the sinner, and commands miracles of tenderness from a heart that till now had been hard as stone, and miracles of resolution from a will that till now has been as unstable as water—no, not one such Gospel-babe that is not an archangel in spiritual power and in saving influence, when compared with the calculating machines called moral philosophers, though the understandings of Bacon, and Newton, and Aristotle, were all in their pay—who would make men virtuous, law-abiding, useful, and happy, by showing them how very good it is to be good, and how very amiable to be amiable, and how very happy to be happy! Men must have tremendous and divine motives to touch their dead hearts and vitalize their torpid wills, before they will experience the moral miracle of rising from the graves of selfishness in which they mostly lie buried. And religion is the only power that ever did or ever will accomplish this work. Love does it for a day, a month, for most—aye, forever for some—but then it becomes religion. But Christ in his Gospel has done it, and is doing it, for millions, because he is Love embodied in a holy life, and bleeding in a sacred death; because he is God's love come down to plead with, and re-create and save, God's child—who knows not he has a heart of heavenly fire, a will of angelic power, till Christ's voice scatters the sins and follies that bury them from sight, and reveals them, by their own light and might, to the astonished consciousness of their now redeemed and emancipated subject and possessor.

My brethren, it is too obvious for argument, that any scheme that leaves out of the plan of human life or social progress such an agency as this, leaves the sun out of the heavens, the oxygen out of the air, the meaning out of the world. A desert island, with every thing found upon it ready for man's use and enjoyment, except a spark of fire—but that forever to be excepted—would not be a more dreary and desolate abode! Better the icy caves of the Northern pole, with fire and fuel at hand, than the spontaneous tropic without them. Better ignorance, crudity, and want, of every other description, with the sole illumination of true and vital religion, than the best and costliest and eldest civilization of the globe, with God's throne vacant, the cross without its bleeding weight, and the human conscience and will deprived of the inspiration and salvation of the religion that alone can meet the weakness, and want, and sinfulness of man!

Nay, it is in the memory, and on the influence of the pious generations that once believed, and loved, and prayed, and wrestled, and conquered—it is as the heirs of a devout ancestry, that a few are able to live now upon the capital of the religious past, without adding to the store of faith in their blood and habits and tastes! From the spiritual heights to which they have been lifted by their believing predecessors, they look down upon the multitude, and say, "Why keep these dogmas and customs and rites and prayers a-going any longer? Don't you see we are up here—good, pure, intelligent, orderly people? *We* have no further occasion for these old scaling-ladders of faith and prayer and sacred customs. Pray, break them up! Religion was a good thing once, but prayers and creeds and beliefs and piety had their long day. Now it is enough to do good and to be good. We are good, and we do good, you must acknowledge. Imitate us, ye simple people, and you shall all be content yourselves, and make all others so."

Ah, ye amiable, well-meaning souls, we acknowledge your essential purity and excellence! Nay, we should gladly fill the world with copies of your moral worth. But we cannot forget to consider how you got where you are, nor to speculate where you would have been, if your parents and grandparents had thought and felt as you do! We cannot but reflect, that religion had a far larger hand in your making than it has in your talking, and is even now more operative in your hearts and wills than it is in your theories. In short, we perceive, that having used the ladders of faith and religious obedience to attain your present moral position, you would persuade the world, which is not at all on your moral level, to abandon all ladders, on the strength of the fact that *you* do not require them; a fact without pertinency to them. You are simply asking them to fly, where you yourselves never flew, but only crept. First, fly yourselves to the elevation next above you—which, if you ever reach it, it can only be by the old means—and then you may persuade us to trust to wings which we do not possess, and to fling away what God has given us—the humbler ways and means of an obedient religious discipline.

Because religion is *true*, and has divine commands for you and over you—because it is life and power, heart and will, and can alone supply you with motives and impulse for a noble and a true life—because, too, it is method, implement, rule, lending a daily guidance, support and discipline—by each and all these considerations, I beg you to discard the error of the day which would seduce you from a simple faith, and leave you, under the pretence of an advanced, a more rational, and more useful style of belief, stripped of the glory, the consolation, and the inspiration of the religion of Christ.

October 2, 1859.

THE END.

www.ingramcontent.com/pod-product-compliance
Lightning Source LLC
LaVergne TN
LVHW021134110826
845150LV00005B/1029

* 9 7 8 1 4 2 5 5 4 9 5 1 0 *